THE TALL TALES OF ROBERT SILVERADO

SIBERIAN INVASION!

WRITTEN & ILLUSTRATED BY:

MATTHEW R. ENLOW

TEXT DESIGN BY:

ANA MARIA WRIGHT

Date: 10/5/15

MODELS:

MATTHEW WRIGHT; ADRIANA ENLOW; CESAR CAMPODONICO;

CHRIS WRIGHT; MATTHEW BRODTMAN; JAMES LOWNEY; A

SPECIAL THANKS TO:
GOD
ADRIANA & ALI ENLOW; MATTHEW & ANA WRIGHT; CESAR
CAMPODONICO & FAMILY; MICHAEL ENLOW & FAMILY; CHRIS WRIGHT;
MATTHEW BRODTMAN; JAMES LOWNEY; LEE & TESS PAGE; ROBERT &
MAUREEN ENLOW; HECTOR & ANA ALVA; DAVID & MARCIA WRIGHT

Likes us on:
www.facebook.com/EnlowArts

FOR ALI

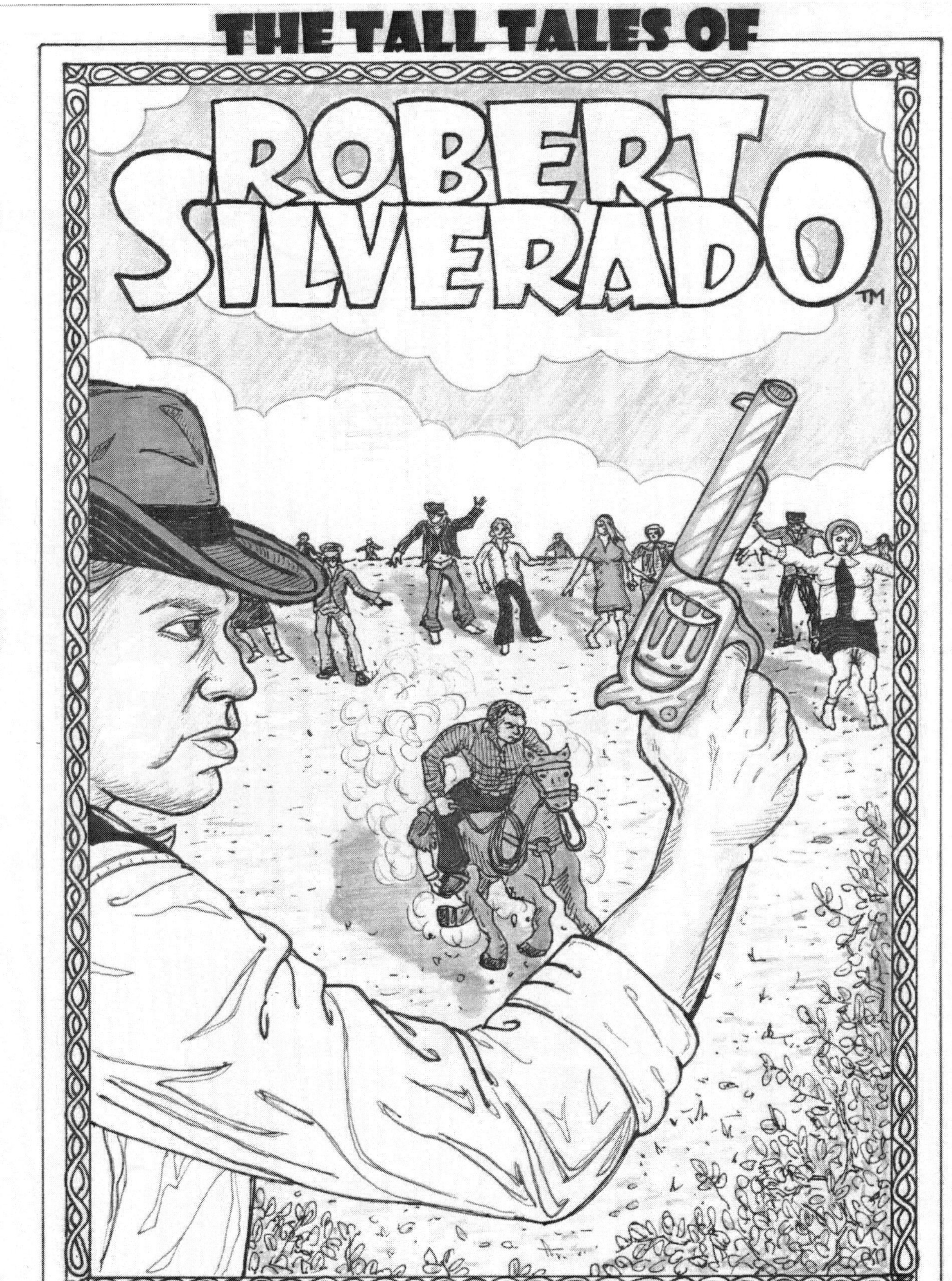
THE TALL TALES OF
ROBERT SILVERADO™

THE TALL TALES OF

ROBERT SILVERADO ™

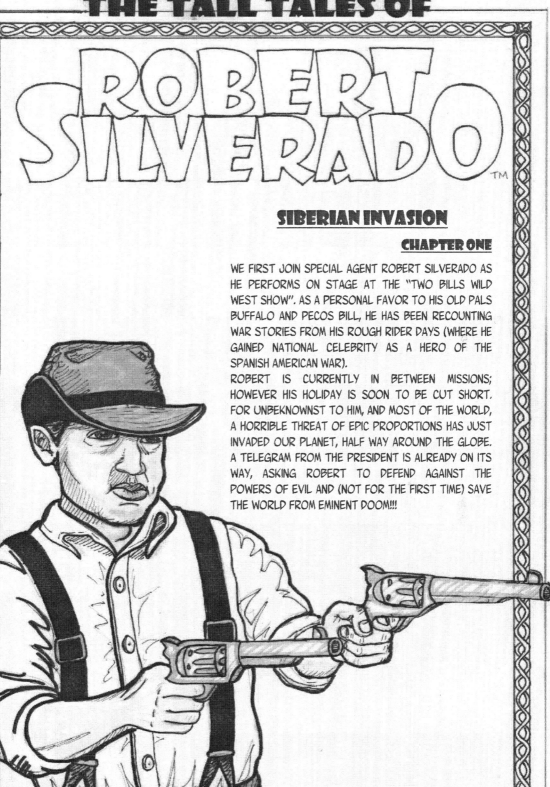

SIBERIAN INVASION

CHAPTER ONE

WE FIRST JOIN SPECIAL AGENT ROBERT SILVERADO AS HE PERFORMS ON STAGE AT THE "TWO BILLS WILD WEST SHOW". AS A PERSONAL FAVOR TO HIS OLD PALS BUFFALO AND PECOS BILL, HE HAS BEEN RECOUNTING WAR STORIES FROM HIS ROUGH RIDER DAYS (WHERE HE GAINED NATIONAL CELEBRITY AS A HERO OF THE SPANISH AMERICAN WAR).

ROBERT IS CURRENTLY IN BETWEEN MISSIONS; HOWEVER HIS HOLIDAY IS SOON TO BE CUT SHORT. FOR UNBEKNOWNST TO HIM, AND MOST OF THE WORLD, A HORRIBLE THREAT OF EPIC PROPORTIONS HAS JUST INVADED OUR PLANET, HALF WAY AROUND THE GLOBE. A TELEGRAM FROM THE PRESIDENT IS ALREADY ON ITS WAY, ASKING ROBERT TO DEFEND AGAINST THE POWERS OF EVIL AND (NOT FOR THE FIRST TIME) SAVE THE WORLD FROM EMINENT DOOM!!!

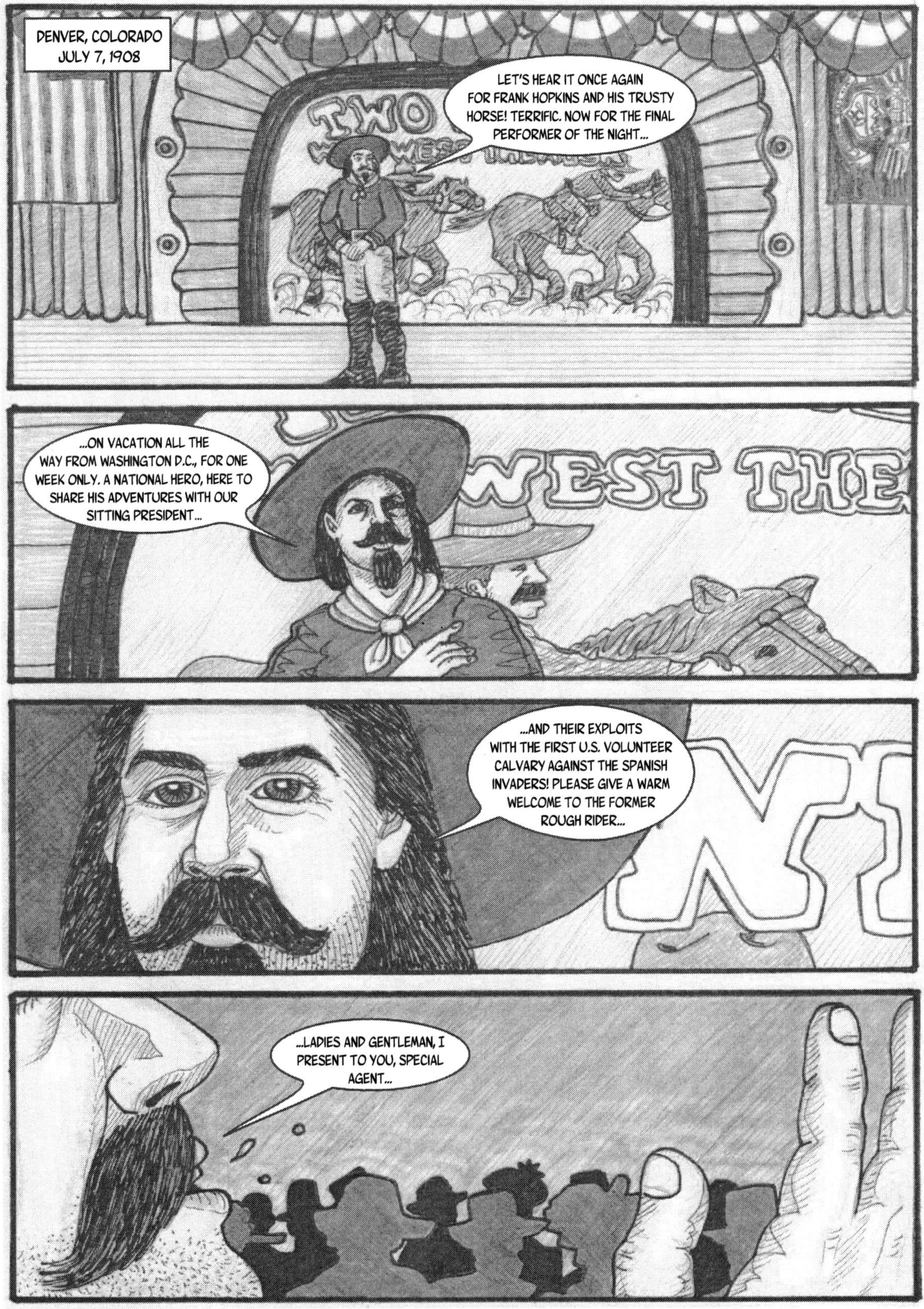
DENVER, COLORADO
JULY 7, 1908
LET'S HEAR IT ONCE AGAIN FOR FRANK HOPKINS AND HIS TRUSTY HORSE! TERRIFIC. NOW FOR THE FINAL PERFORMER OF THE NIGHT...
TWO
...ON VACATION ALL THE WAY FROM WASHINGTON D.C., FOR ONE WEEK ONLY. A NATIONAL HERO, HERE TO SHARE HIS ADVENTURES WITH OUR SITTING PRESIDENT...
WEST THE
...AND THEIR EXPLOITS WITH THE FIRST U.S. VOLUNTEER CALVARY AGAINST THE SPANISH INVADERS! PLEASE GIVE A WARM WELCOME TO THE FORMER ROUGH RIDER...
...LADIES AND GENTLEMAN, I PRESENT TO YOU, SPECIAL AGENT...

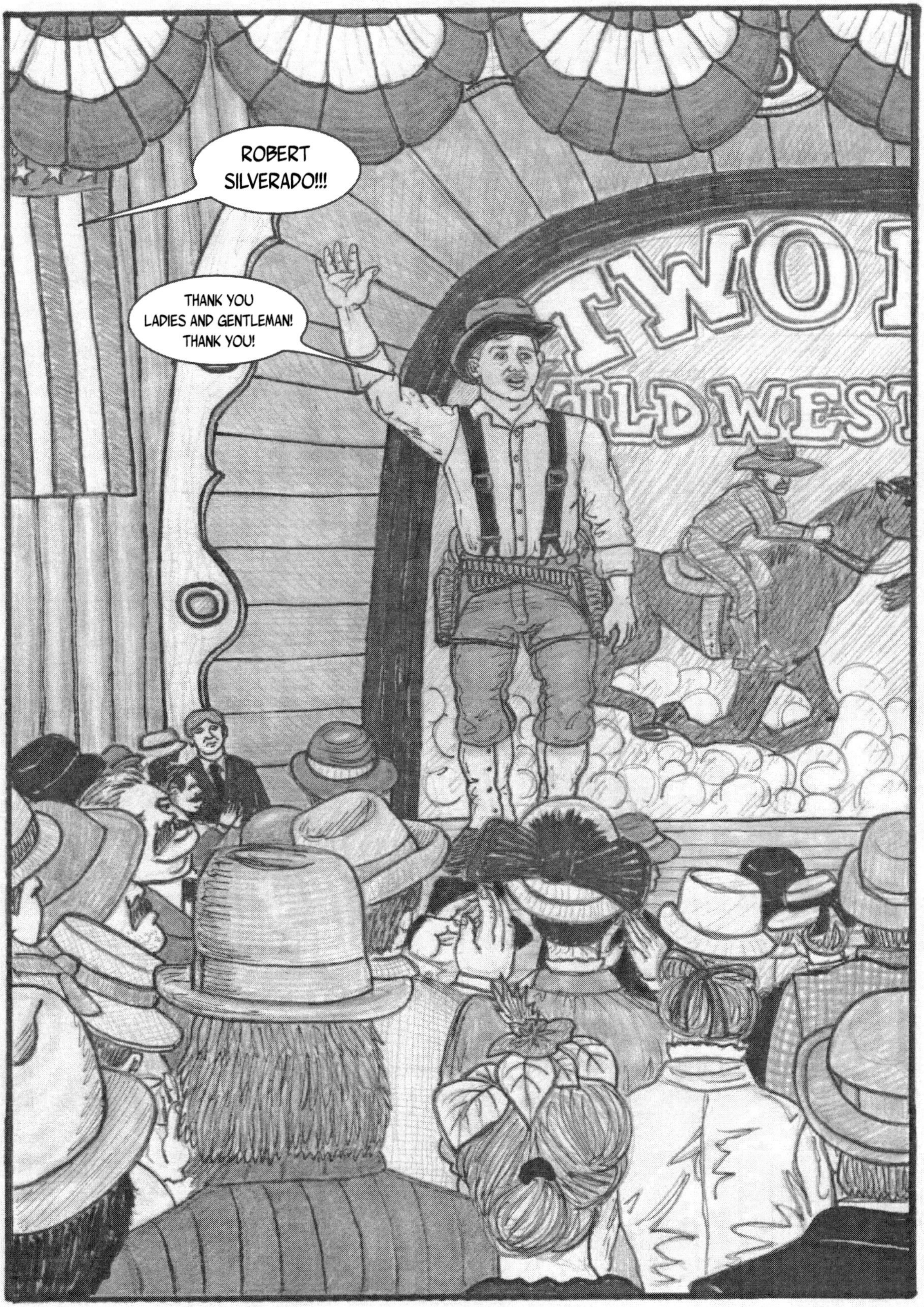
ROBERT SILVERADO!!!
THANK YOU LADIES AND GENTLEMAN! THANK YOU!
WILD WEST

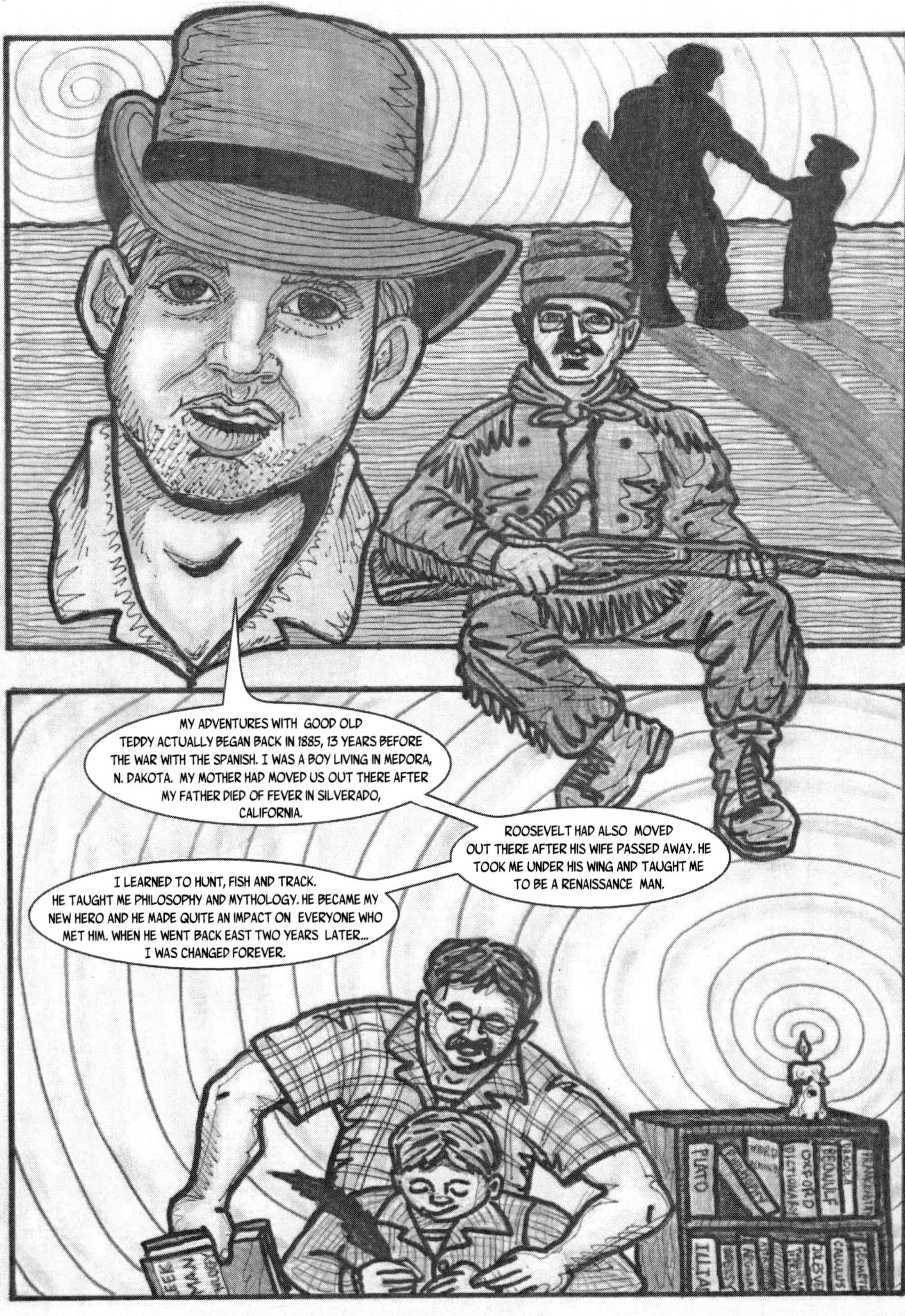
MY ADVENTURES WITH GOOD OLD TEDDY ACTUALLY BEGAN BACK IN 1885, 13 YEARS BEFORE THE WAR WITH THE SPANISH. I WAS A BOY LIVING IN MEDORA, N. DAKOTA. MY MOTHER HAD MOVED US OUT THERE AFTER MY FATHER DIED OF FEVER IN SILVERADO, CALIFORNIA.
ROOSEVELT HAD ALSO MOVED OUT THERE AFTER HIS WIFE PASSED AWAY. HE TOOK ME UNDER HIS WING AND TAUGHT ME TO BE A RENAISSANCE MAN.
I LEARNED TO HUNT, FISH AND TRACK. HE TAUGHT ME PHILOSOPHY AND MYTHOLOGY. HE BECAME MY NEW HERO AND HE MADE QUITE AN IMPACT ON EVERYONE WHO MET HIM. WHEN HE WENT BACK EAST TWO YEARS LATER... I WAS CHANGED FOREVER.
PLATO
OXFORD DICTIONARY
BEOWULF

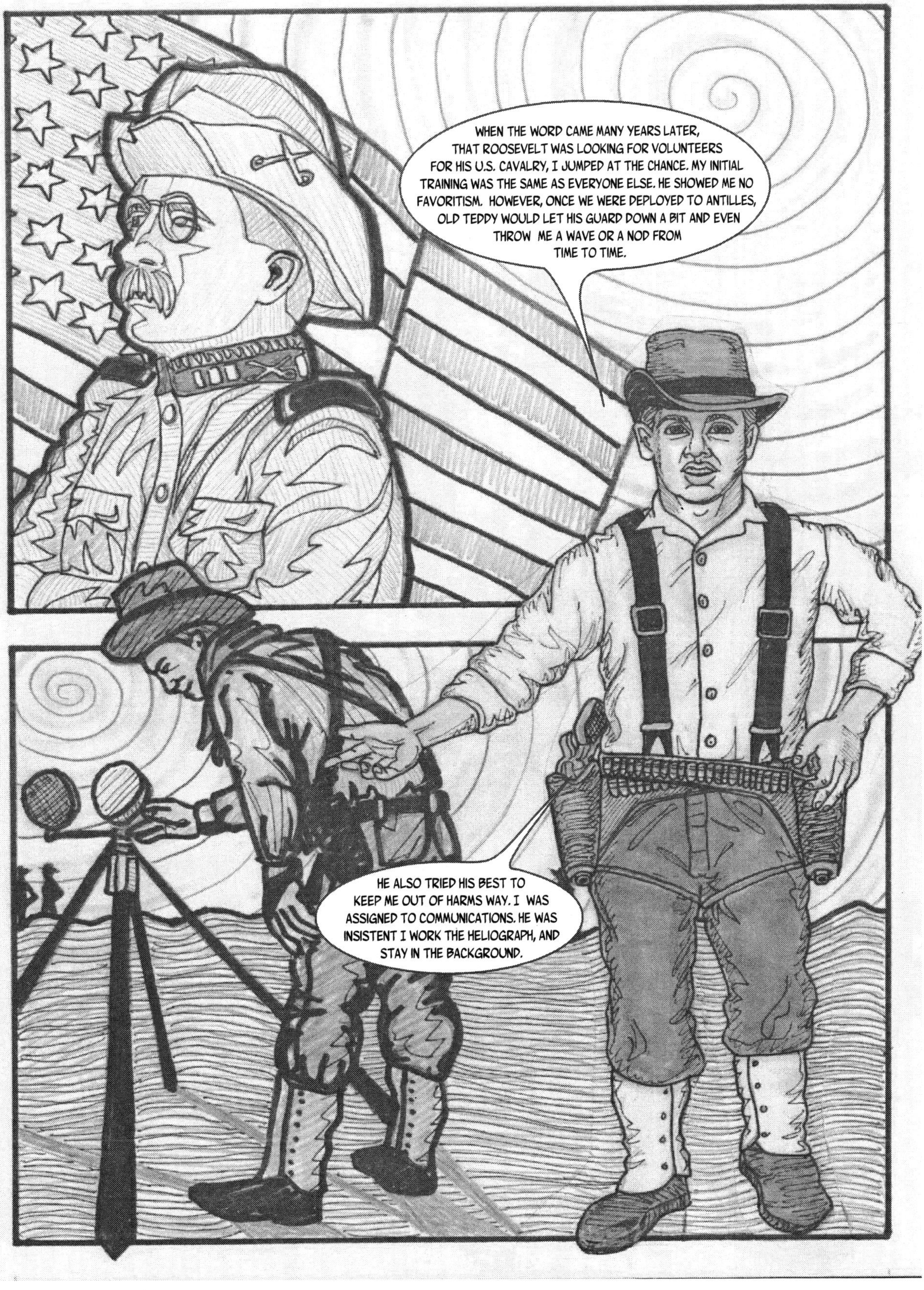
WHEN THE WORD CAME MANY YEARS LATER, THAT ROOSEVELT WAS LOOKING FOR VOLUNTEERS FOR HIS U.S. CAVALRY, I JUMPED AT THE CHANCE. MY INITIAL TRAINING WAS THE SAME AS EVERYONE ELSE. HE SHOWED ME NO FAVORITISM. HOWEVER, ONCE WE WERE DEPLOYED TO ANTILLES, OLD TEDDY WOULD LET HIS GUARD DOWN A BIT AND EVEN THROW ME A WAVE OR A NOD FROM TIME TO TIME.
HE ALSO TRIED HIS BEST TO KEEP ME OUT OF HARMS WAY. I WAS ASSIGNED TO COMMUNICATIONS. HE WAS INSISTENT I WORK THE HELIOGRAPH, AND STAY IN THE BACKGROUND.

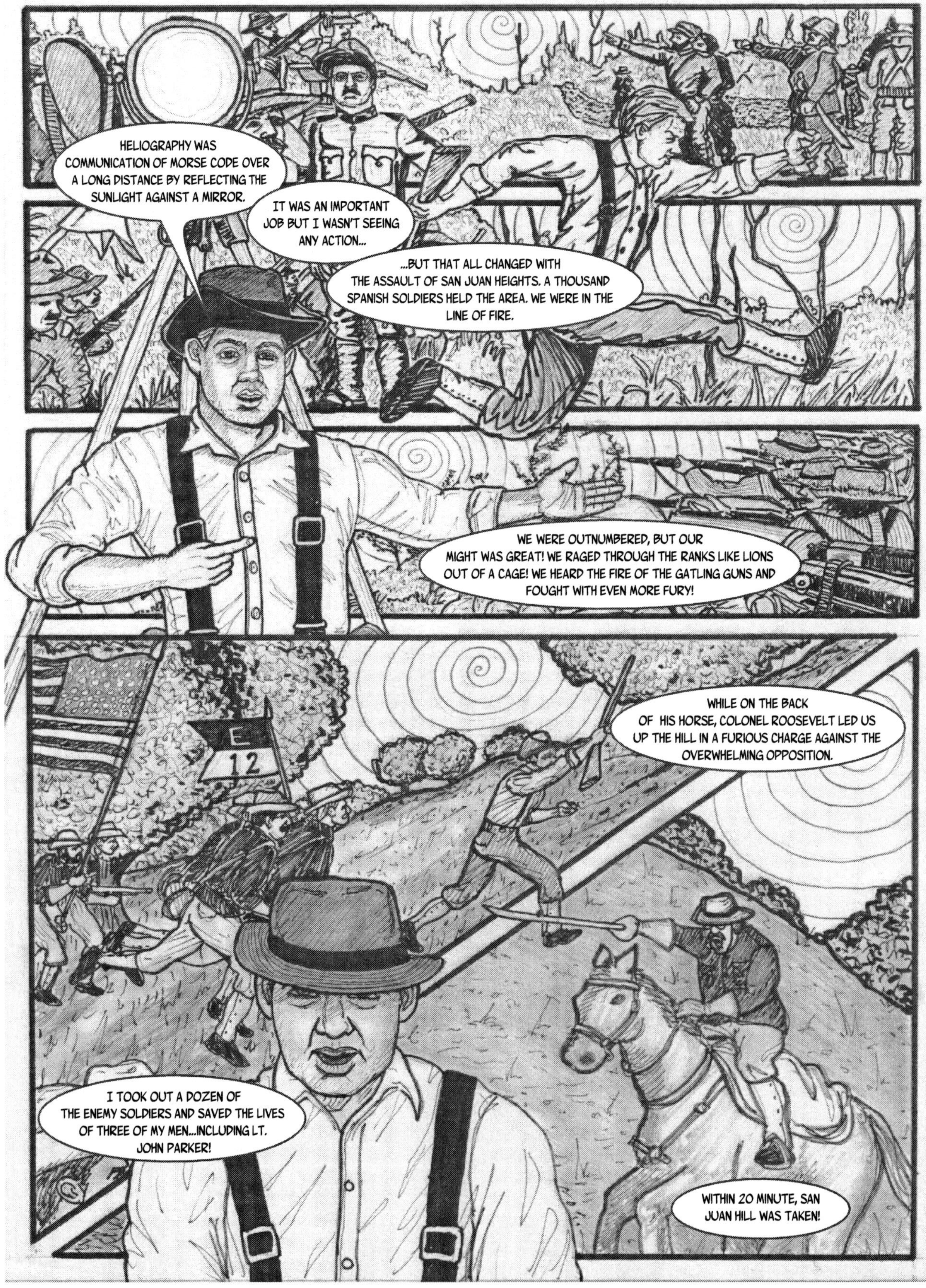

HELIOGRAPHY WAS COMMUNICATION OF MORSE CODE OVER A LONG DISTANCE BY REFLECTING THE SUNLIGHT AGAINST A MIRROR.
IT WAS AN IMPORTANT JOB BUT I WASN'T SEEING ANY ACTION...
...BUT THAT ALL CHANGED WITH THE ASSAULT OF SAN JUAN HEIGHTS. A THOUSAND SPANISH SOLDIERS HELD THE AREA. WE WERE IN THE LINE OF FIRE.
WE WERE OUTNUMBERED, BUT OUR MIGHT WAS GREAT! WE RAGED THROUGH THE RANKS LIKE LIONS OUT OF A CAGE! WE HEARD THE FIRE OF THE GATLING GUNS AND FOUGHT WITH EVEN MORE FURY!
E
12
WHILE ON THE BACK OF HIS HORSE, COLONEL ROOSEVELT LED US UP THE HILL IN A FURIOUS CHARGE AGAINST THE OVERWHELMING OPPOSITION.
I TOOK OUT A DOZEN OF THE ENEMY SOLDIERS AND SAVED THE LIVES OF THREE OF MY MEN...INCLUDING LT. JOHN PARKER!
WITHIN 20 MINUTE, SAN JUAN HILL WAS TAKEN!

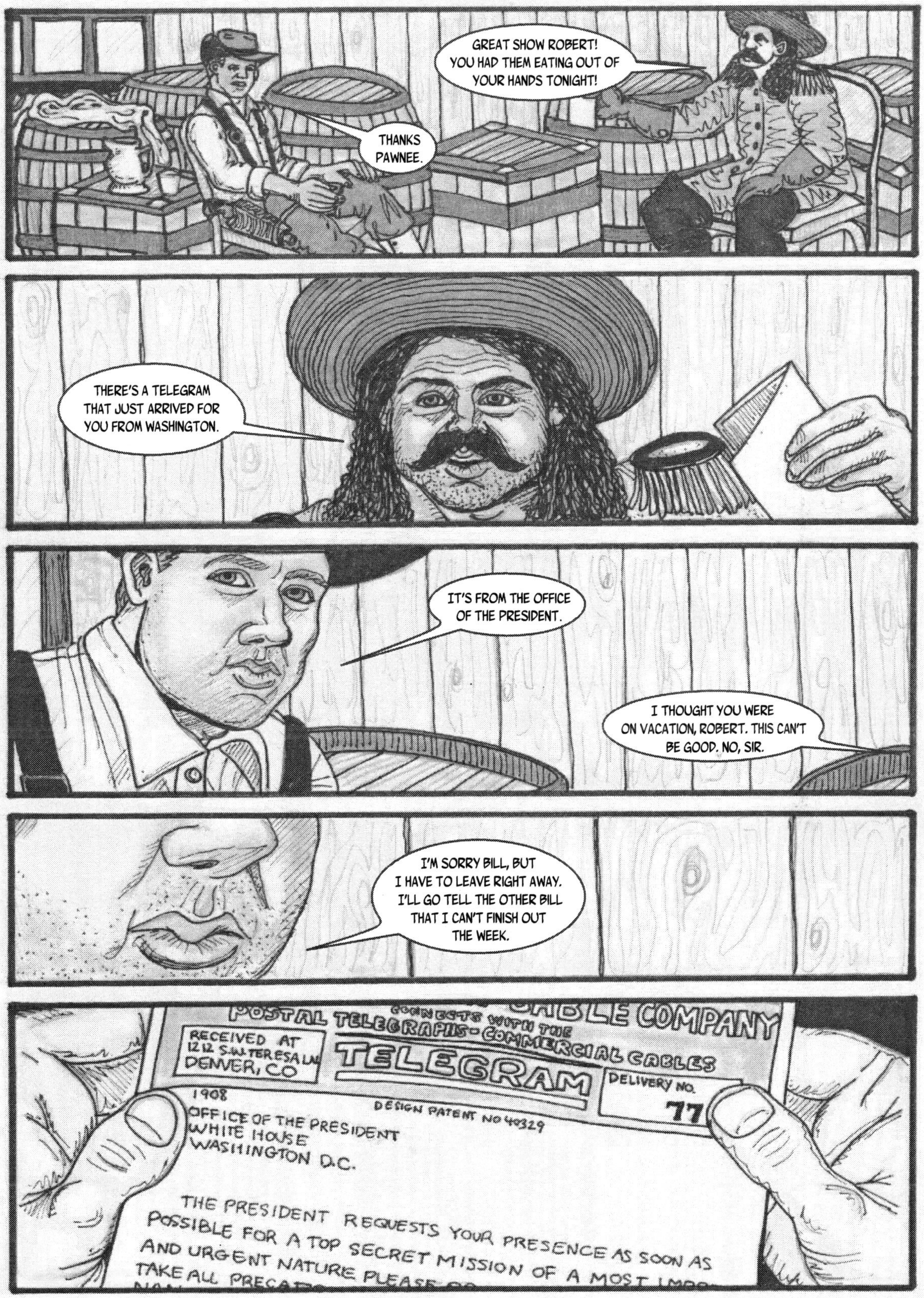
GREAT SHOW ROBERT! YOU HAD THEM EATING OUT OF YOUR HANDS TONIGHT!
THANKS PAWNEE.
THERE'S A TELEGRAM THAT JUST ARRIVED FOR YOU FROM WASHINGTON.
IT'S FROM THE OFFICE OF THE PRESIDENT.
I THOUGHT YOU WERE ON VACATION, ROBERT. THIS CAN'T BE GOOD. NO, SIR.
I'M SORRY BILL, BUT I HAVE TO LEAVE RIGHT AWAY. I'LL GO TELL THE OTHER BILL THAT I CAN'T FINISH OUT THE WEEK.
POSTAL
CABLES
RECEIVED AT
DENVER, CO
TELEGRAM
DELIVERY NO.
77
1908
DESIGN PATENT NO 40329
OFFICE OF THE PRESIDENT
WHITE HOUSE
WASHINGTON D.C.
THE PRESIDENT REQUESTS YOUR PRESENCE AS SOON AS
POSSIBLE FOR A TOP SECRET MISSION OF A MOST
AND URGENT NATURE
TAKE ALL

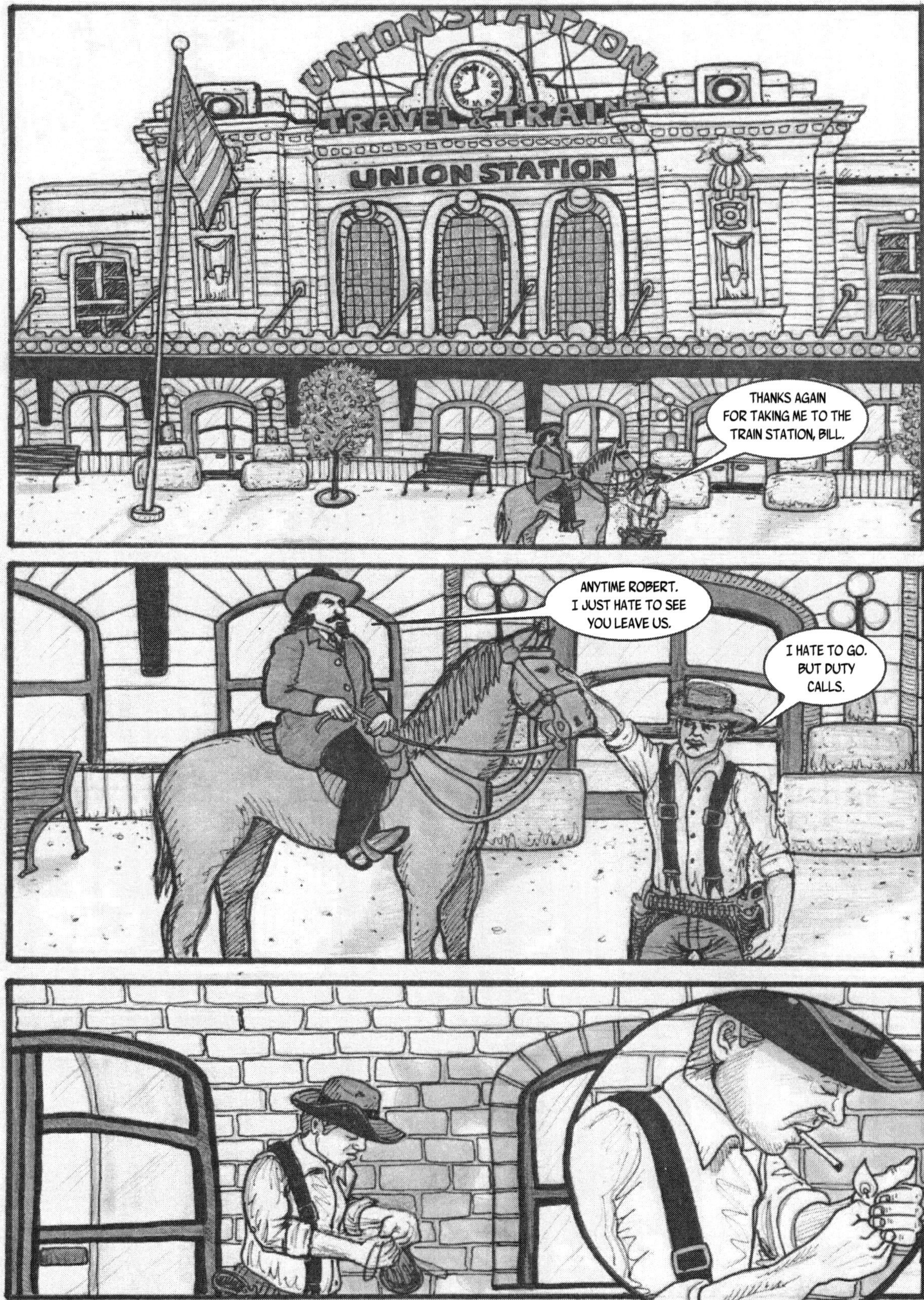
UNION STATION
TRAVEL & TRAIN
UNION STATION
THANKS AGAIN FOR TAKING ME TO THE TRAIN STATION, BILL.
ANYTIME ROBERT. I JUST HATE TO SEE YOU LEAVE US.
I HATE TO GO. BUT DUTY CALLS.

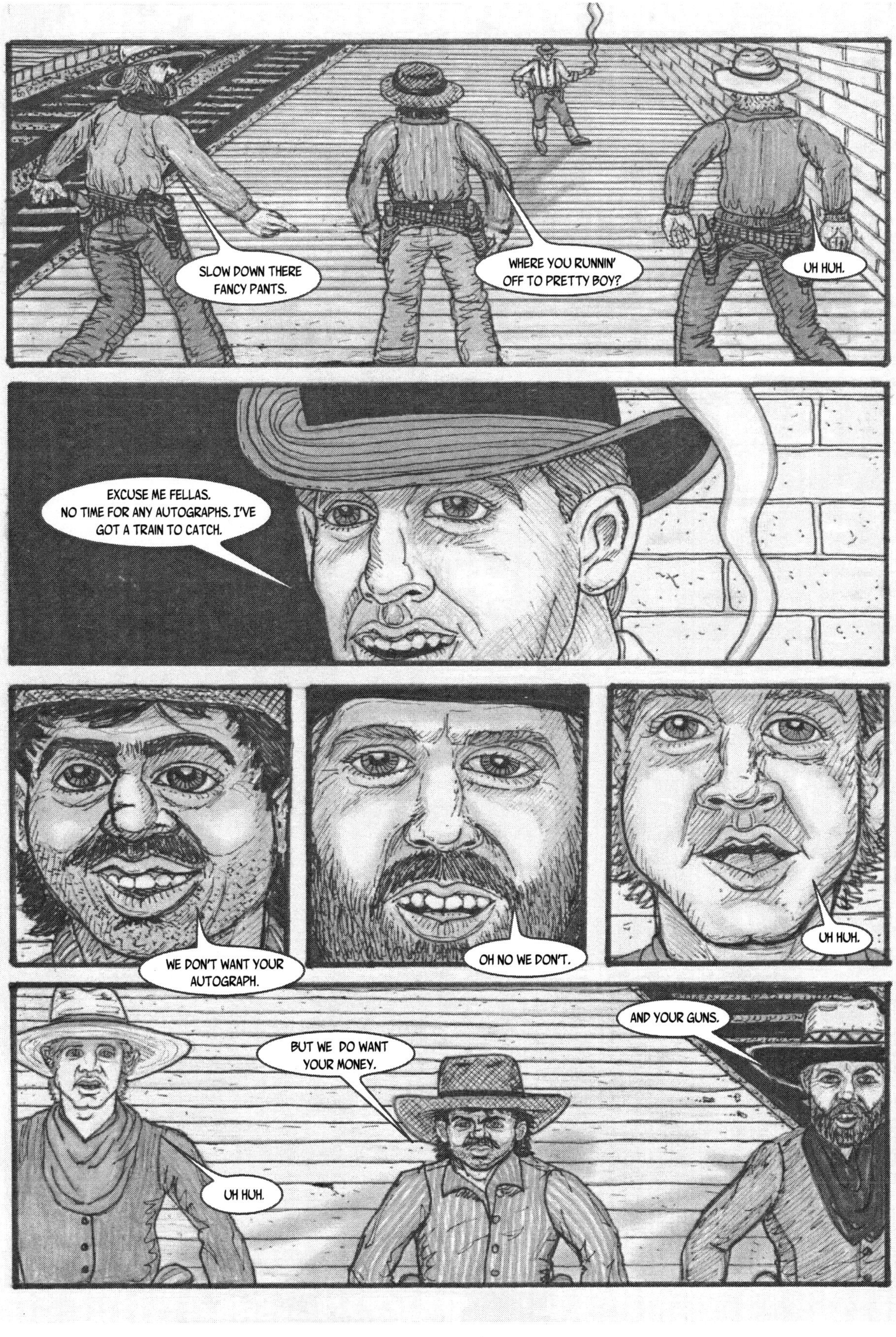
SLOW DOWN THERE FANCY PANTS.
WHERE YOU RUNNIN' OFF TO PRETTY BOY?
UH HUH.
EXCUSE ME FELLAS. NO TIME FOR ANY AUTOGRAPHS. I'VE GOT A TRAIN TO CATCH.
WE DON'T WANT YOUR AUTOGRAPH.
OH NO WE DON'T.
UH HUH.
BUT WE DO WANT YOUR MONEY.
AND YOUR GUNS.
UH HUH.

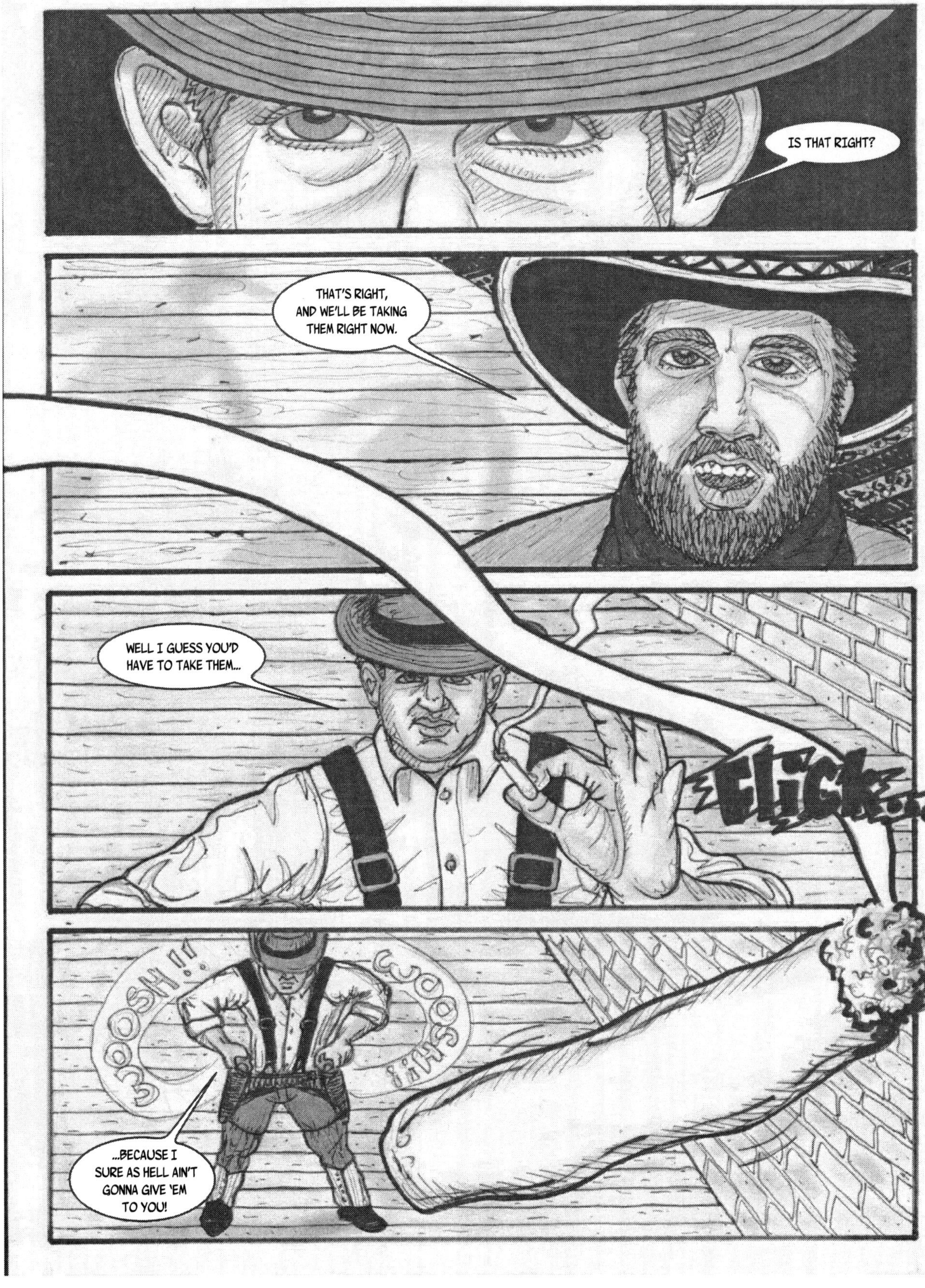
IS THAT RIGHT?
THAT'S RIGHT, AND WE'LL BE TAKING THEM RIGHT NOW.
WELL I GUESS YOU'D HAVE TO TAKE THEM...
FLICK
WOOSH !!
WOOSH!!
...BECAUSE I SURE AS HELL AIN'T GONNA GIVE 'EM TO YOU!

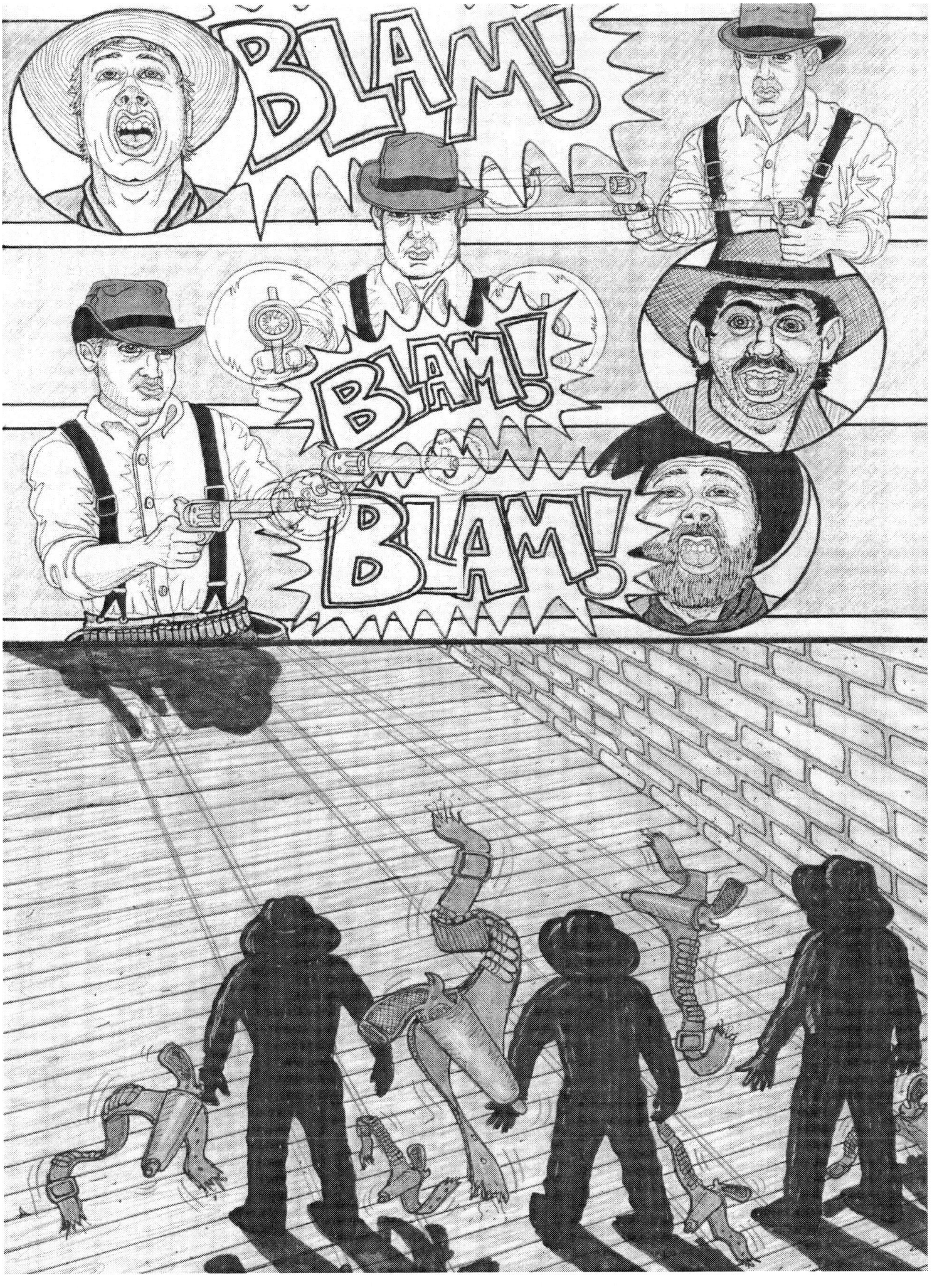
BLAM!
BLAM!
BLAM!

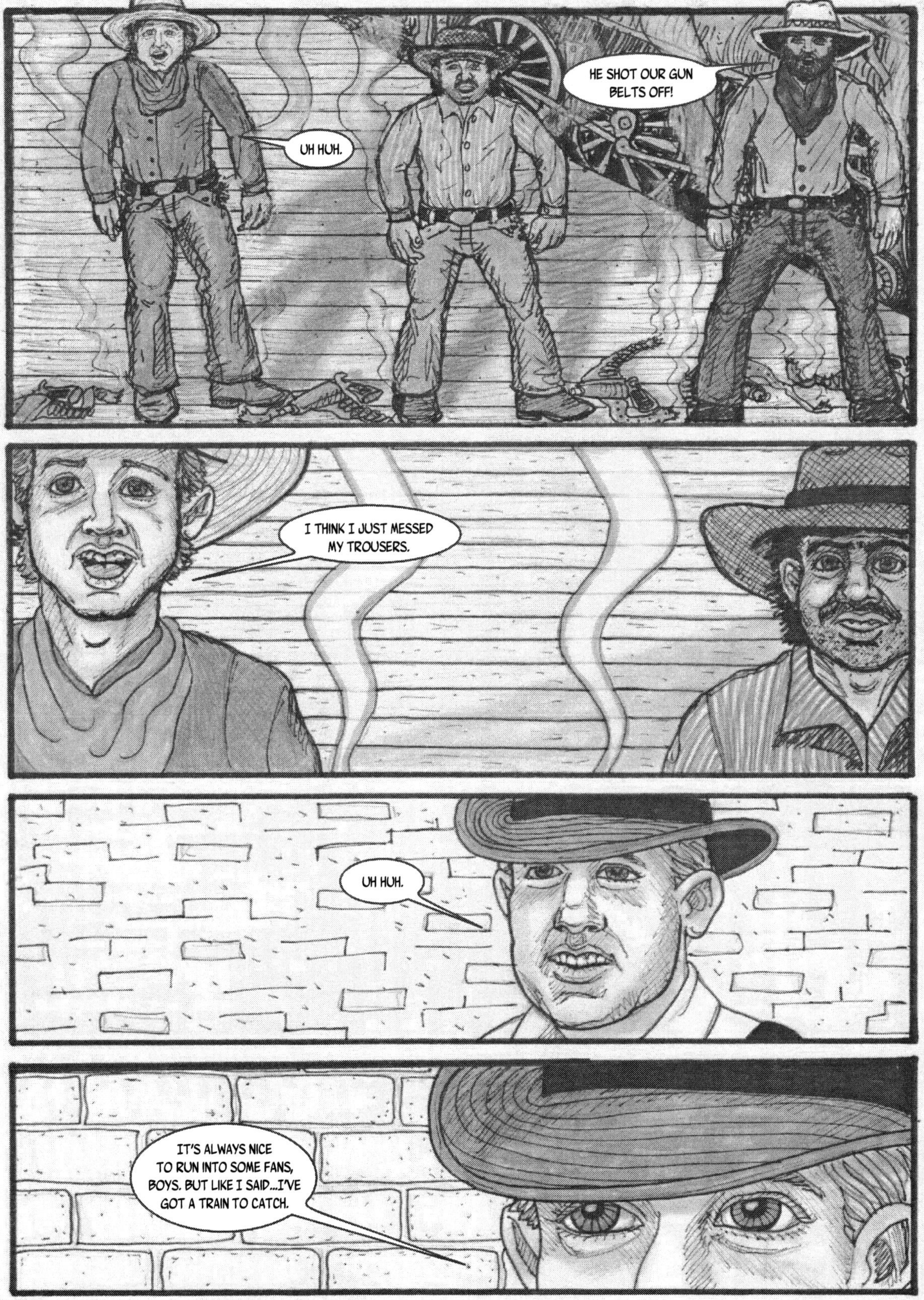
HE SHOT OUR GUN BELTS OFF!
UH HUH.
I THINK I JUST MESSED MY TROUSERS.
UH HUH.
IT'S ALWAYS NICE TO RUN INTO SOME FANS, BOYS. BUT LIKE I SAID...I'VE GOT A TRAIN TO CATCH.

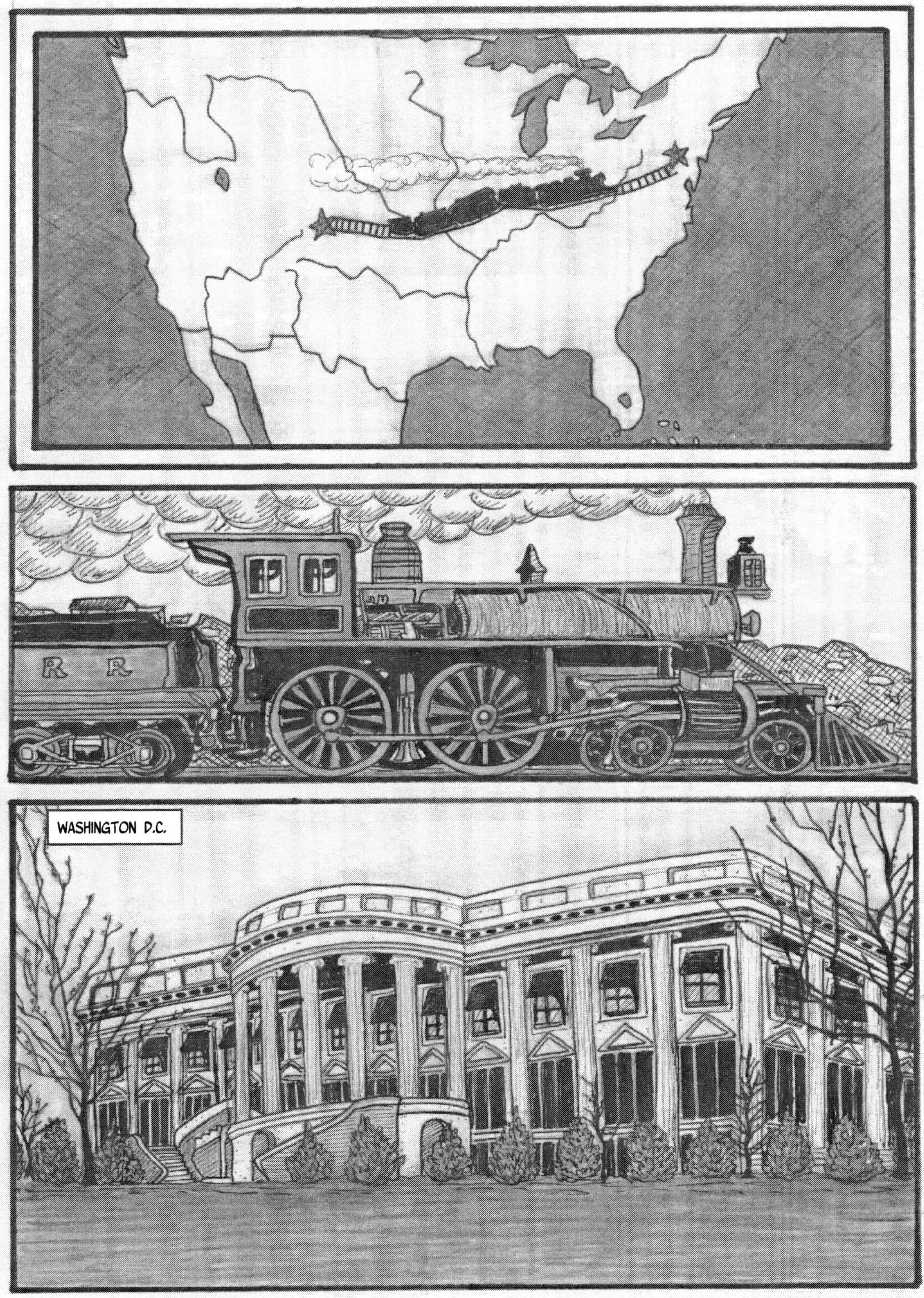
R R
WASHINGTON D.C.

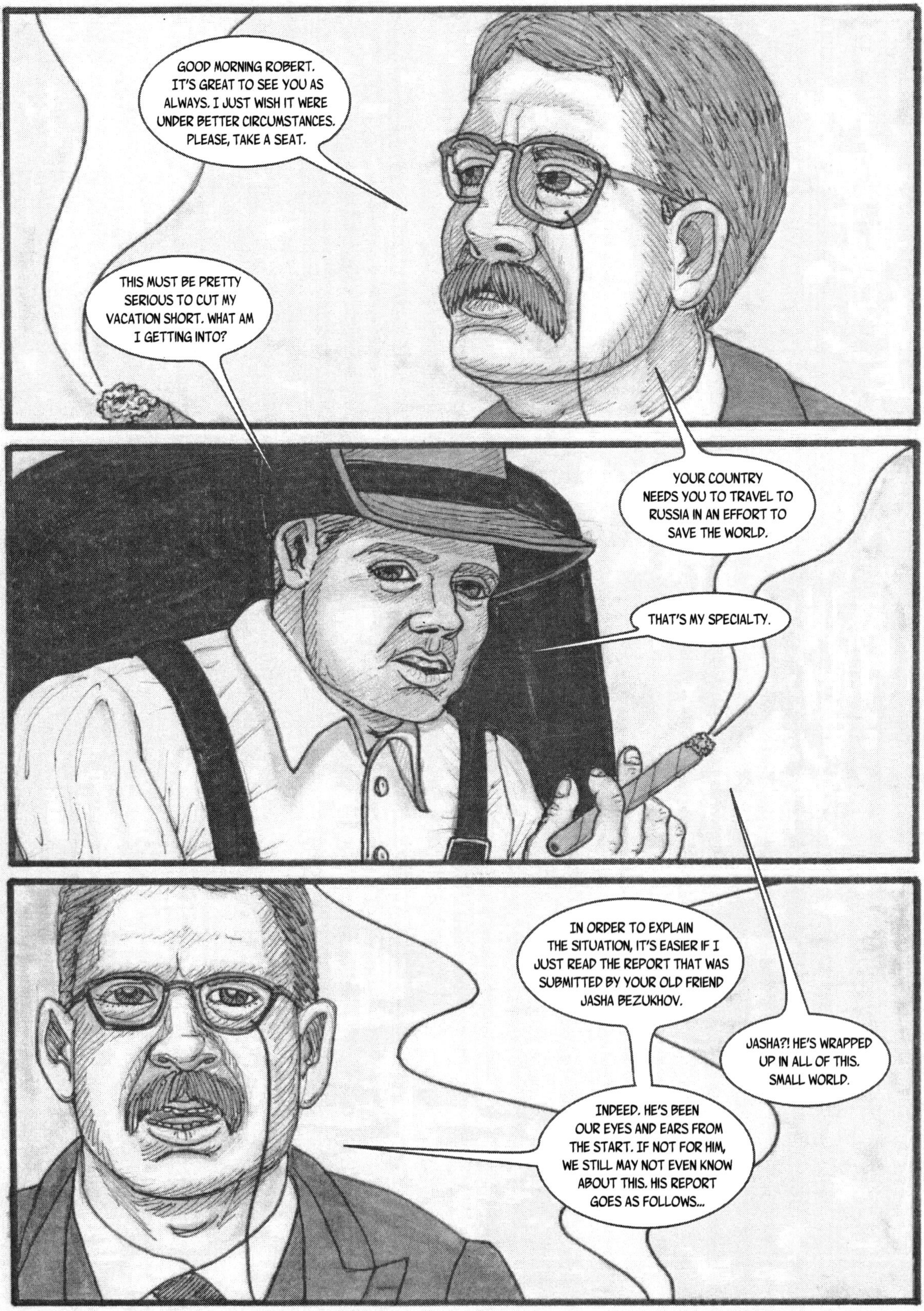
GOOD MORNING ROBERT. IT'S GREAT TO SEE YOU AS ALWAYS. I JUST WISH IT WERE UNDER BETTER CIRCUMSTANCES. PLEASE, TAKE A SEAT.
THIS MUST BE PRETTY SERIOUS TO CUT MY VACATION SHORT. WHAT AM I GETTING INTO?
YOUR COUNTRY NEEDS YOU TO TRAVEL TO RUSSIA IN AN EFFORT TO SAVE THE WORLD.
THAT'S MY SPECIALTY.
IN ORDER TO EXPLAIN THE SITUATION, IT'S EASIER IF I JUST READ THE REPORT THAT WAS SUBMITTED BY YOUR OLD FRIEND JASHA BEZUKHOV.
JASHA?! HE'S WRAPPED UP IN ALL OF THIS. SMALL WORLD.
INDEED. HE'S BEEN OUR EYES AND EARS FROM THE START. IF NOT FOR HIM, WE STILL MAY NOT EVEN KNOW ABOUT THIS. HIS REPORT GOES AS FOLLOWS...

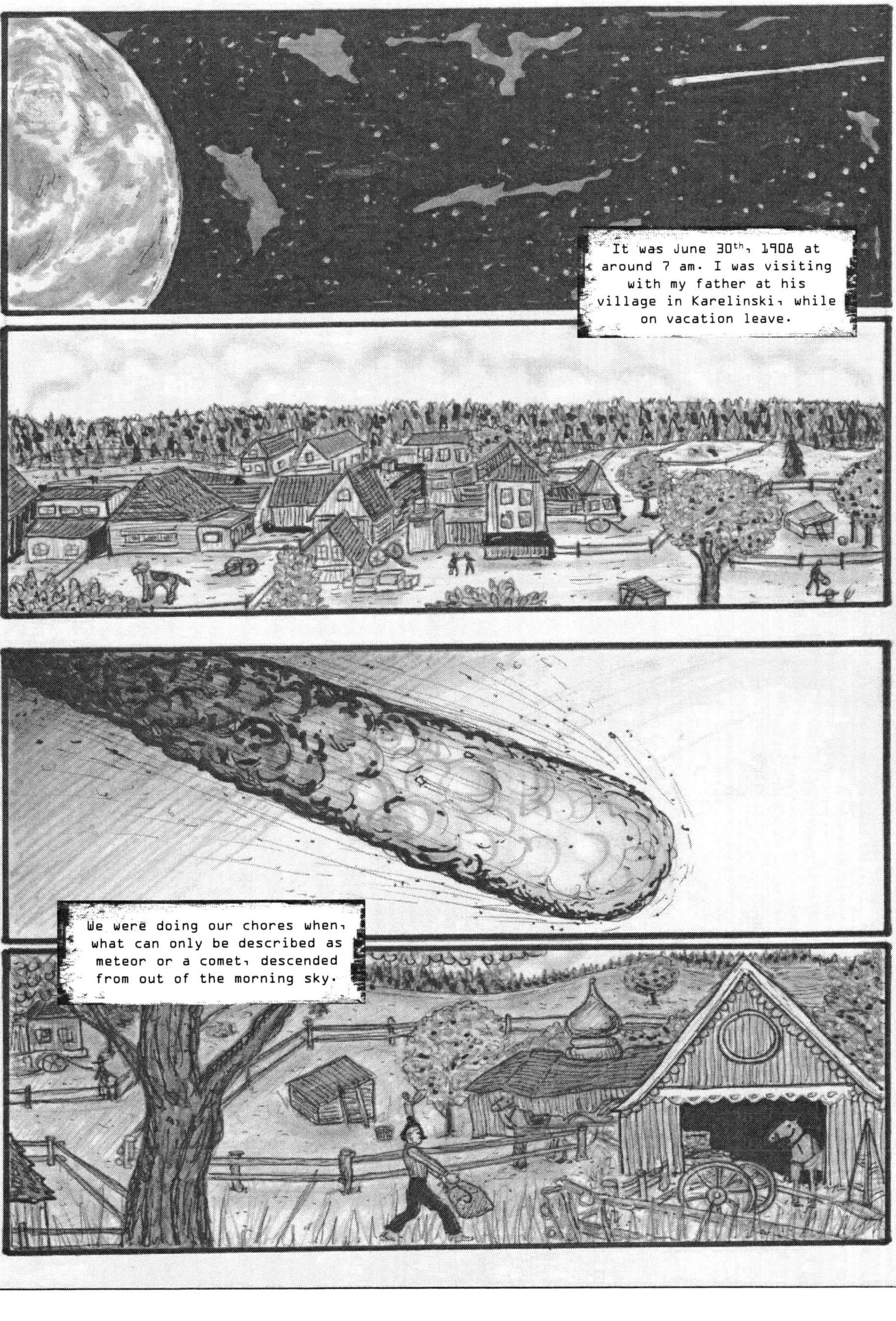
It was June 30th, 1908 at around 7 am. I was visiting with my father at his village in Karelinski, while on vacation leave.
We were doing our chores when, what can only be described as meteor or a comet, descended from out of the morning sky.

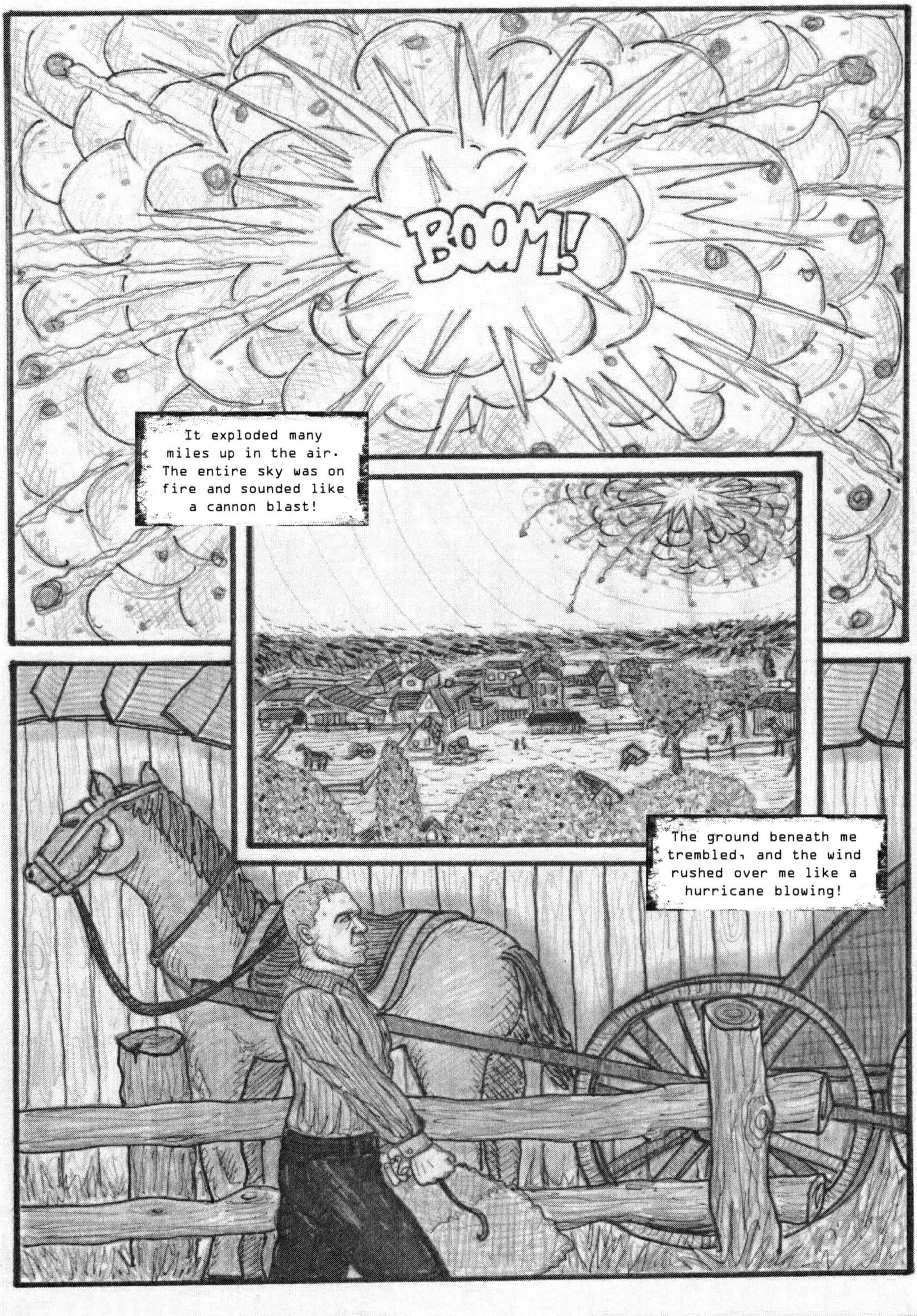
BOOM!
It exploded many miles up in the air. The entire sky was on fire and sounded like a cannon blast!
The ground beneath me trembled, and the wind rushed over me like a hurricane blowing!

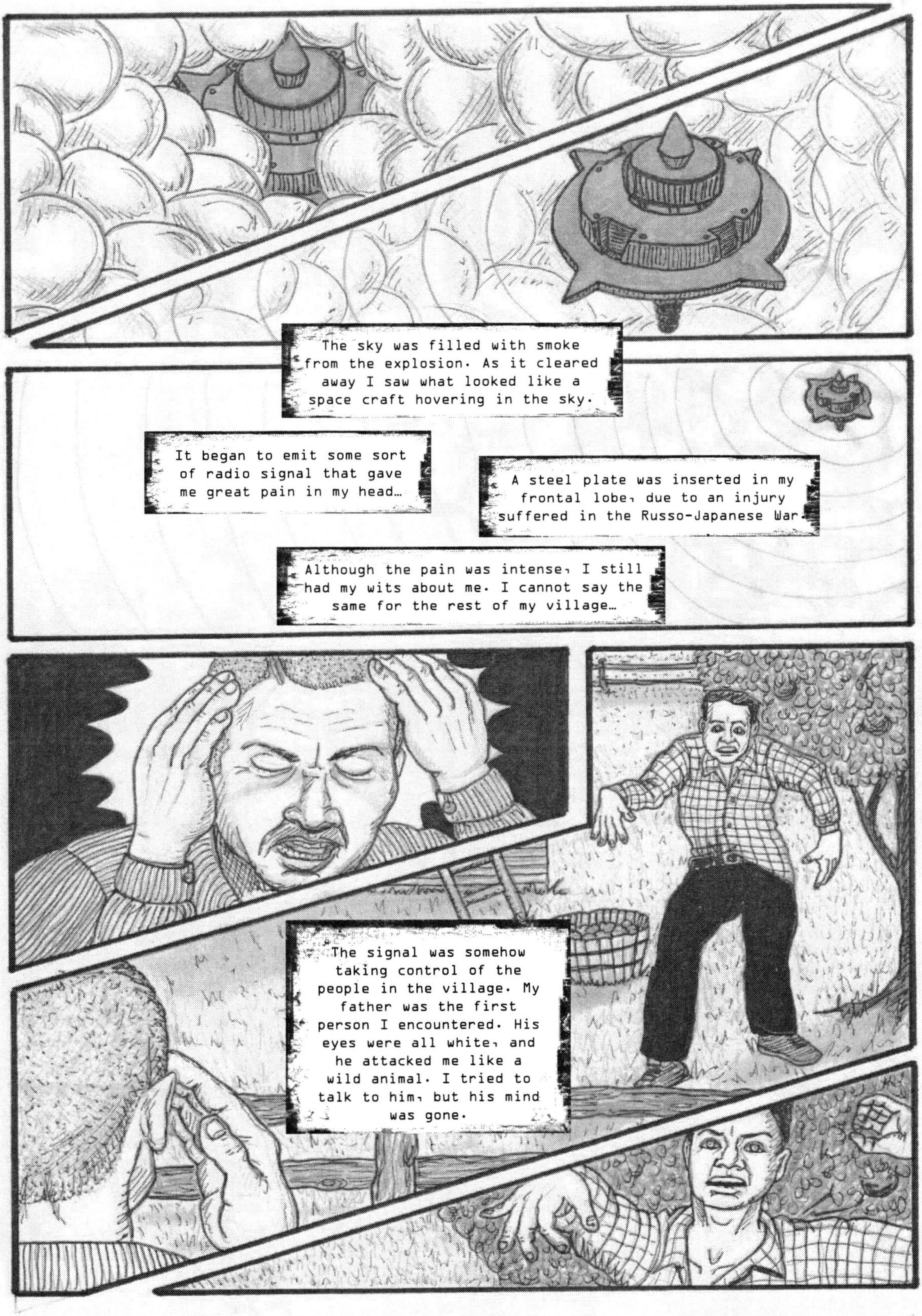
The sky was filled with smoke from the explosion. As it cleared away I saw what looked like a space craft hovering in the sky.
It began to emit some sort of radio signal that gave me great pain in my head...
A steel plate was inserted in my frontal lobe, due to an injury suffered in the Russo-Japanese War.
Although the pain was intense, I still had my wits about me. I cannot say the same for the rest of my village...
The signal was somehow taking control of the people in the village. My father was the first person I encountered. His eyes were all white, and he attacked me like a wild animal. I tried to talk to him, but his mind was gone.

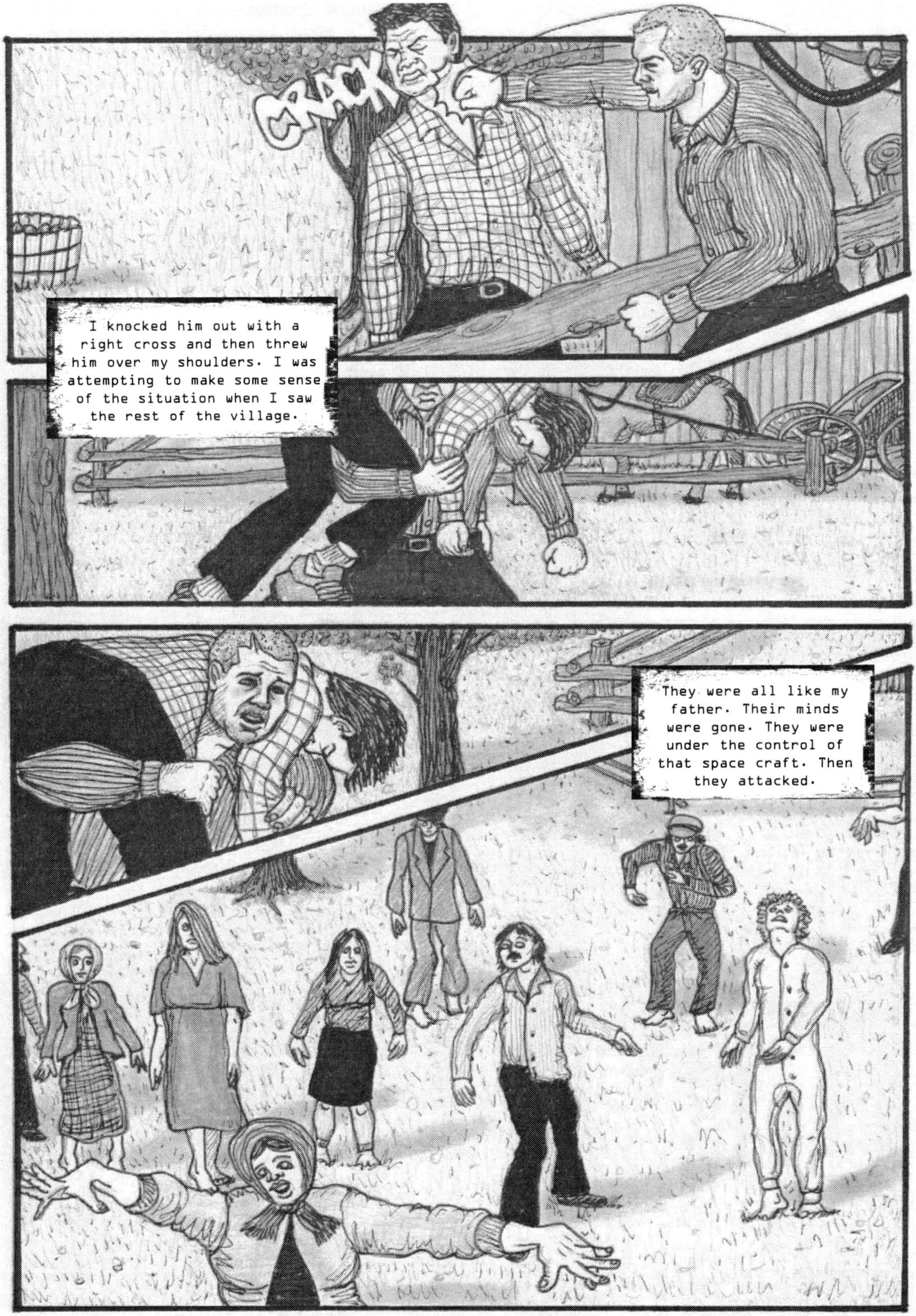
I knocked him out with a right cross and then threw him over my shoulders. I was attempting to make some sense of the situation when I saw the rest of the village.
They were all like my father. Their minds were gone. They were under the control of that space craft. Then they attacked.

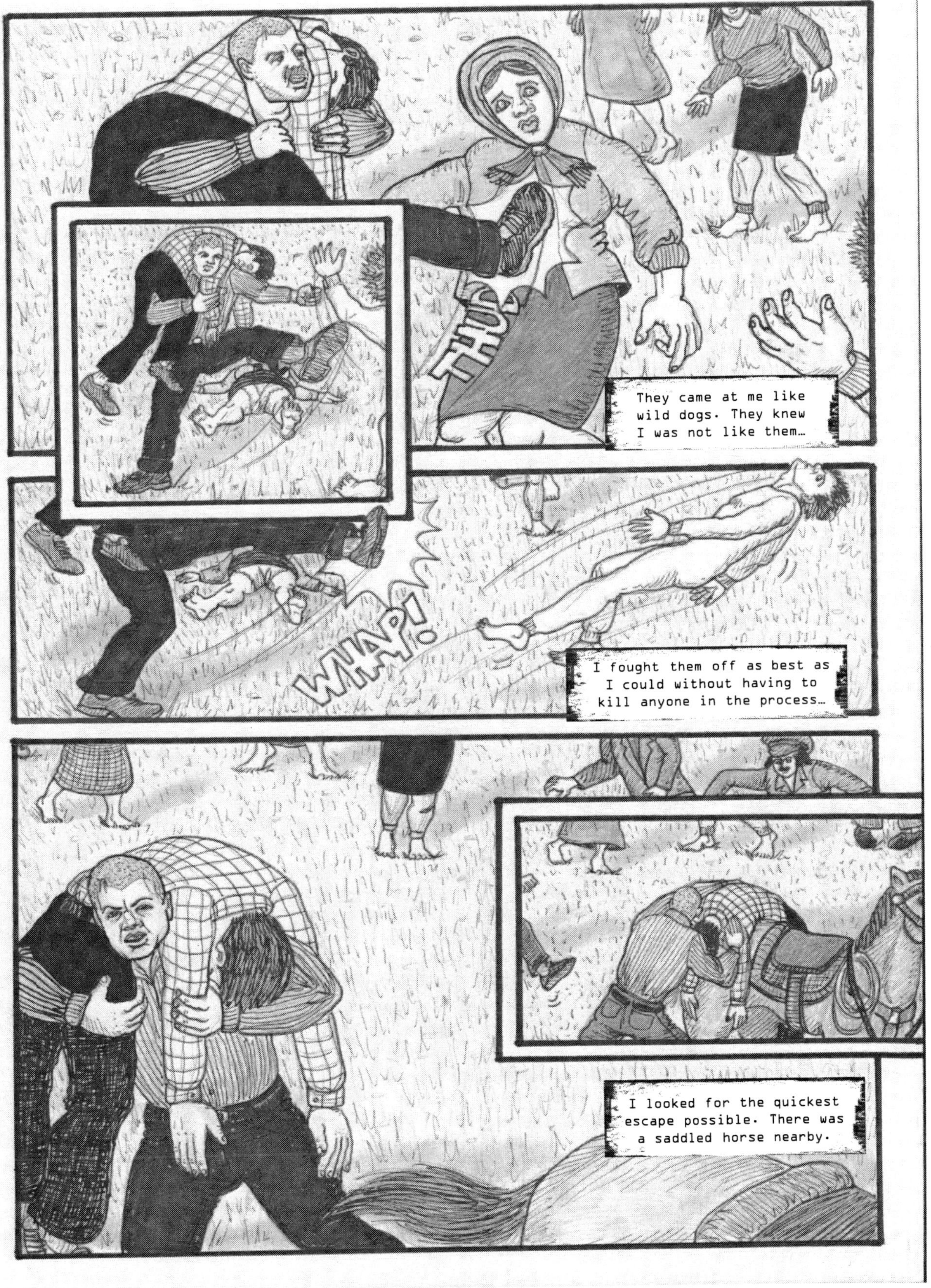
THUD
They came at me like wild dogs. They knew I was not like them…
WHAP!
I fought them off as best as I could without having to kill anyone in the process…
I looked for the quickest escape possible. There was a saddled horse nearby.

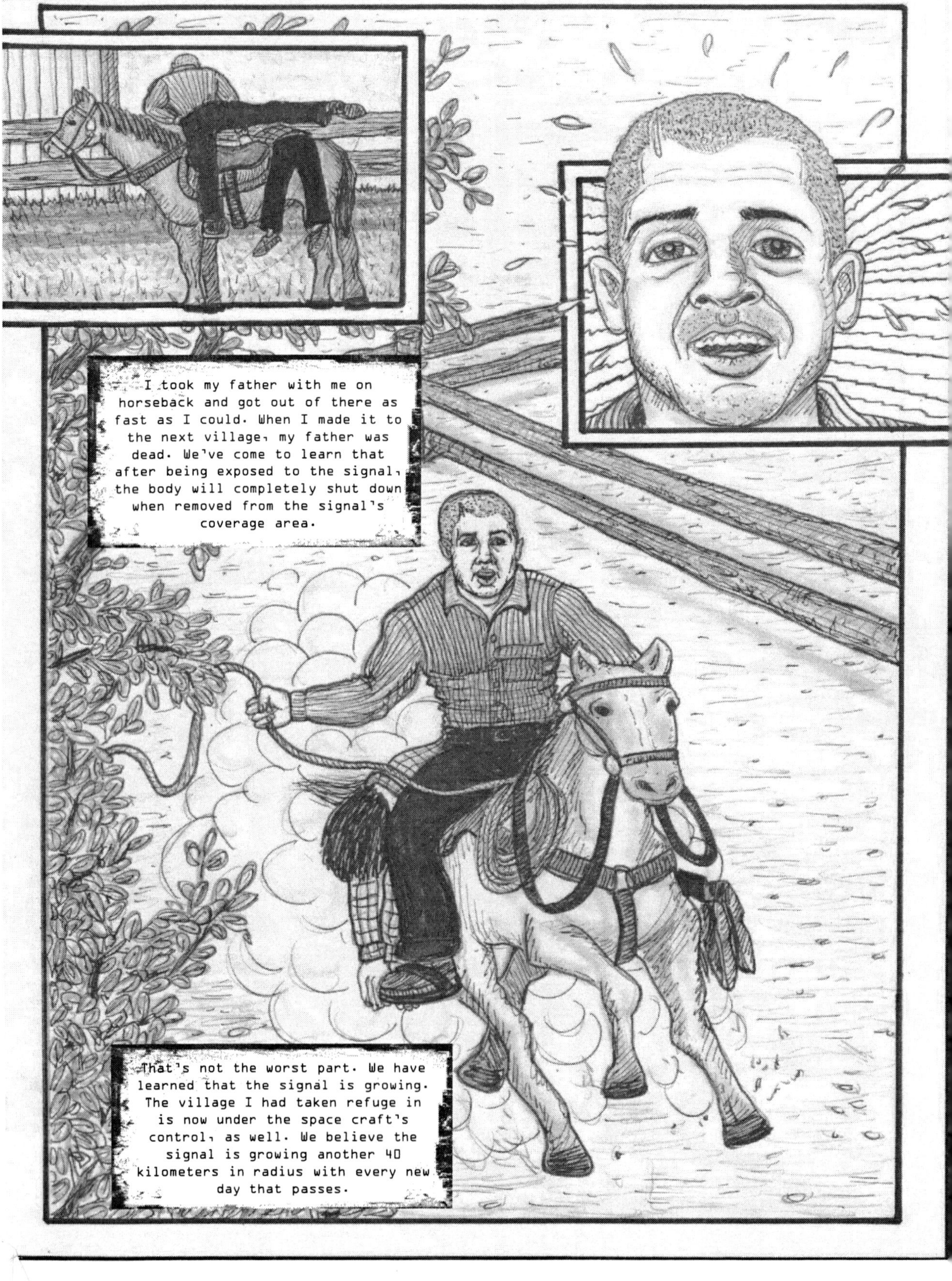
I took my father with me on horseback and got out of there as fast as I could. When I made it to the next village, my father was dead. We've come to learn that after being exposed to the signal, the body will completely shut down when removed from the signal's coverage area.
That's not the worst part. We have learned that the signal is growing. The village I had taken refuge in is now under the space craft's control, as well. We believe the signal is growing another 40 kilometers in radius with every new day that passes.

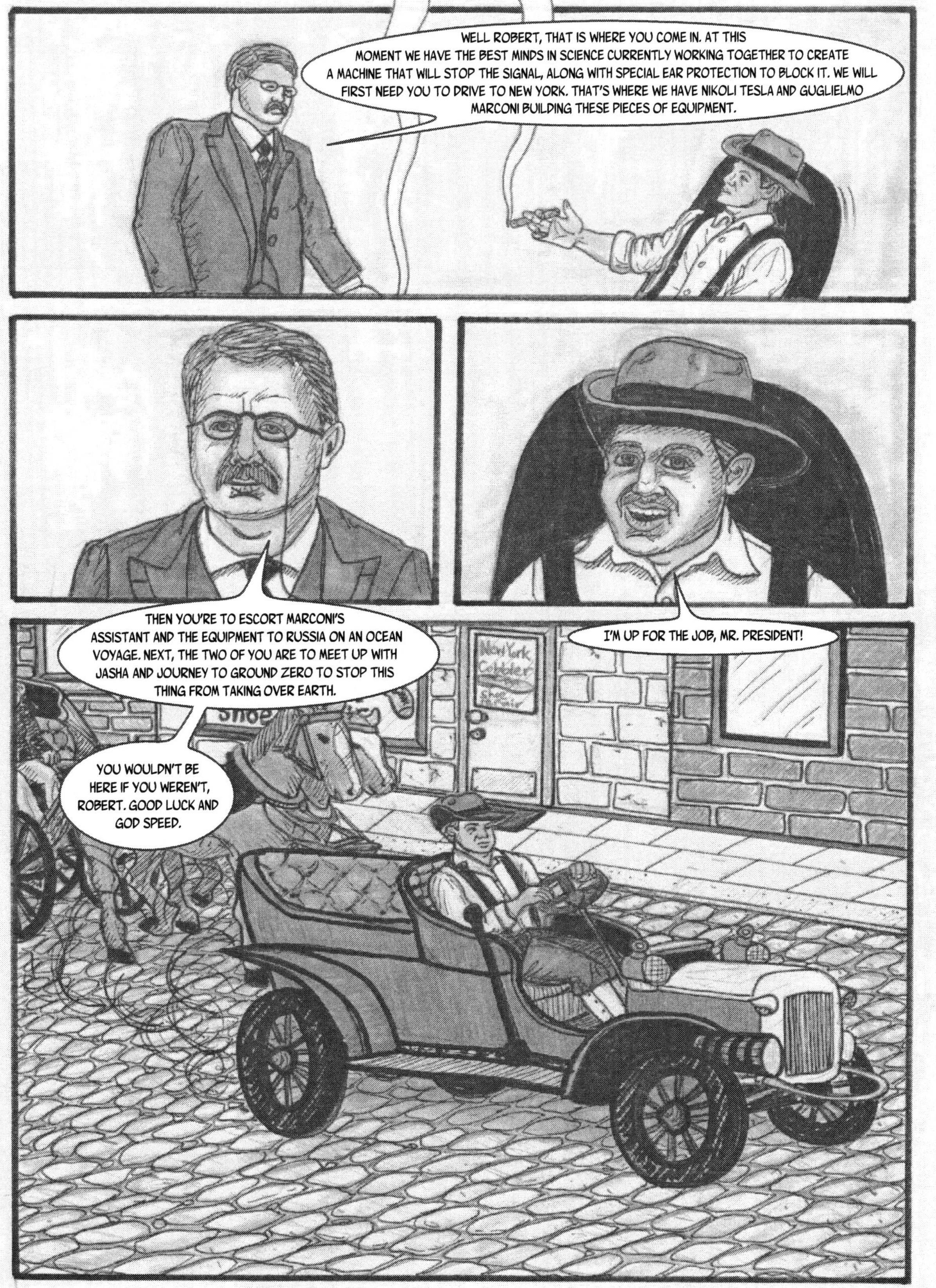
WELL ROBERT, THAT IS WHERE YOU COME IN. AT THIS MOMENT WE HAVE THE BEST MINDS IN SCIENCE CURRENTLY WORKING TOGETHER TO CREATE A MACHINE THAT WILL STOP THE SIGNAL, ALONG WITH SPECIAL EAR PROTECTION TO BLOCK IT. WE WILL FIRST NEED YOU TO DRIVE TO NEW YORK. THAT'S WHERE WE HAVE NIKOLI TESLA AND GUGLIELMO MARCONI BUILDING THESE PIECES OF EQUIPMENT.
THEN YOU'RE TO ESCORT MARCONI'S ASSISTANT AND THE EQUIPMENT TO RUSSIA ON AN OCEAN VOYAGE. NEXT, THE TWO OF YOU ARE TO MEET UP WITH JASHA AND JOURNEY TO GROUND ZERO TO STOP THIS THING FROM TAKING OVER EARTH.
I'M UP FOR THE JOB, MR. PRESIDENT!
YOU WOULDN'T BE HERE IF YOU WEREN'T, ROBERT. GOOD LUCK AND GOD SPEED.
New York Cobbler

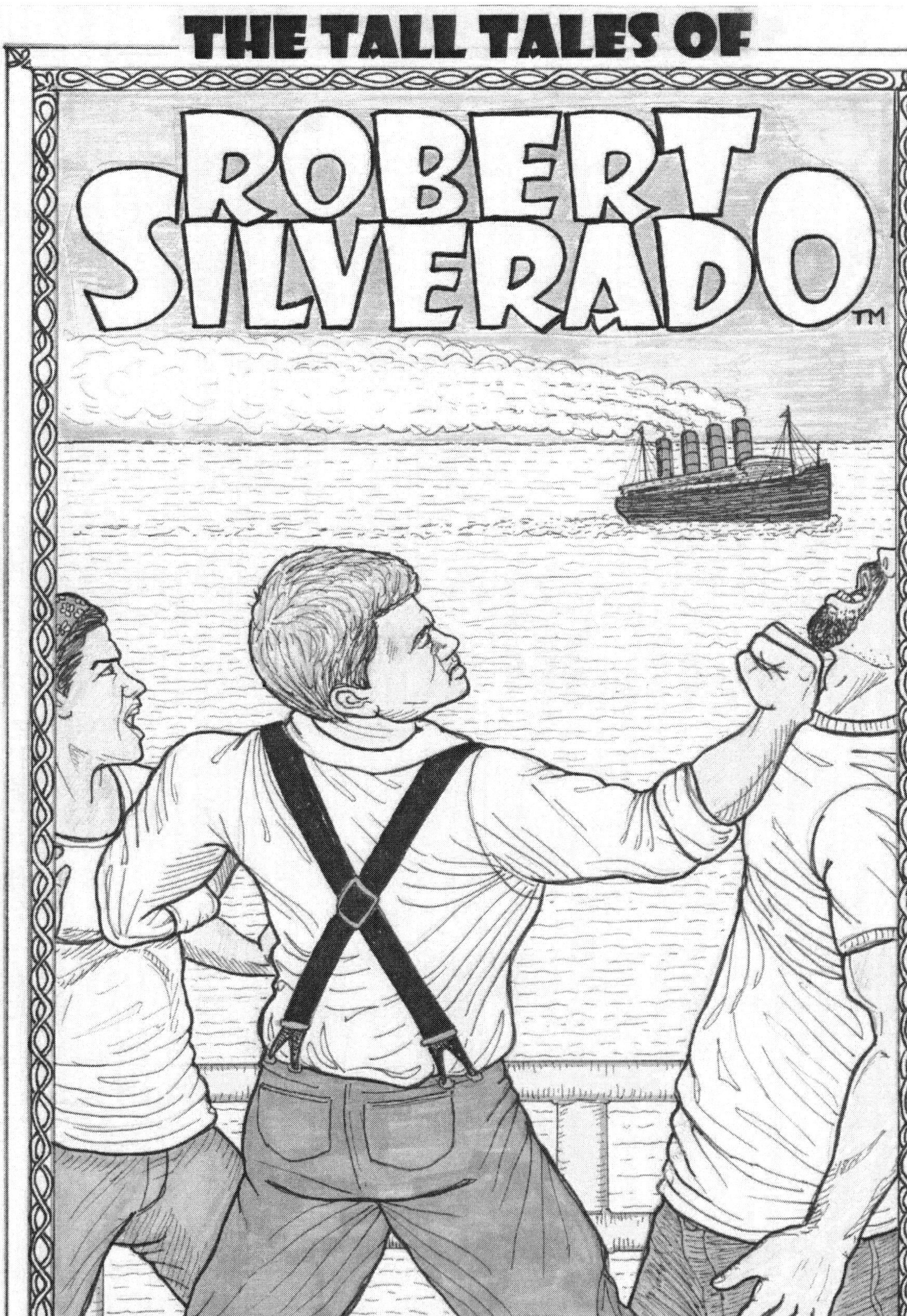
THE TALL TALES OF
ROBERT
SILVERADO™

THE TALL TALES OF

ROBERT SILVERADO

SIBERIAN INVASION

CHAPTER TWO

AFTER HIS LONG DRIVE FROM OUR NATION'S CAPITAL, SPECIAL AGENT ROBERT SILVERADO FINALLY ARRIVES IN WARDENCLYFFE, NEW YORK, AT THE LABORATORY OF NIKOLA TESLA. THIS WILL BE THE FIRST STOP ON HIS MISSION TO SAVE THE EARTH FROM AN OUTER-WORLDLY THREAT THAT IS CURRENTLY REEKING DEADLY HAVOC OVER SIBERIA, RUSSIA.

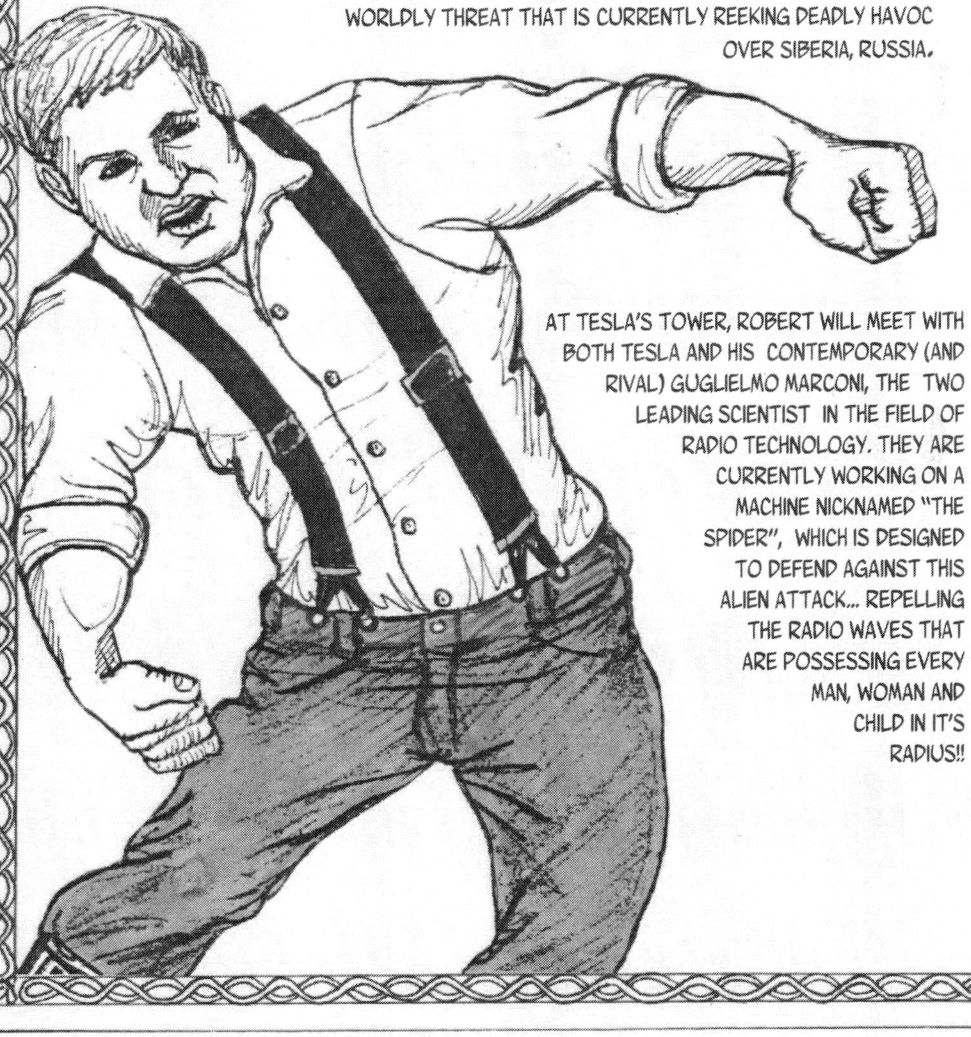

AT TESLA'S TOWER, ROBERT WILL MEET WITH BOTH TESLA AND HIS CONTEMPORARY (AND RIVAL) GUGLIELMO MARCONI, THE TWO LEADING SCIENTIST IN THE FIELD OF RADIO TECHNOLOGY. THEY ARE CURRENTLY WORKING ON A MACHINE NICKNAMED "THE SPIDER", WHICH IS DESIGNED TO DEFEND AGAINST THIS ALIEN ATTACK... REPELLING THE RADIO WAVES THAT ARE POSSESSING EVERY MAN, WOMAN AND CHILD IN IT'S RADIUS!!

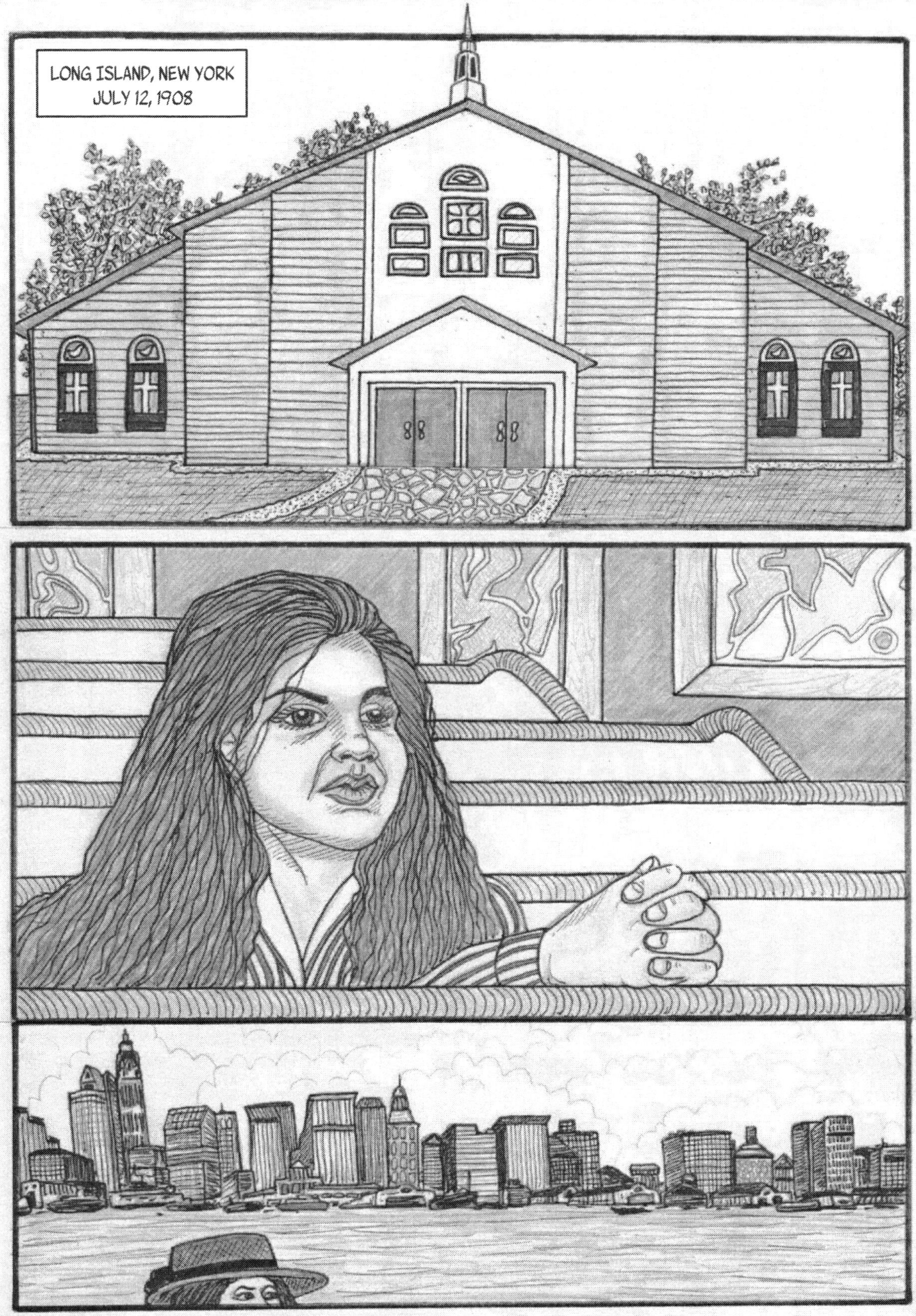
LONG ISLAND, NEW YORK
JULY 12, 1908

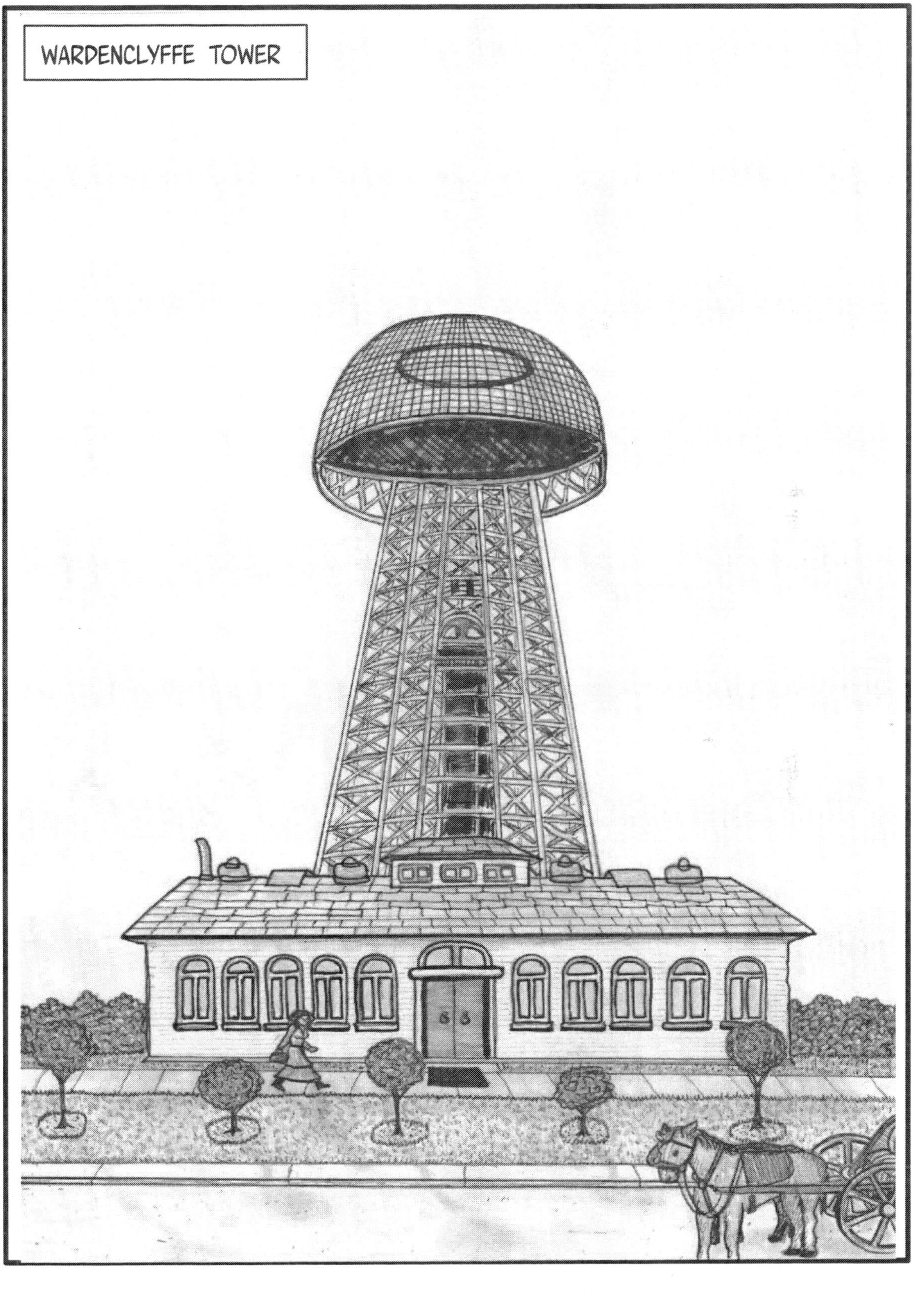
WARDENCLYFFE TOWER

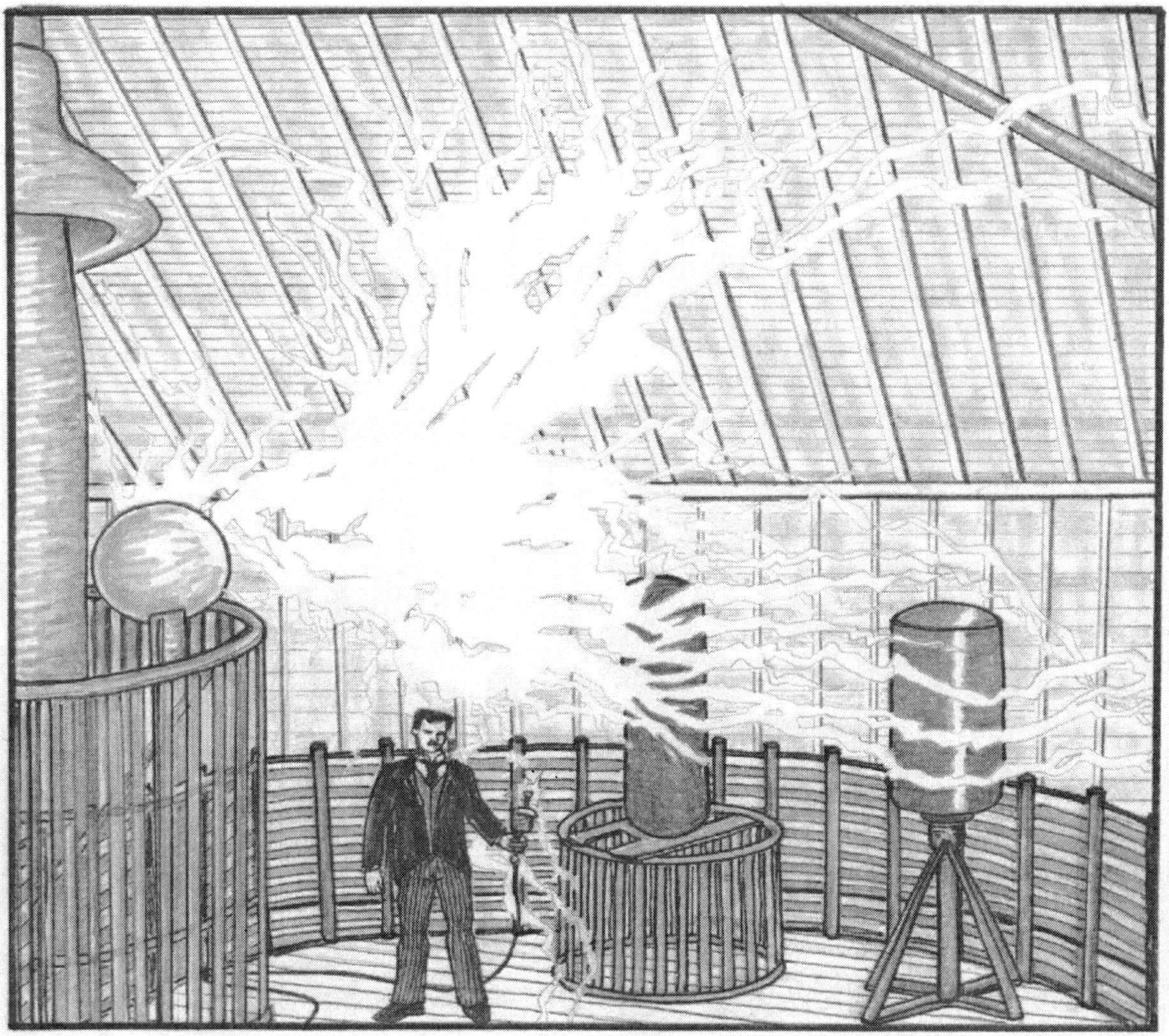

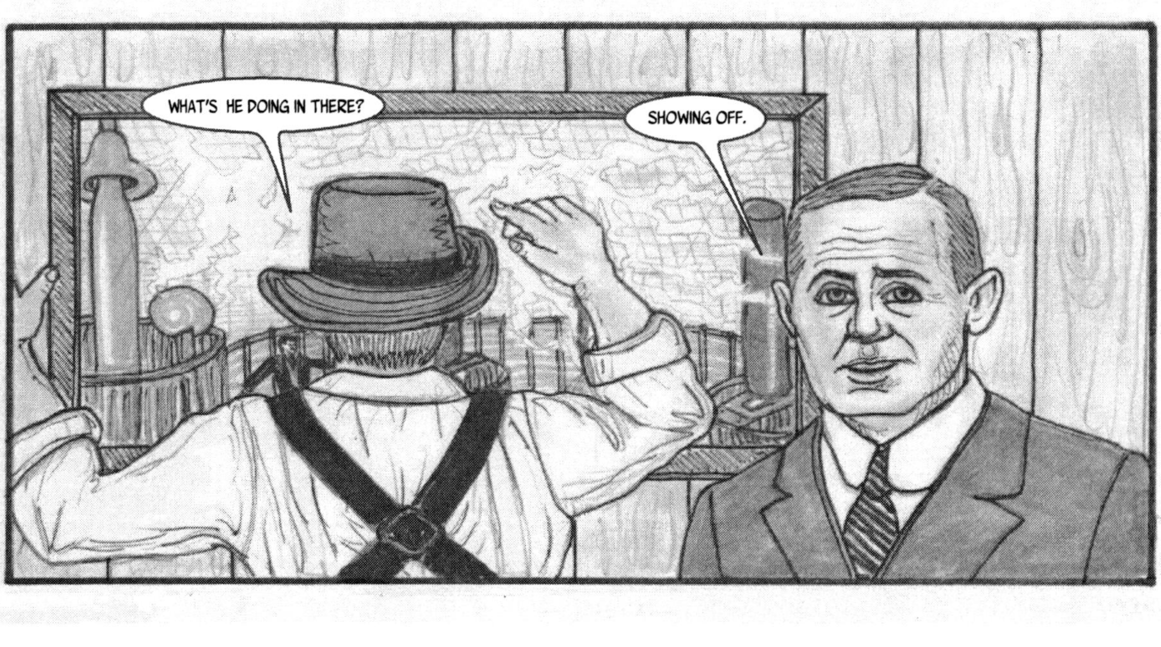
WHAT'S HE DOING IN THERE?
SHOWING OFF.

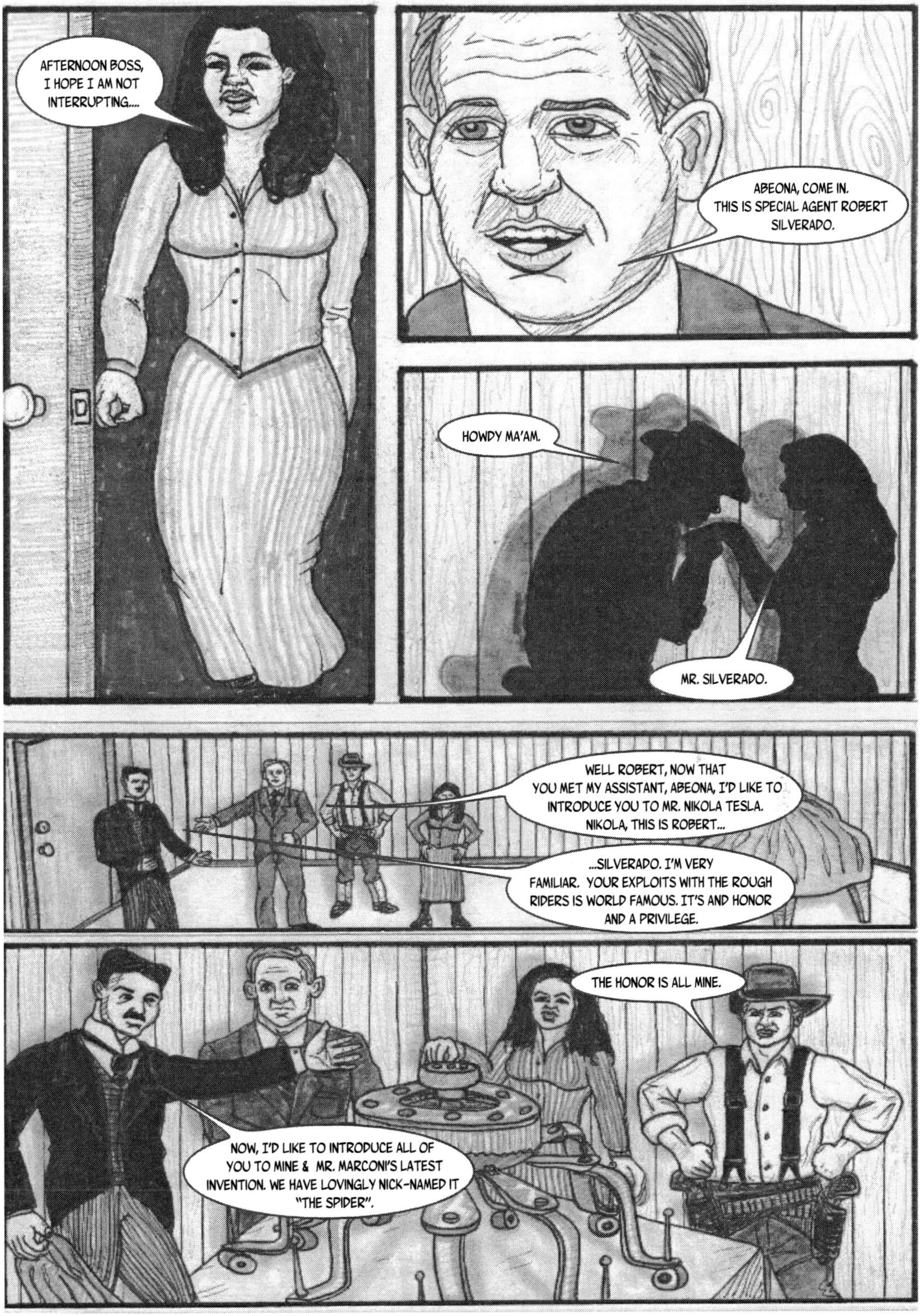
AFTERNOON BOSS, I HOPE I AM NOT INTERRUPTING....
ABEONA, COME IN. THIS IS SPECIAL AGENT ROBERT SILVERADO.
HOWDY MA'AM.
MR. SILVERADO.
WELL ROBERT, NOW THAT YOU MET MY ASSISTANT, ABEONA, I'D LIKE TO INTRODUCE YOU TO MR. NIKOLA TESLA. NIKOLA, THIS IS ROBERT...
...SILVERADO. I'M VERY FAMILIAR. YOUR EXPLOITS WITH THE ROUGH RIDERS IS WORLD FAMOUS. IT'S AND HONOR AND A PRIVILEGE.
THE HONOR IS ALL MINE.
NOW, I'D LIKE TO INTRODUCE ALL OF YOU TO MINE & MR. MARCONI'S LATEST INVENTION. WE HAVE LOVINGLY NICK-NAMED IT "THE SPIDER".

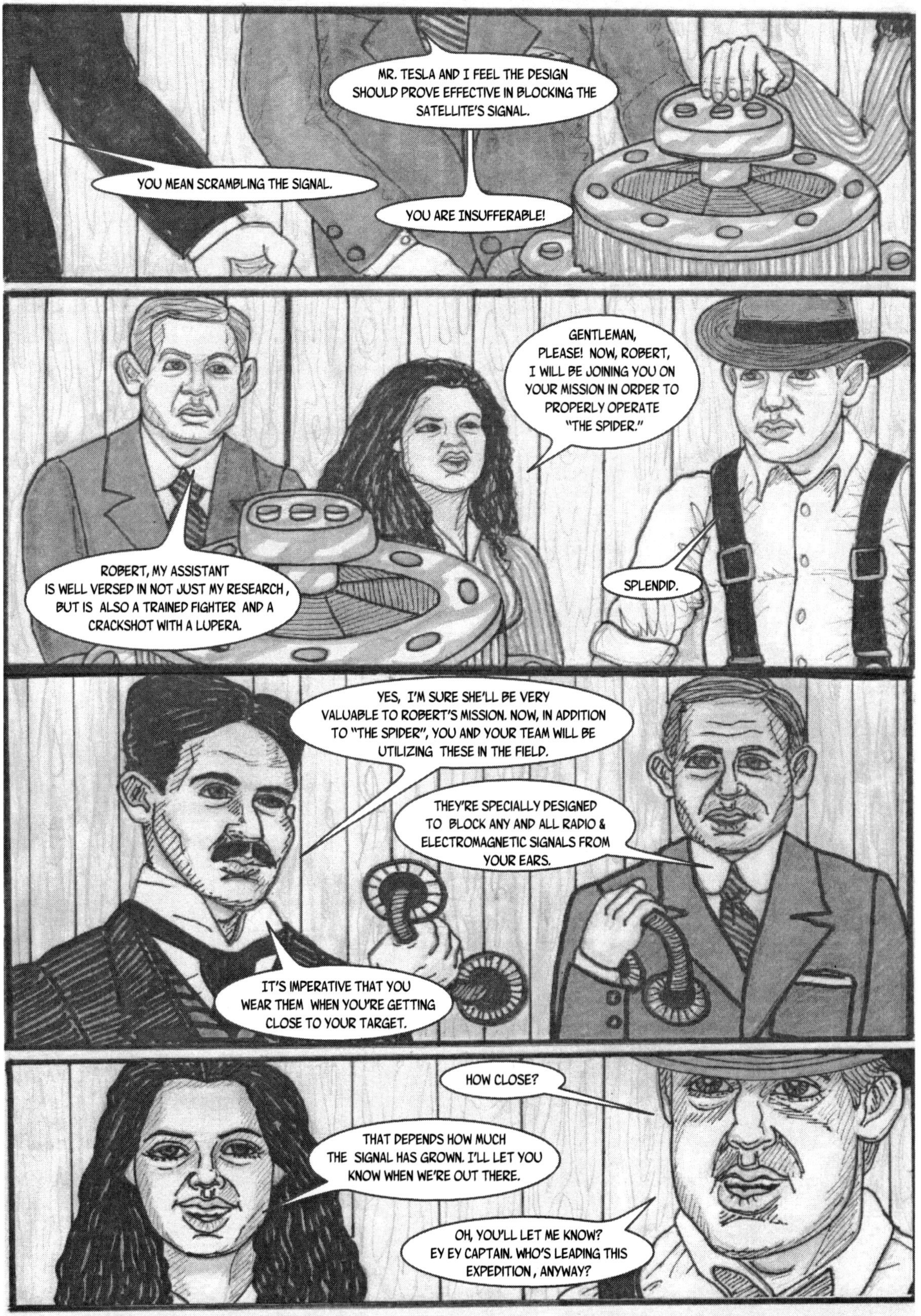
MR. TESLA AND I FEEL THE DESIGN SHOULD PROVE EFFECTIVE IN BLOCKING THE SATELLITE'S SIGNAL.
YOU MEAN SCRAMBLING THE SIGNAL.
YOU ARE INSUFFERABLE!
ROBERT, MY ASSISTANT IS WELL VERSED IN NOT JUST MY RESEARCH , BUT IS ALSO A TRAINED FIGHTER AND A CRACKSHOT WITH A LUPERA.
GENTLEMAN, PLEASE! NOW, ROBERT, I WILL BE JOINING YOU ON YOUR MISSION IN ORDER TO PROPERLY OPERATE "THE SPIDER."
SPLENDID.
YES, I'M SURE SHE'LL BE VERY VALUABLE TO ROBERT'S MISSION. NOW, IN ADDITION TO "THE SPIDER", YOU AND YOUR TEAM WILL BE UTILIZING THESE IN THE FIELD.
THEY'RE SPECIALLY DESIGNED TO BLOCK ANY AND ALL RADIO & ELECTROMAGNETIC SIGNALS FROM YOUR EARS.
IT'S IMPERATIVE THAT YOU WEAR THEM WHEN YOU'RE GETTING CLOSE TO YOUR TARGET.
HOW CLOSE?
THAT DEPENDS HOW MUCH THE SIGNAL HAS GROWN. I'LL LET YOU KNOW WHEN WE'RE OUT THERE.
OH, YOU'LL LET ME KNOW? EY EY CAPTAIN. WHO'S LEADING THIS EXPEDITION , ANYWAY?

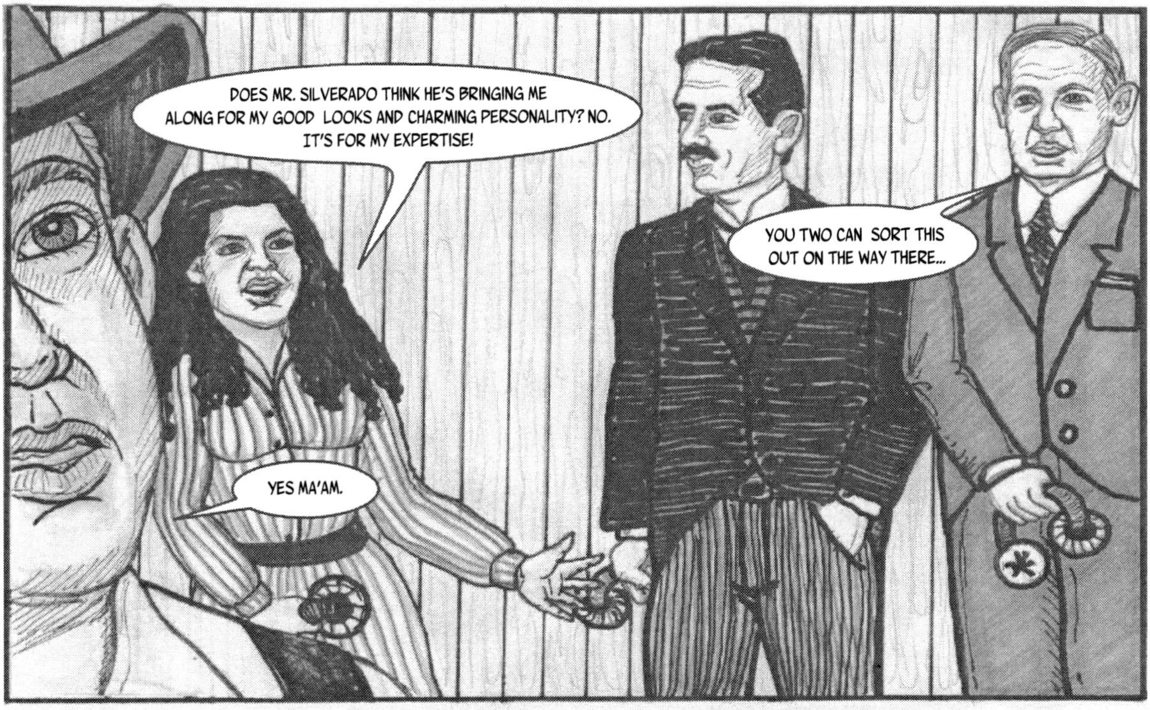
DOES MR. SILVERADO THINK HE'S BRINGING ME ALONG FOR MY GOOD LOOKS AND CHARMING PERSONALITY? NO. IT'S FOR MY EXPERTISE!
YOU TWO CAN SORT THIS OUT ON THE WAY THERE...
YES MA'AM.

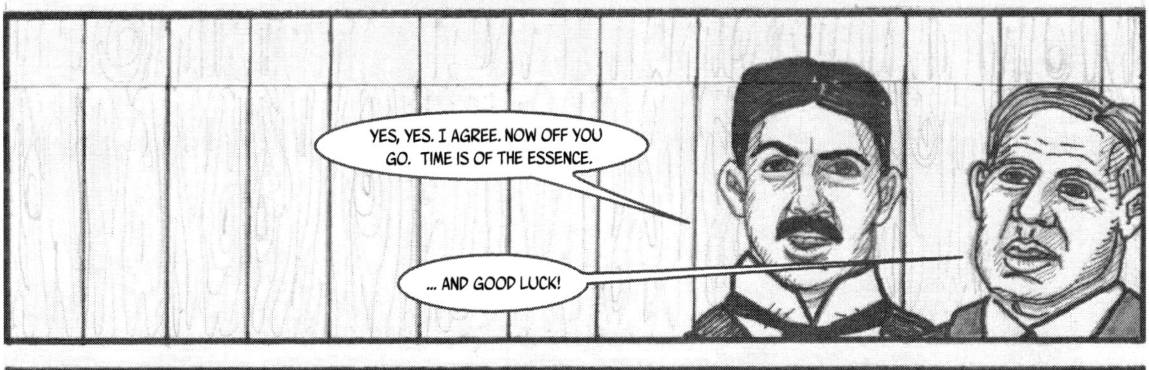
YES, YES. I AGREE. NOW OFF YOU GO. TIME IS OF THE ESSENCE.
... AND GOOD LUCK!

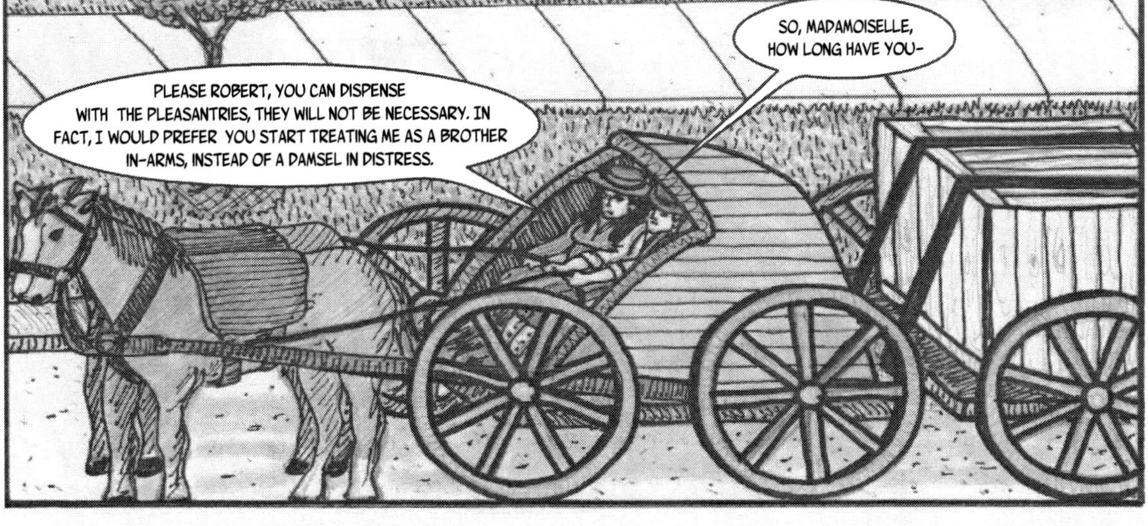
SO, MADAMOISELLE, HOW LONG HAVE YOU-
PLEASE ROBERT, YOU CAN DISPENSE WITH THE PLEASANTRIES, THEY WILL NOT BE NECESSARY. IN FACT, I WOULD PREFER YOU START TREATING ME AS A BROTHER IN-ARMS, INSTEAD OF A DAMSEL IN DISTRESS.

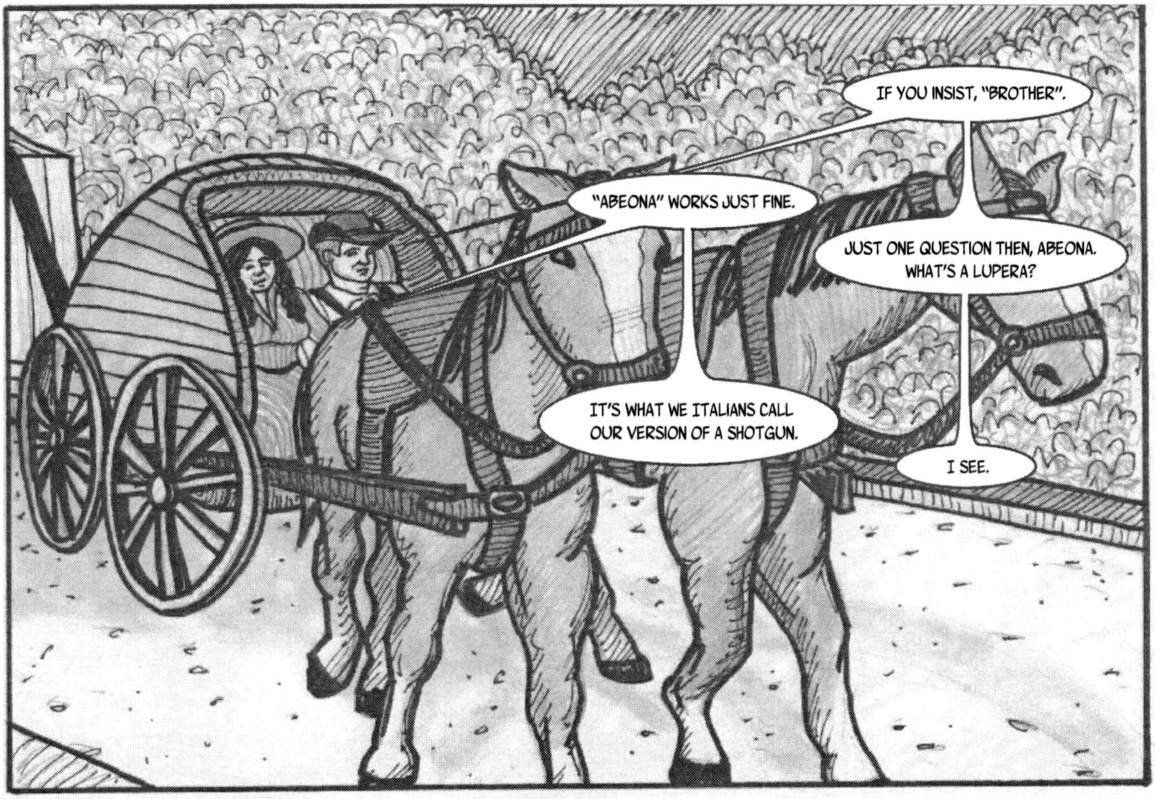
IF YOU INSIST, "BROTHER".
"ABEONA" WORKS JUST FINE.
JUST ONE QUESTION THEN, ABEONA. WHAT'S A LUPERA?
IT'S WHAT WE ITALIANS CALL OUR VERSION OF A SHOTGUN.
I SEE.

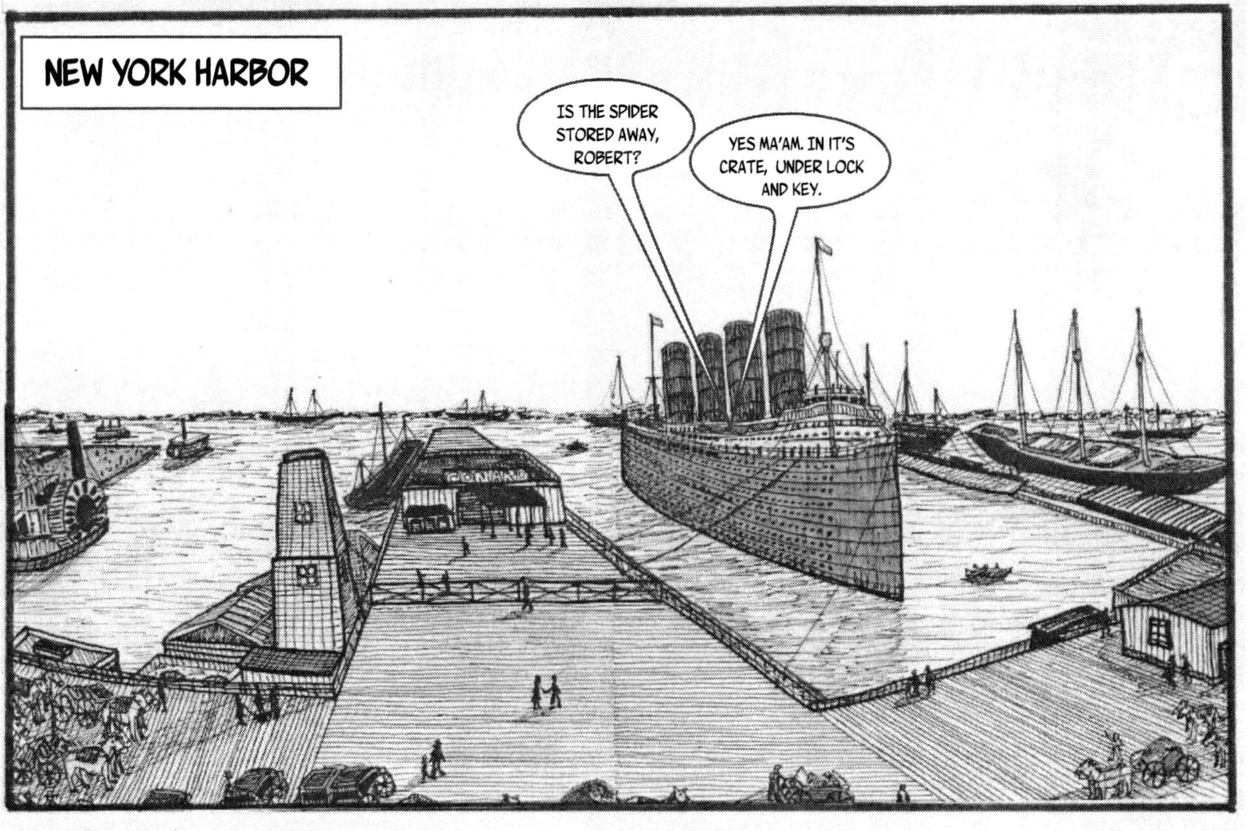
NEW YORK HARBOR
IS THE SPIDER STORED AWAY, ROBERT?
YES MA'AM. IN IT'S CRATE, UNDER LOCK AND KEY.

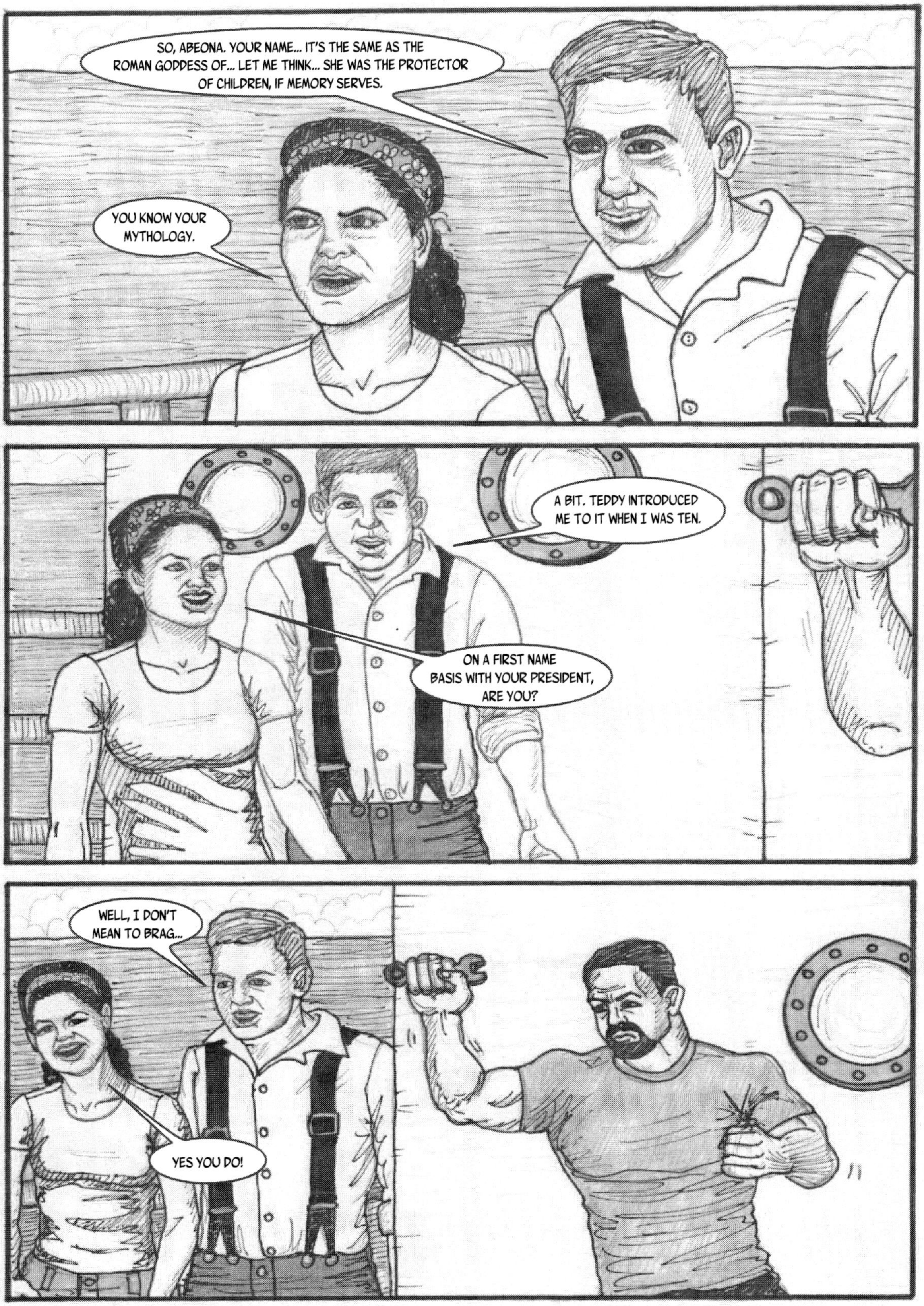

SO, ABEONA. YOUR NAME... IT'S THE SAME AS THE ROMAN GODDESS OF... LET ME THINK... SHE WAS THE PROTECTOR OF CHILDREN, IF MEMORY SERVES.
YOU KNOW YOUR MYTHOLOGY.
A BIT. TEDDY INTRODUCED ME TO IT WHEN I WAS TEN.
ON A FIRST NAME BASIS WITH YOUR PRESIDENT, ARE YOU?
WELL, I DON'T MEAN TO BRAG...
YES YOU DO!

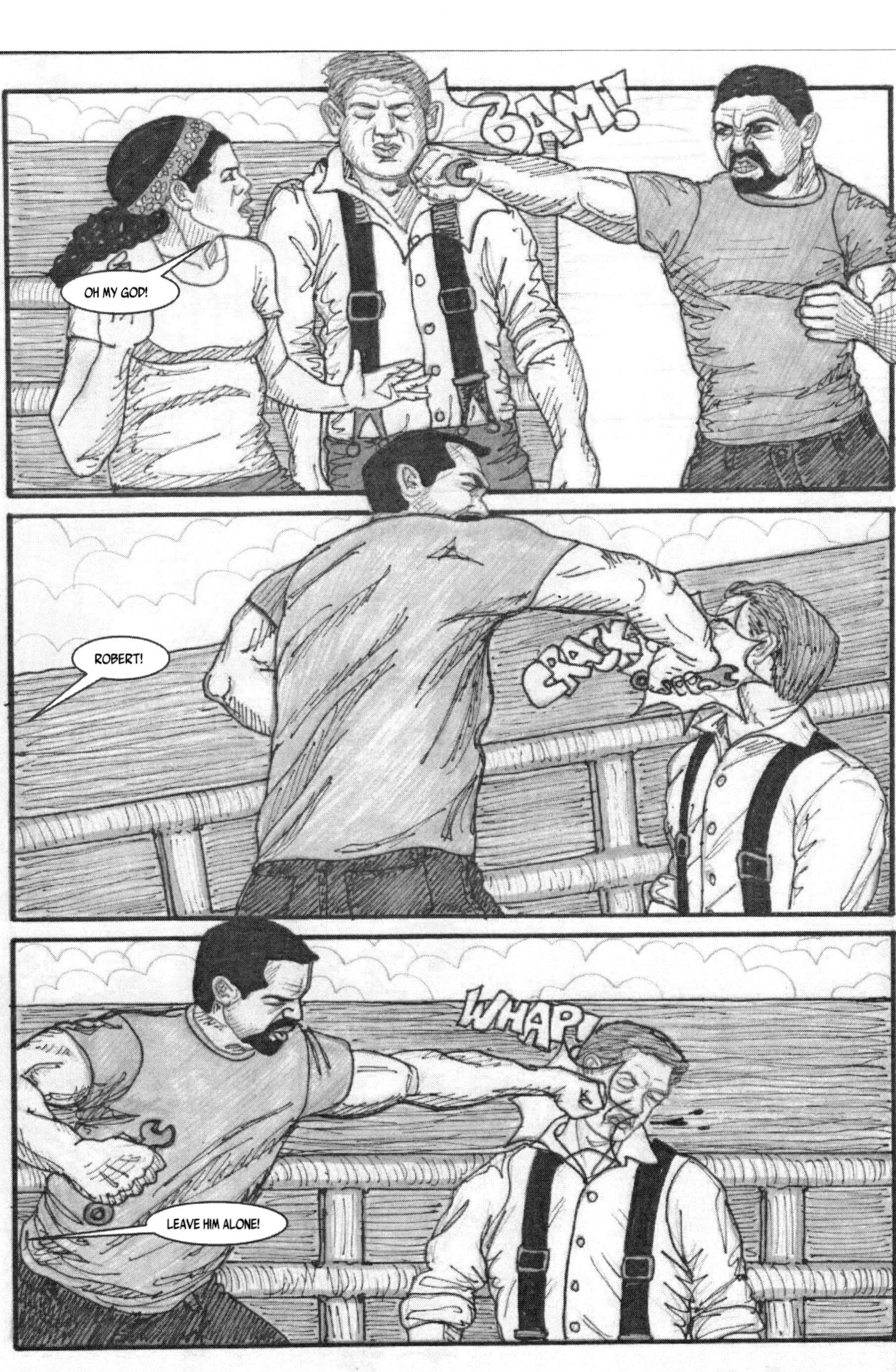
BAM!
OH MY GOD!
ROBERT!
WHAP!
LEAVE HIM ALONE!

I SAID LEAVE HIM...
ALONE!!
THUD!
UGH!
TAKE THAT YOU BASTARD!

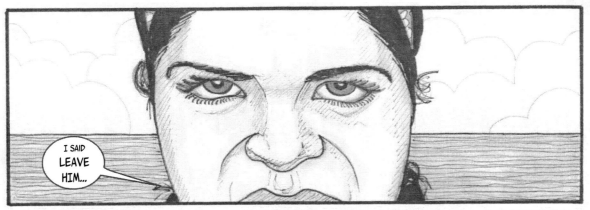

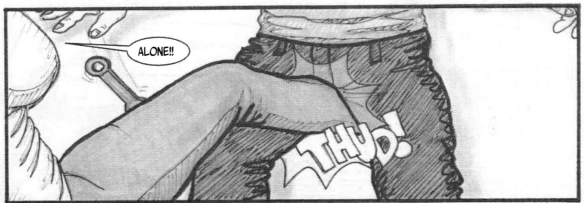

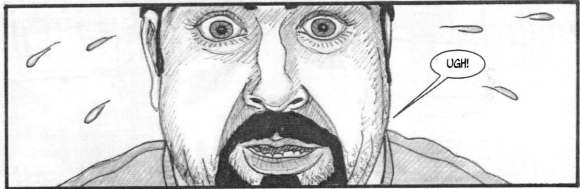

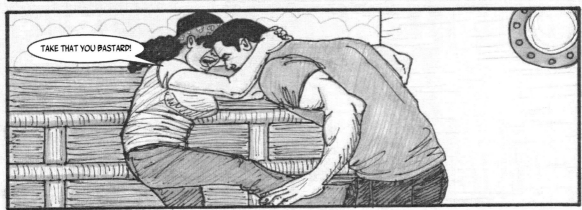

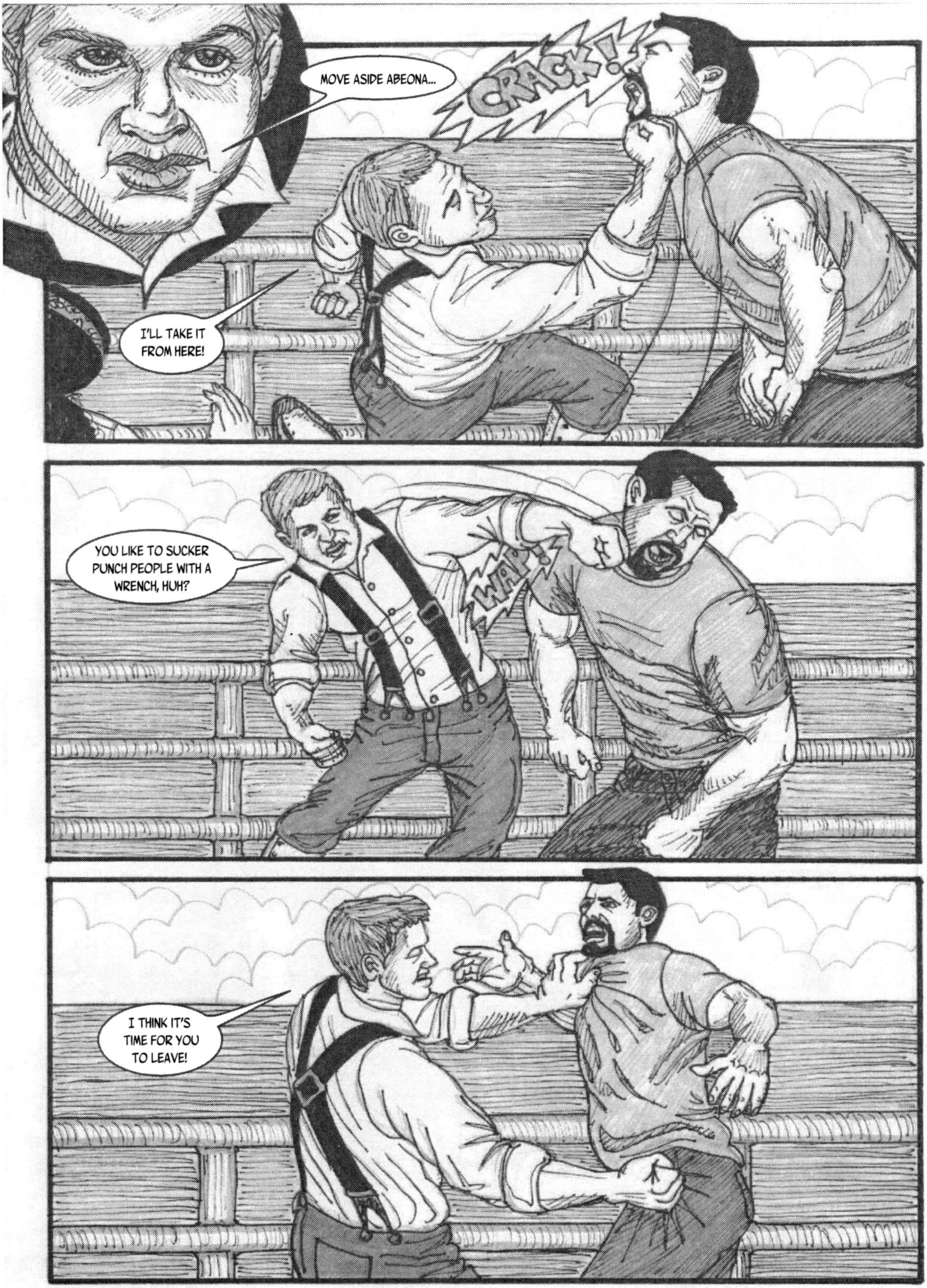
MOVE ASIDE ABEONA...
I'LL TAKE IT FROM HERE!
CRACK!
YOU LIKE TO SUCKER PUNCH PEOPLE WITH A WRENCH, HUH?
I THINK IT'S TIME FOR YOU TO LEAVE!

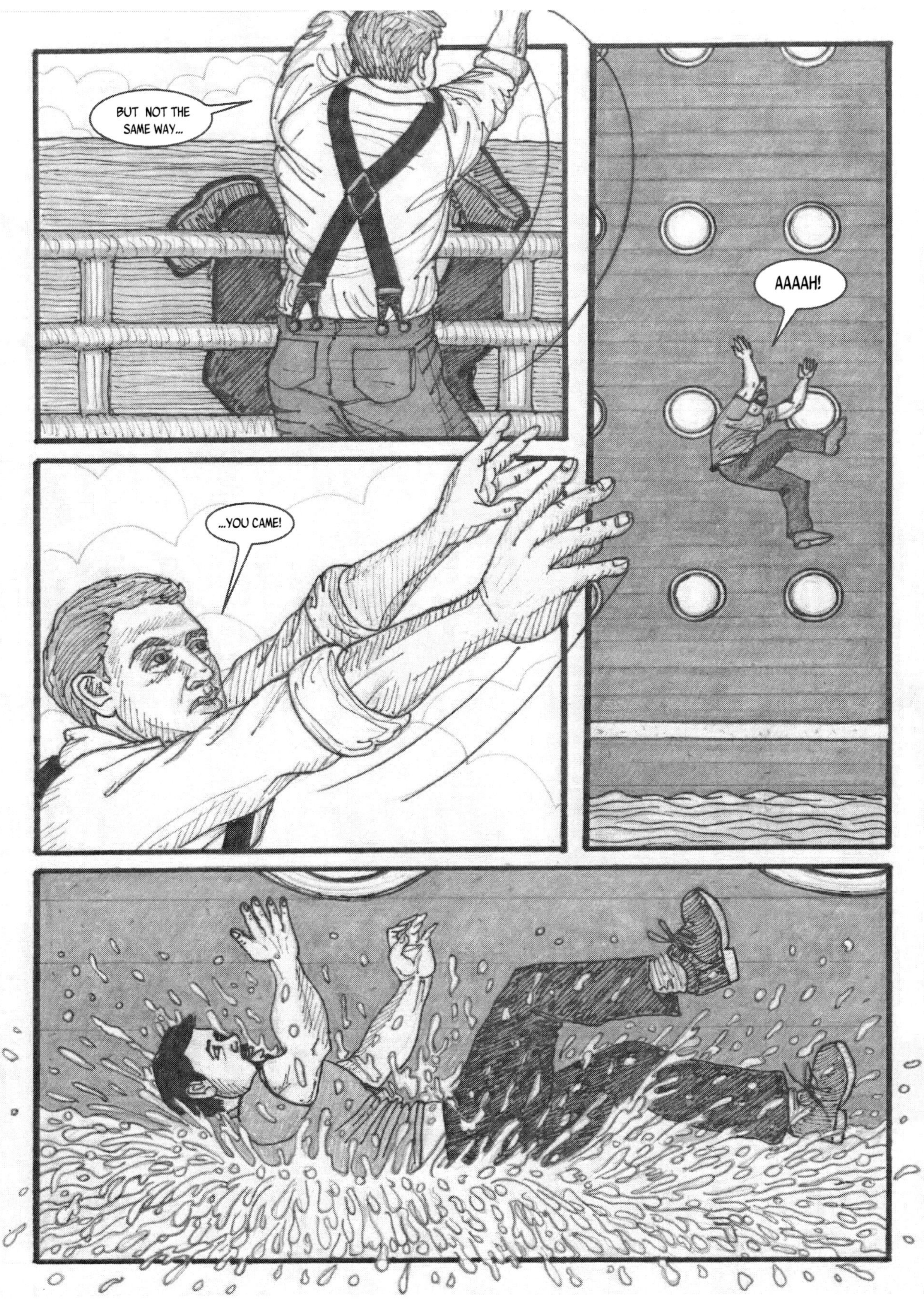
BUT NOT THE SAME WAY...
AAAAH!
...YOU CAME!

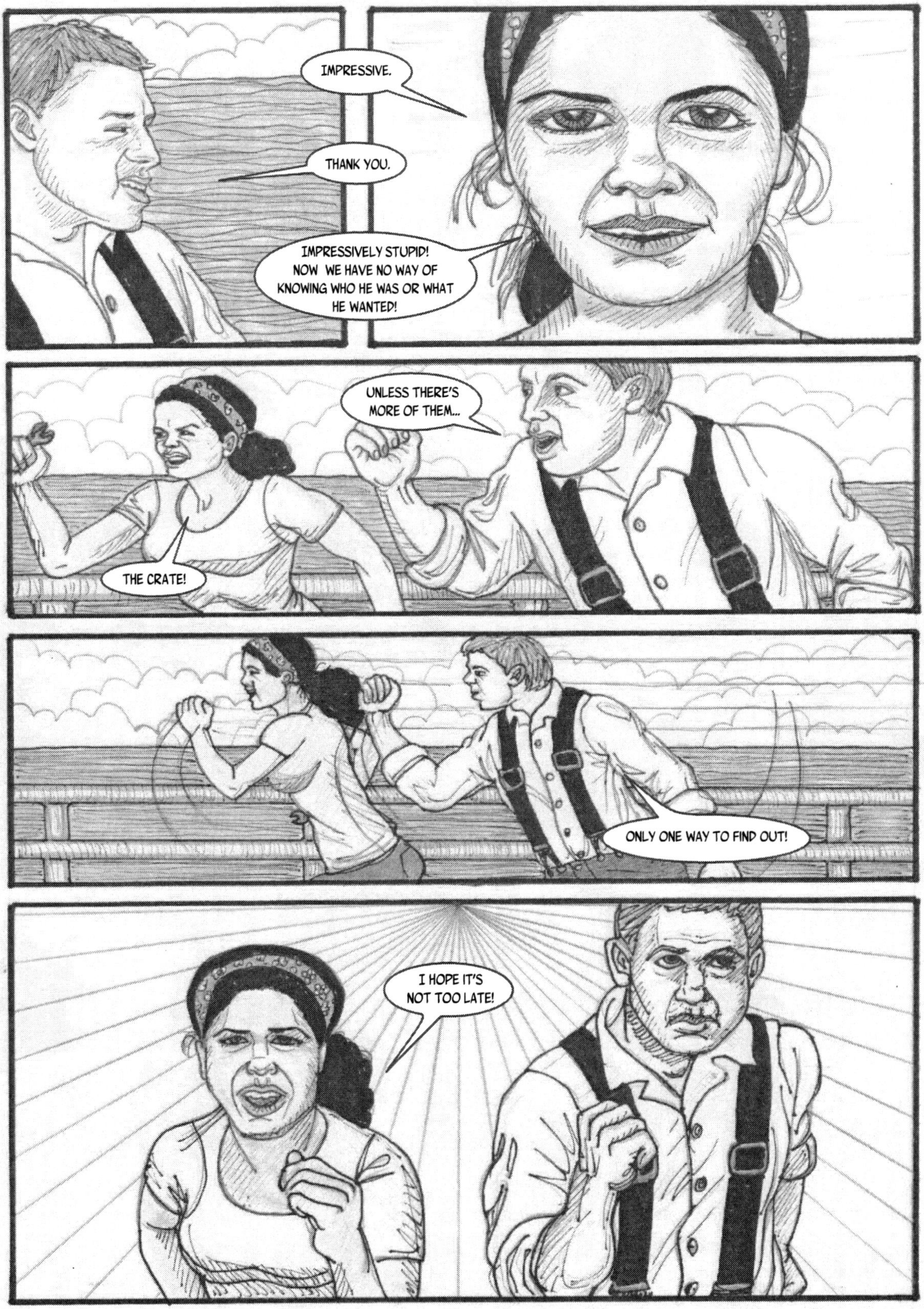
IMPRESSIVE.
THANK YOU.
IMPRESSIVELY STUPID! NOW WE HAVE NO WAY OF KNOWING WHO HE WAS OR WHAT HE WANTED!
UNLESS THERE'S MORE OF THEM...
THE CRATE!
ONLY ONE WAY TO FIND OUT!
I HOPE IT'S NOT TOO LATE!

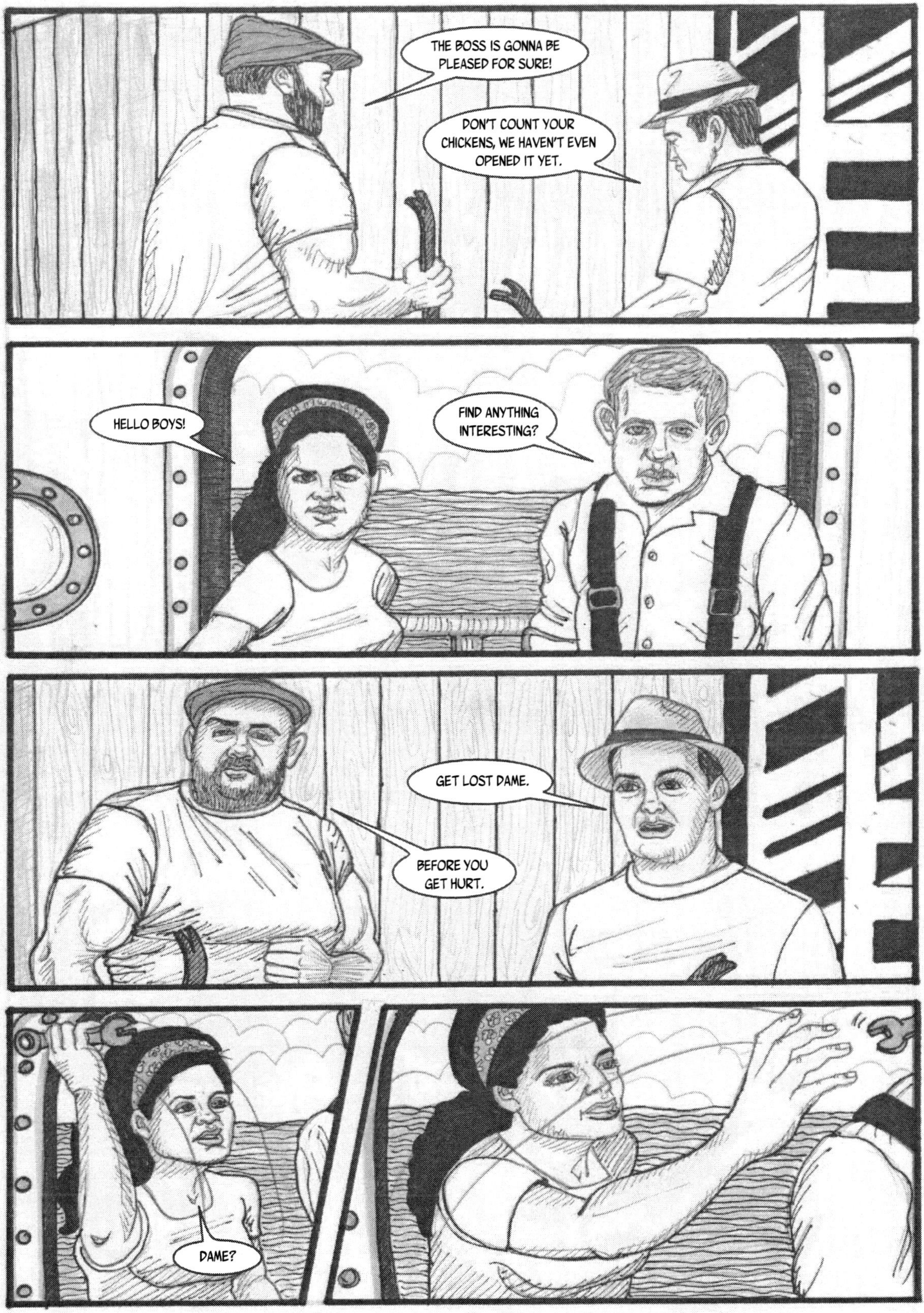
THE BOSS IS GONNA BE PLEASED FOR SURE!
DON'T COUNT YOUR CHICKENS, WE HAVEN'T EVEN OPENED IT YET.
HELLO BOYS!
FIND ANYTHING INTERESTING?
GET LOST DAME.
BEFORE YOU GET HURT.
DAME?

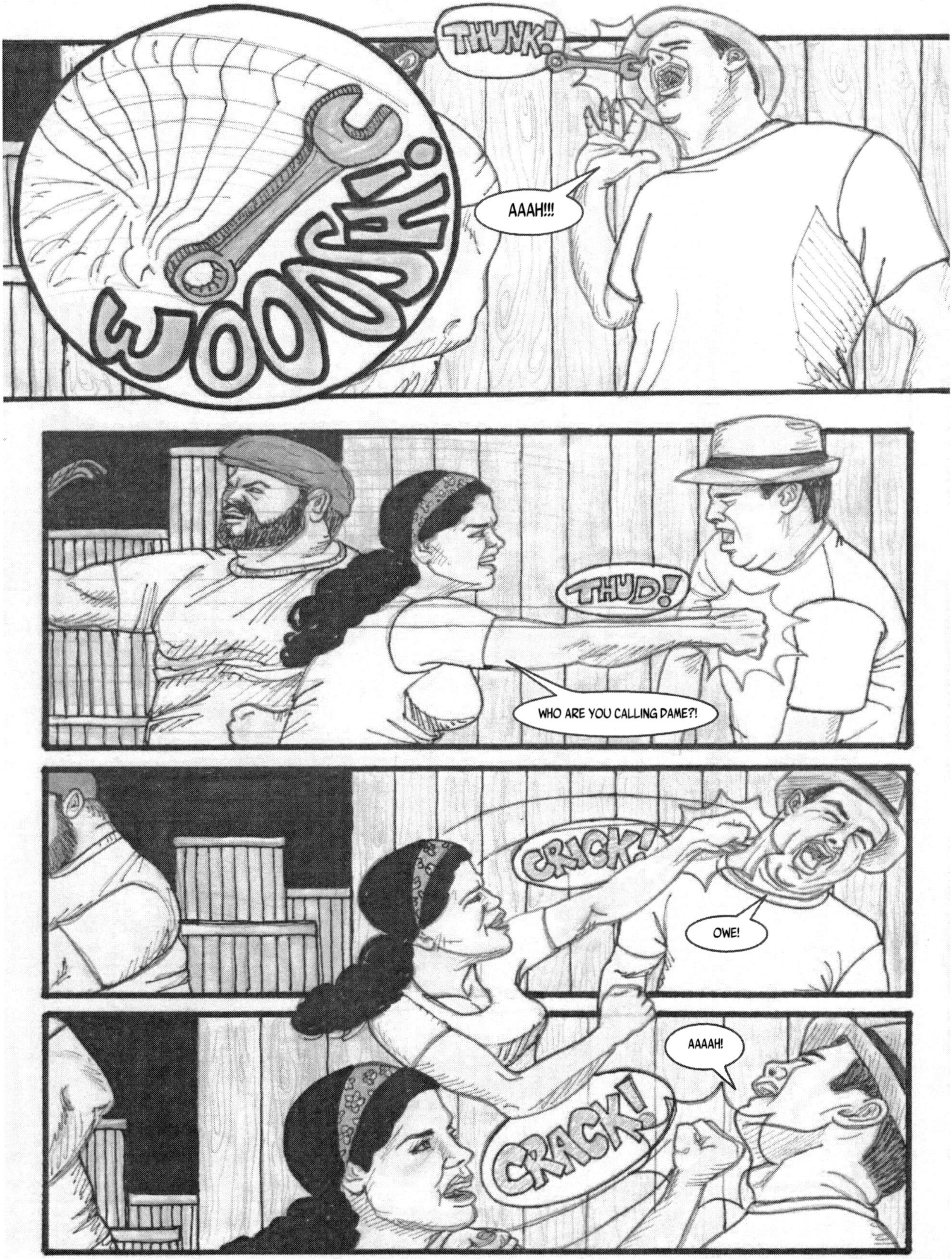
WOOSH!
THUNK!
AAAH!!!
THUD!
WHO ARE YOU CALLING DAME?!
CRACK!
OWE!
AAAAH!
CRACK!

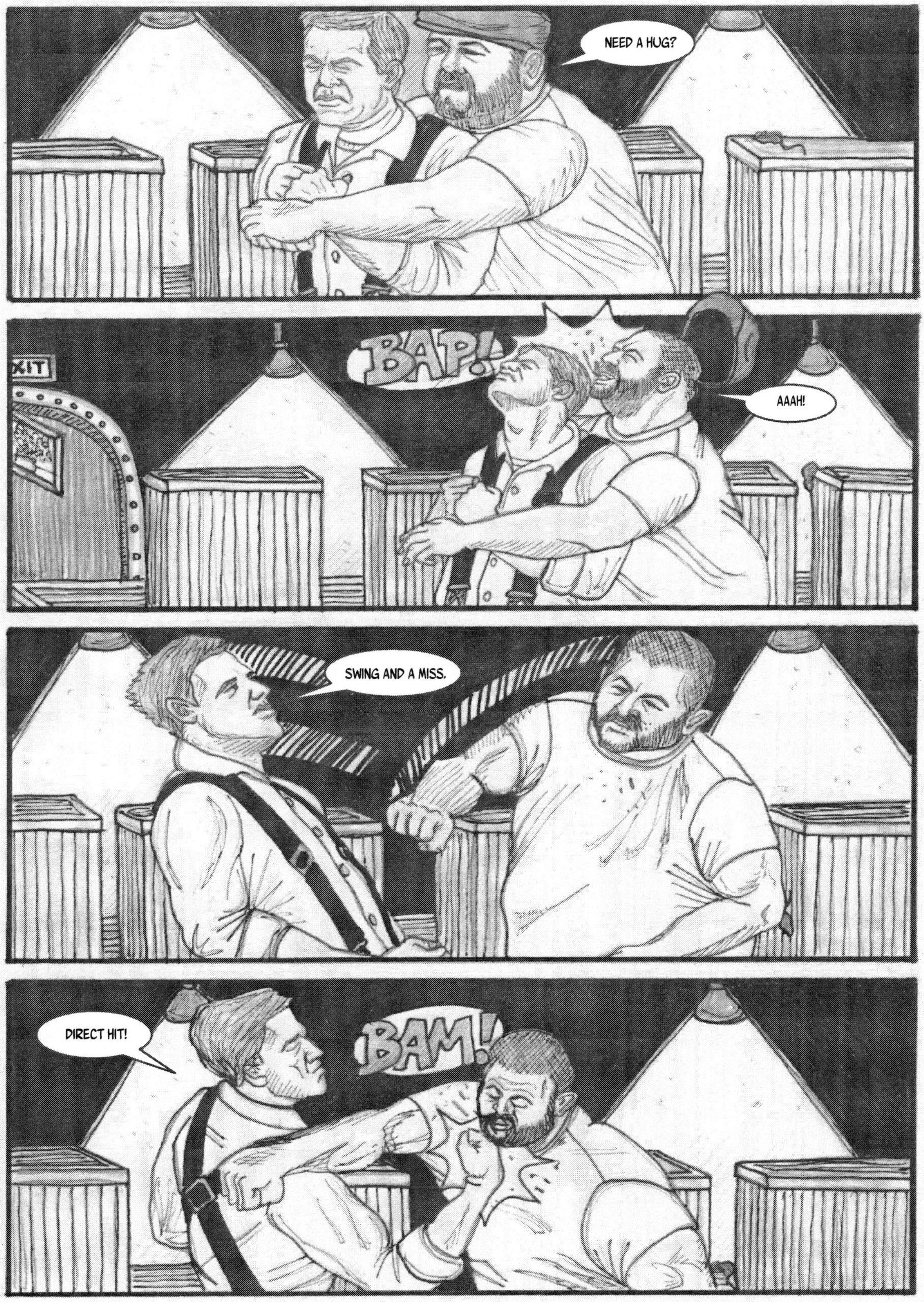
NEED A HUG?
BAP!
AAAH!
XIT
SWING AND A MISS.
DIRECT HIT!
BAM!

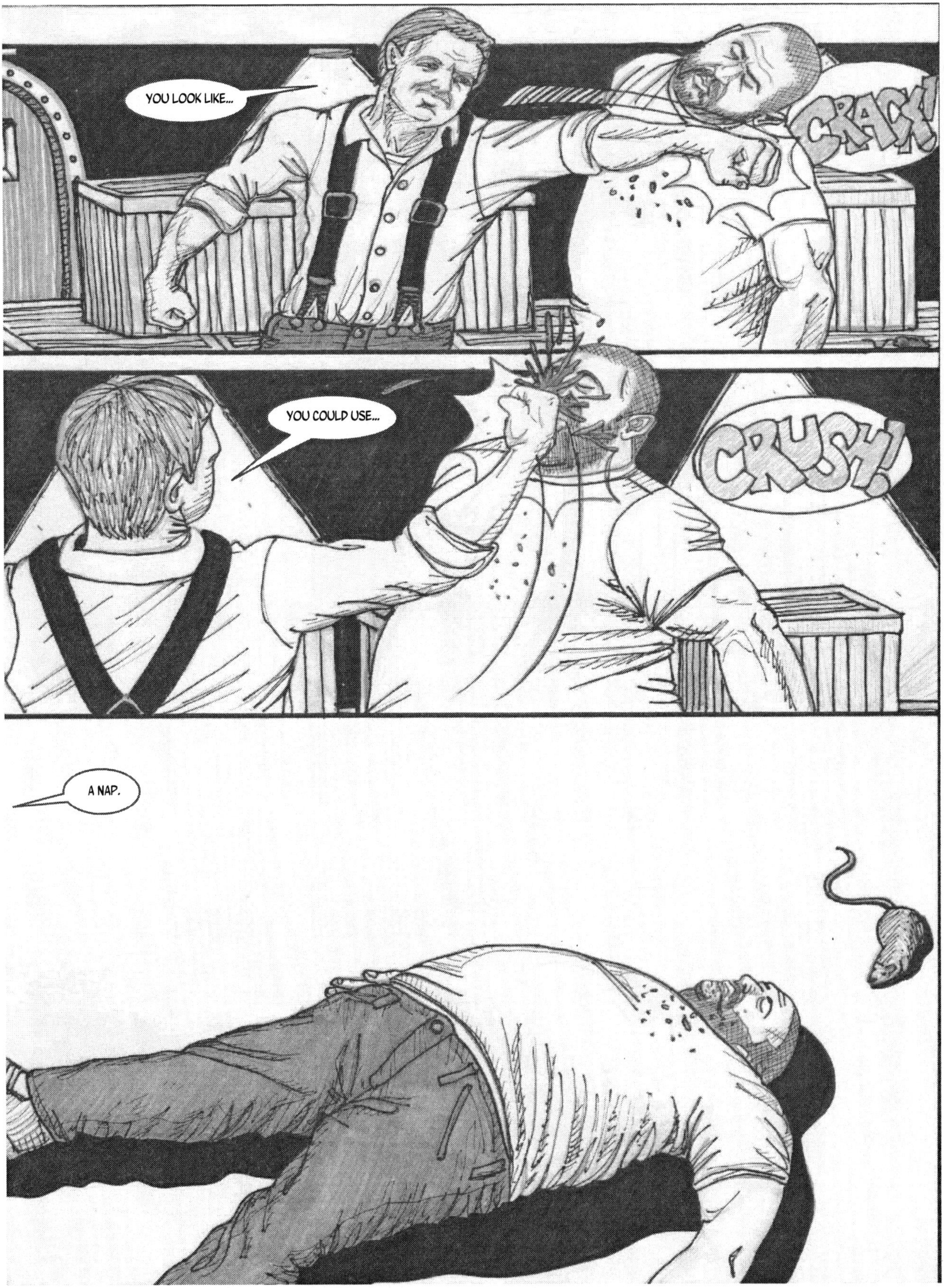
YOU LOOK LIKE...
CRACK!
YOU COULD USE...
CRUSH!
A NAP.

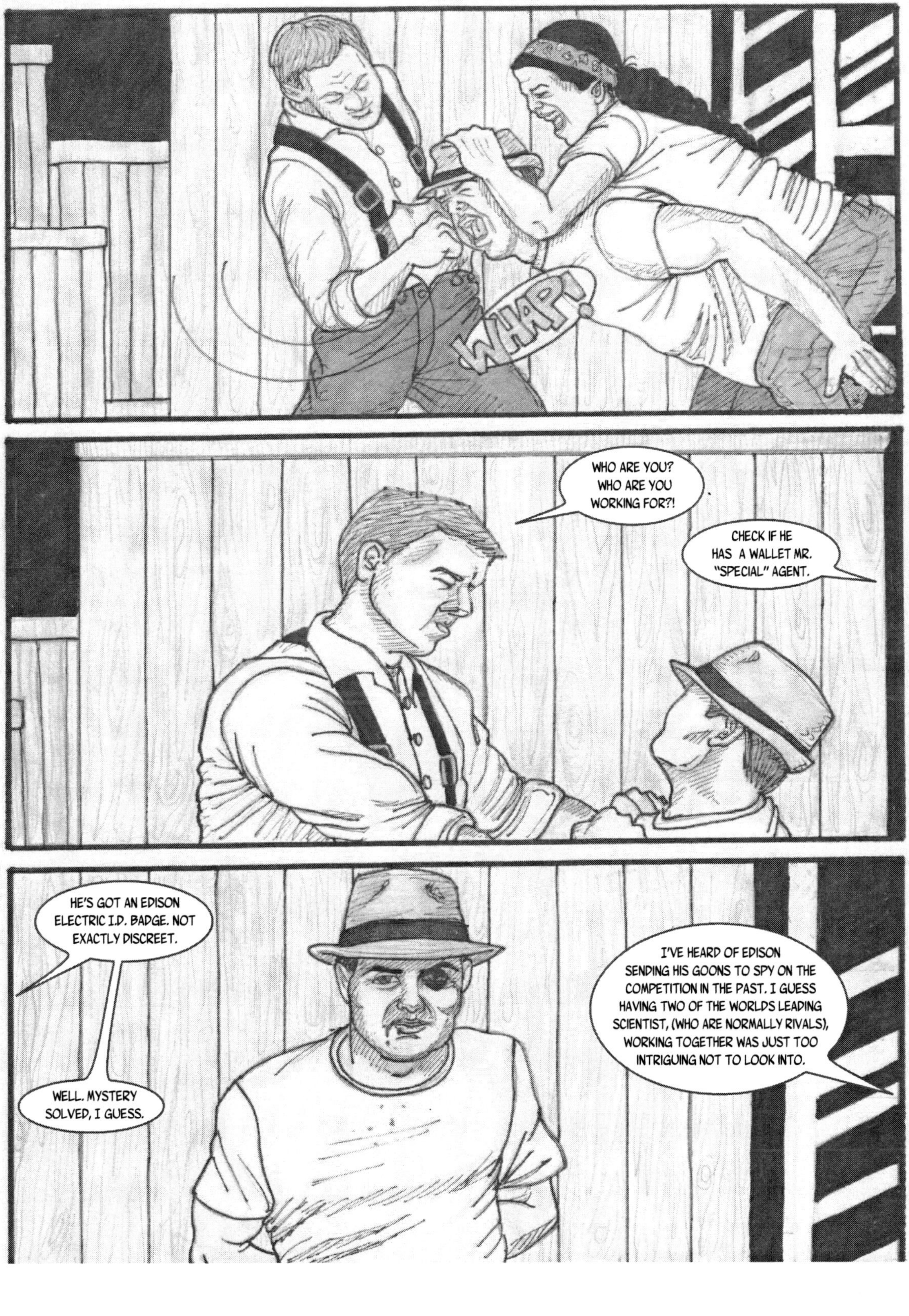
WHAP!
WHO ARE YOU? WHO ARE YOU WORKING FOR?!
CHECK IF HE HAS A WALLET MR. "SPECIAL" AGENT.
HE'S GOT AN EDISON ELECTRIC I.D. BADGE. NOT EXACTLY DISCREET.
WELL. MYSTERY SOLVED, I GUESS.
I'VE HEARD OF EDISON SENDING HIS GOONS TO SPY ON THE COMPETITION IN THE PAST. I GUESS HAVING TWO OF THE WORLDS LEADING SCIENTIST, (WHO ARE NORMALLY RIVALS), WORKING TOGETHER WAS JUST TOO INTRIGUING NOT TO LOOK INTO.

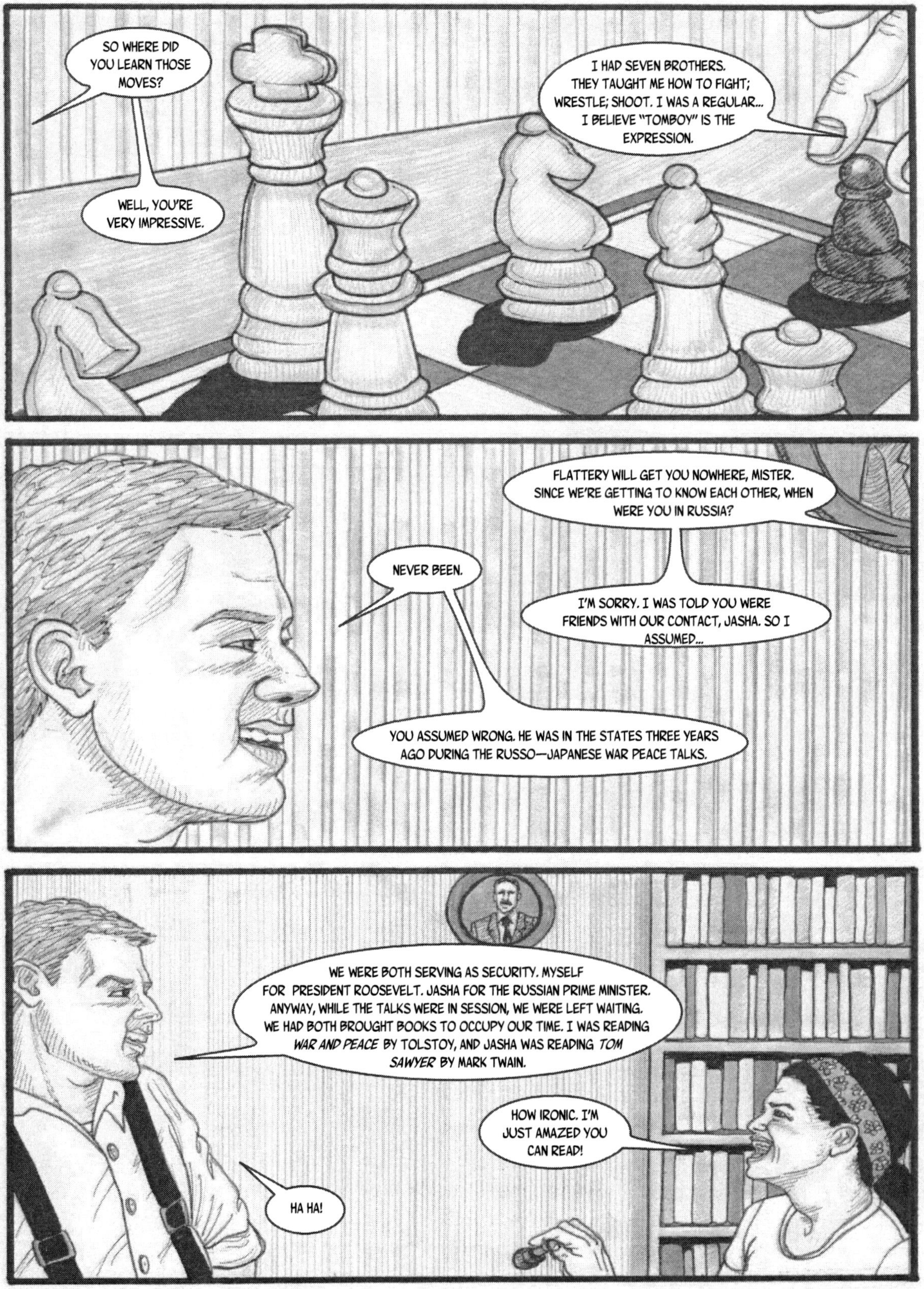
SO WHERE DID YOU LEARN THOSE MOVES?
I HAD SEVEN BROTHERS. THEY TAUGHT ME HOW TO FIGHT; WRESTLE; SHOOT. I WAS A REGULAR... I BELIEVE "TOMBOY" IS THE EXPRESSION.
WELL, YOU'RE VERY IMPRESSIVE.
FLATTERY WILL GET YOU NOWHERE, MISTER. SINCE WE'RE GETTING TO KNOW EACH OTHER, WHEN WERE YOU IN RUSSIA?
NEVER BEEN.
I'M SORRY. I WAS TOLD YOU WERE FRIENDS WITH OUR CONTACT, JASHA. SO I ASSUMED...
YOU ASSUMED WRONG. HE WAS IN THE STATES THREE YEARS AGO DURING THE RUSSO—JAPANESE WAR PEACE TALKS.
WE WERE BOTH SERVING AS SECURITY. MYSELF FOR PRESIDENT ROOSEVELT. JASHA FOR THE RUSSIAN PRIME MINISTER. ANYWAY, WHILE THE TALKS WERE IN SESSION, WE WERE LEFT WAITING. WE HAD BOTH BROUGHT BOOKS TO OCCUPY OUR TIME. I WAS READING *WAR AND PEACE* BY TOLSTOY, AND JASHA WAS READING *TOM SAWYER* BY MARK TWAIN.
HOW IRONIC. I'M JUST AMAZED YOU CAN READ!
HA HA!

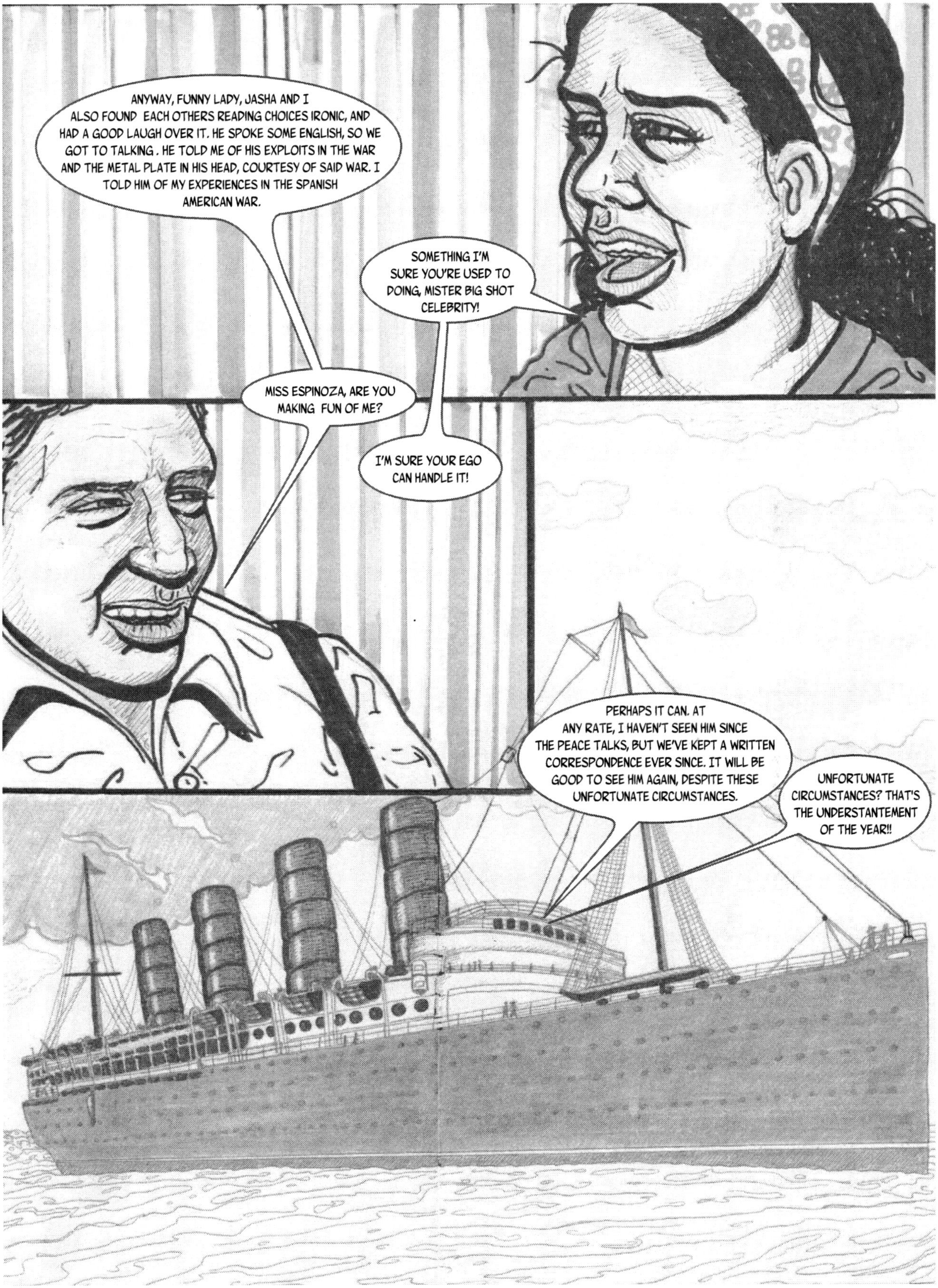
ANYWAY, FUNNY LADY, JASHA AND I ALSO FOUND EACH OTHERS READING CHOICES IRONIC, AND HAD A GOOD LAUGH OVER IT. HE SPOKE SOME ENGLISH, SO WE GOT TO TALKING . HE TOLD ME OF HIS EXPLOITS IN THE WAR AND THE METAL PLATE IN HIS HEAD, COURTESY OF SAID WAR. I TOLD HIM OF MY EXPERIENCES IN THE SPANISH AMERICAN WAR.
SOMETHING I'M SURE YOU'RE USED TO DOING, MISTER BIG SHOT CELEBRITY!
MISS ESPINOZA, ARE YOU MAKING FUN OF ME?
I'M SURE YOUR EGO CAN HANDLE IT!
PERHAPS IT CAN. AT ANY RATE, I HAVEN'T SEEN HIM SINCE THE PEACE TALKS, BUT WE'VE KEPT A WRITTEN CORRESPONDENCE EVER SINCE. IT WILL BE GOOD TO SEE HIM AGAIN, DESPITE THESE UNFORTUNATE CIRCUMSTANCES.
UNFORTUNATE CIRCUMSTANCES? THAT'S THE UNDERSTANTEMENT OF THE YEAR!!

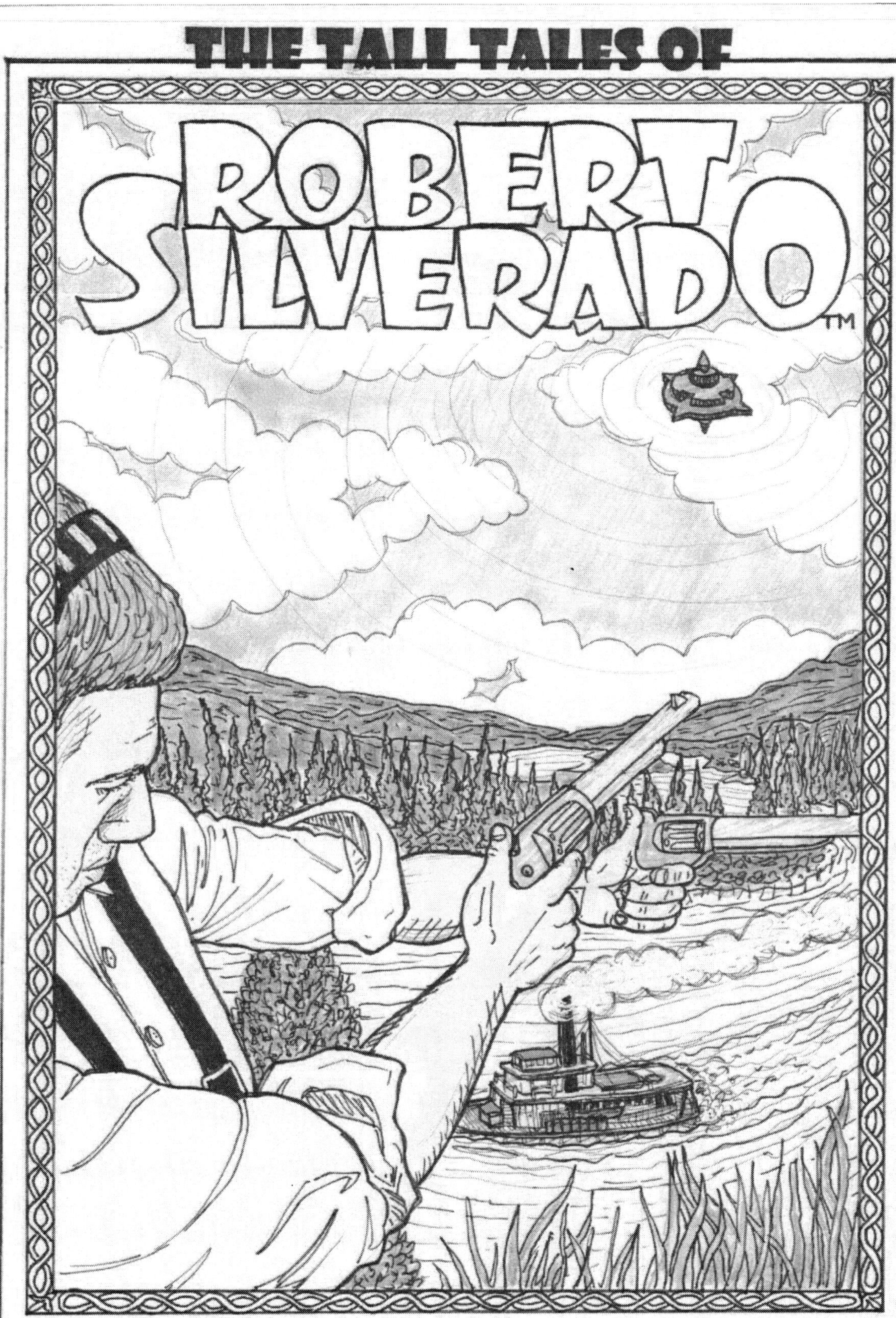
THE TALL TALES OF
ROBERT SILVERADO
TM

THE TALL TALES OF

ROBERT SILVERADO

SIBERIAN INVASION

CHAPTER THREE

AFTER A LONG TRANS-ATLANTIC VOYAGE, SPECIAL AGENT ROBERT SILVERADO, WHO IS ACCOMPANIED BY SCIENTIST ABEONA MARIA ESPINOZA, FINALLY ARRIVES IN SAINT PETERSBURG, RUSSIA. HERE, ROBERT AND HIS COMPANION ARE TO JOIN UP WITH HIS OLD COMRADE, RUSSIAN AGENT JASHA BEZUKHOV , IN AN EFFORT TO TRANSPORT THE "SPIDER" (A MACHINE DESIGNED TO REPEL RADIO WAVES) TO GROUND ZERO OF THE ALIEN ATTACK THAT IS CURRENTLY TAKING OVER NORTHERN RUSSIA. IF NOT SNUFFED OUT SOON, THE SPACECRAFT AND ITS GROWING DEADLY RADIO SIGNAL WILL OVERPOWER EVERY PERSON ON THE PLANET, TURNING THEM INTO MINDLESS, CANNIBAL, KILLING MACHINES!

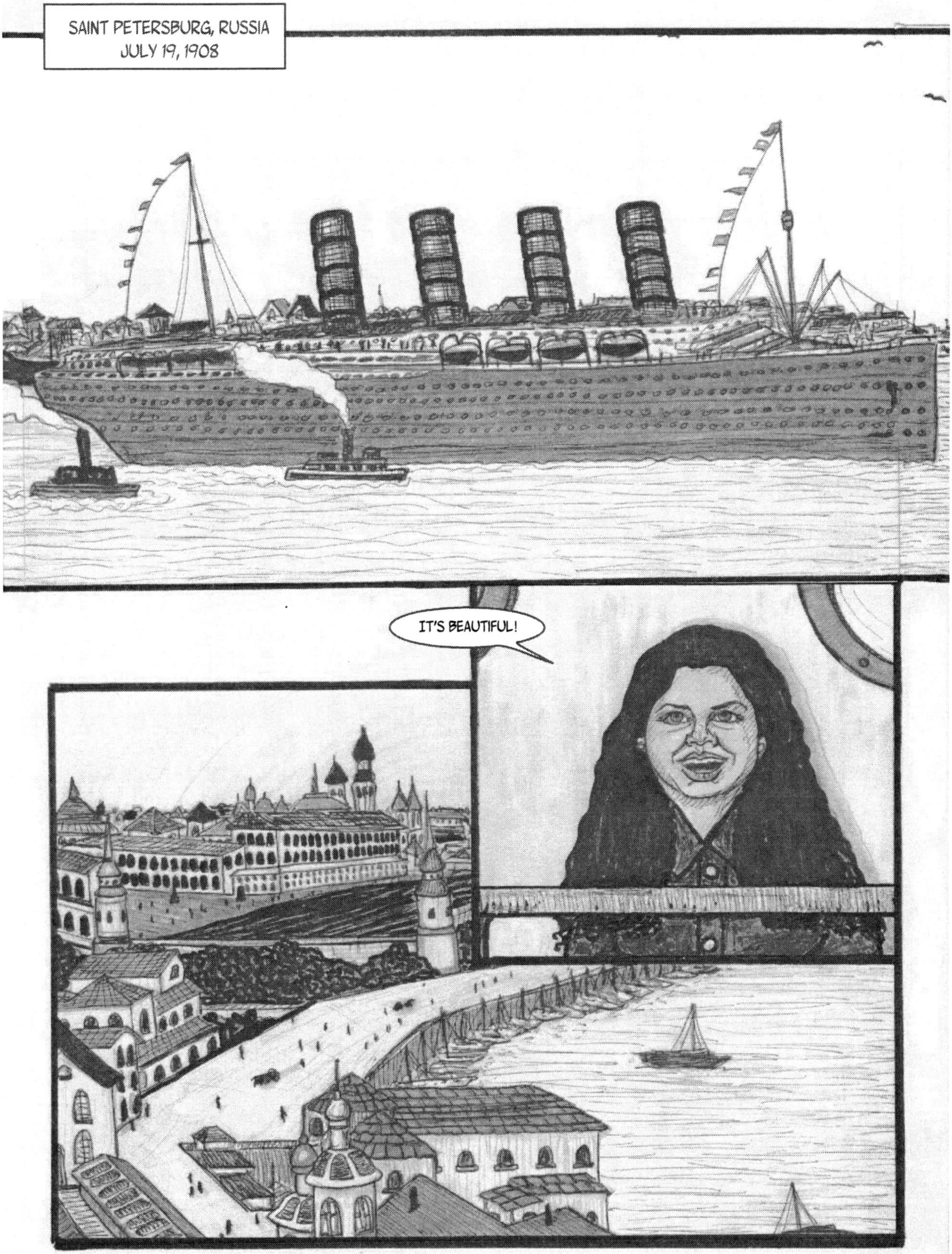
SAINT PETERSBURG, RUSSIA
JULY 19, 1908
IT'S BEAUTIFUL!

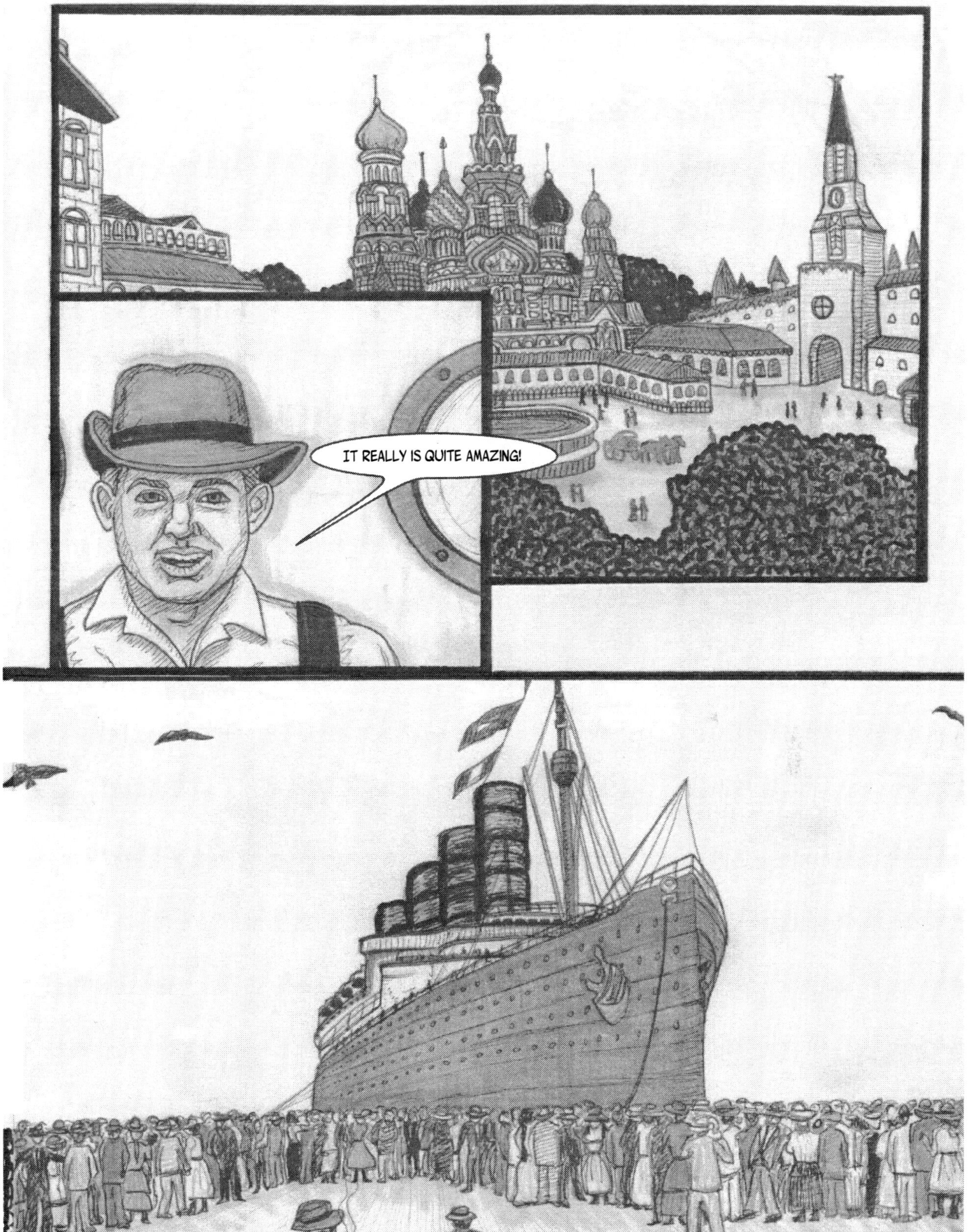
IT REALLY IS QUITE AMAZING!

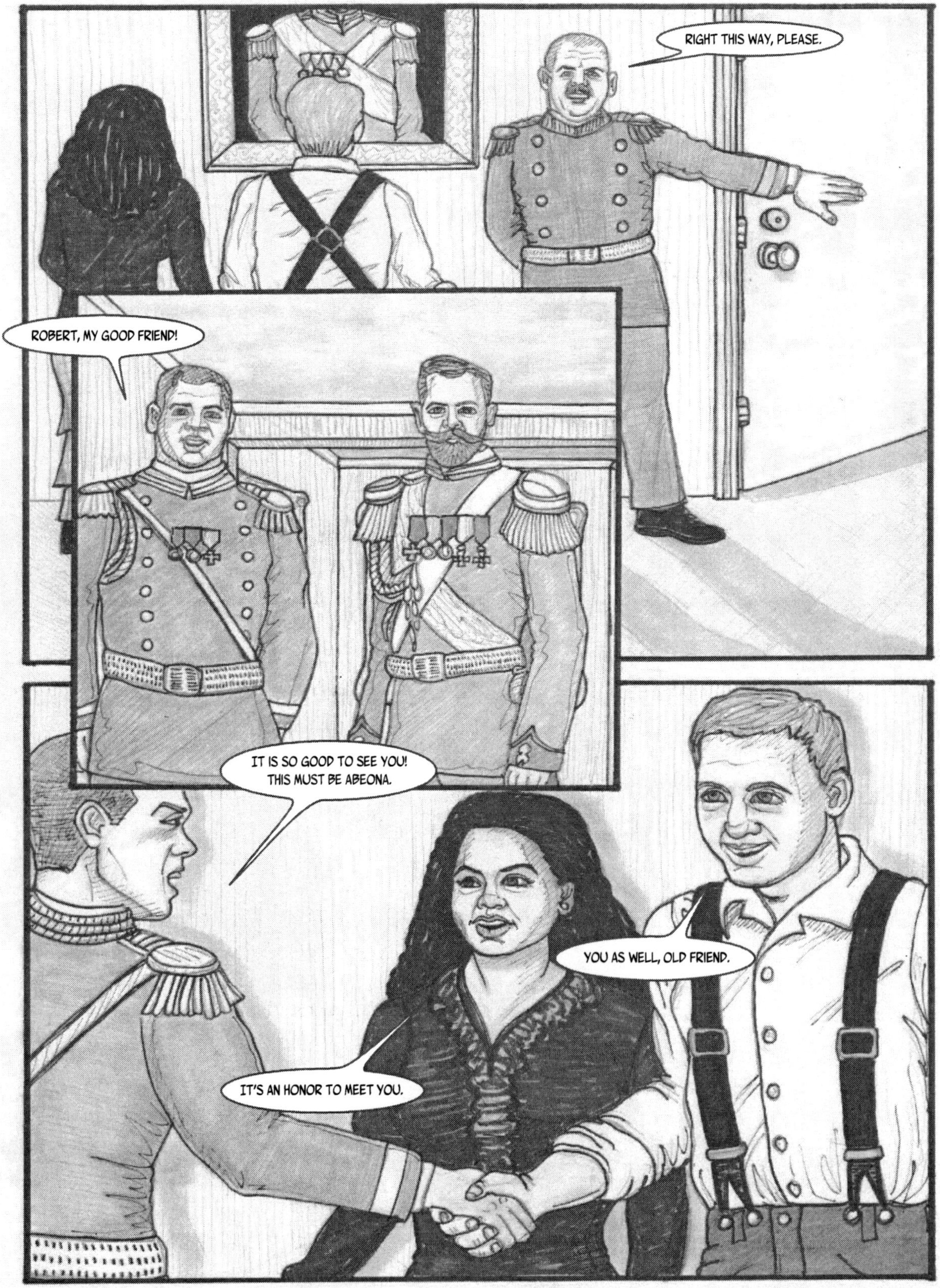
RIGHT THIS WAY, PLEASE.
ROBERT, MY GOOD FRIEND!
IT IS SO GOOD TO SEE YOU! THIS MUST BE ABEONA.
YOU AS WELL, OLD FRIEND.
IT'S AN HONOR TO MEET YOU.

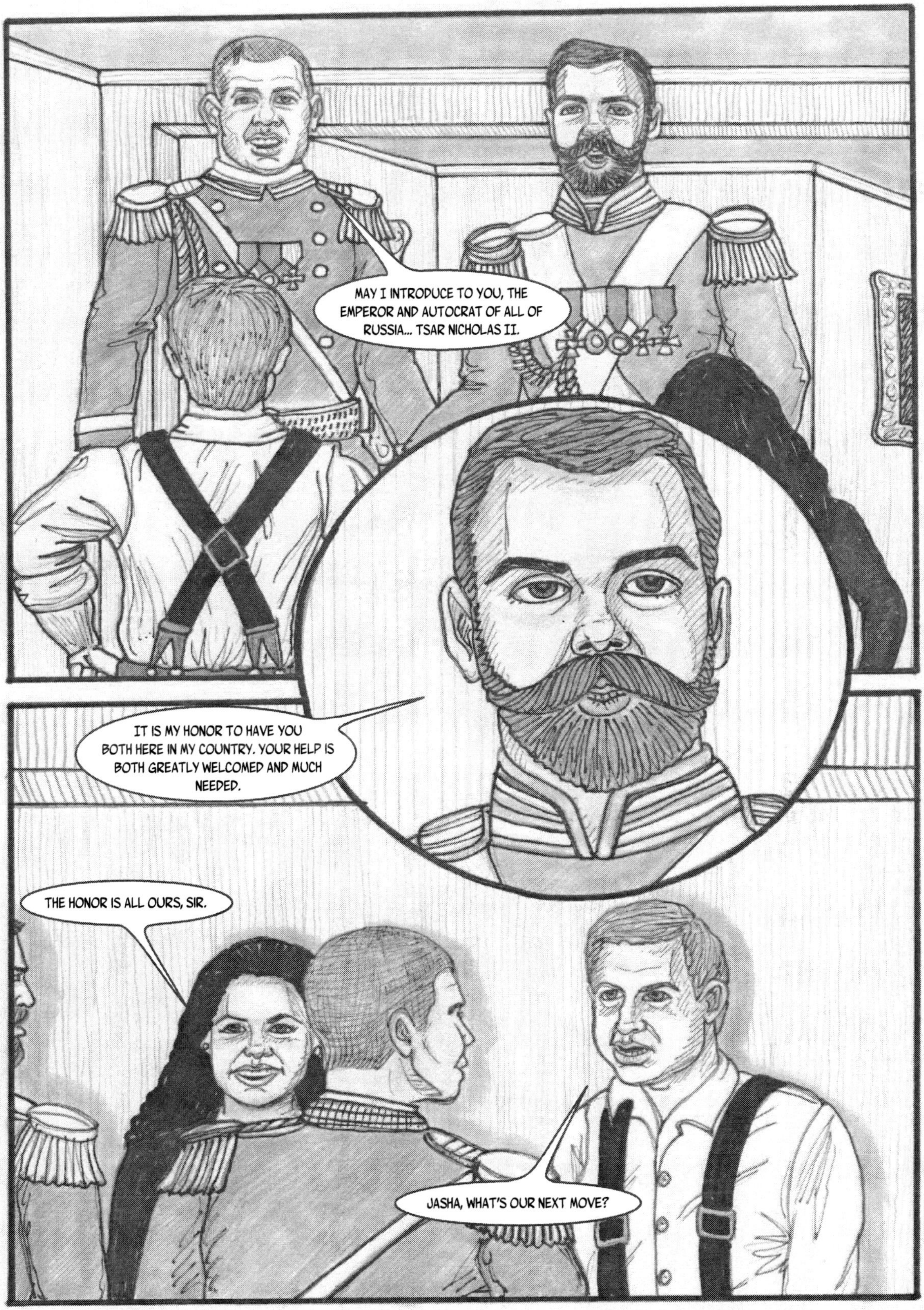

MAY I INTRODUCE TO YOU, THE EMPEROR AND AUTOCRAT OF ALL OF RUSSIA... TSAR NICHOLAS II.
IT IS MY HONOR TO HAVE YOU BOTH HERE IN MY COUNTRY. YOUR HELP IS BOTH GREATLY WELCOMED AND MUCH NEEDED.
THE HONOR IS ALL OURS, SIR.
JASHA, WHAT'S OUR NEXT MOVE?

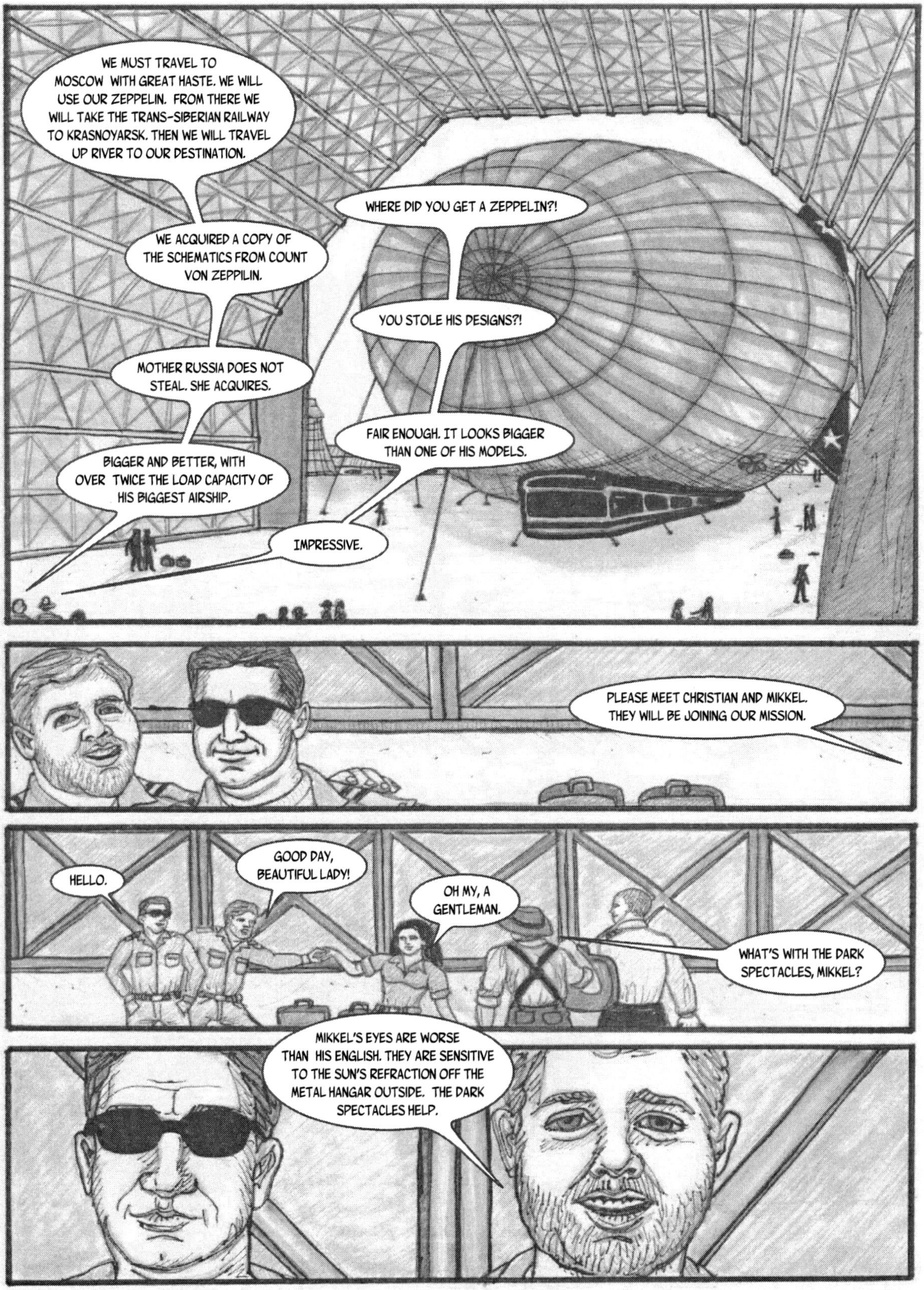
WE MUST TRAVEL TO MOSCOW WITH GREAT HASTE. WE WILL USE OUR ZEPPELIN. FROM THERE WE WILL TAKE THE TRANS-SIBERIAN RAILWAY TO KRASNOYARSK. THEN WE WILL TRAVEL UP RIVER TO OUR DESTINATION.
WHERE DID YOU GET A ZEPPELIN?!
WE ACQUIRED A COPY OF THE SCHEMATICS FROM COUNT VON ZEPPILIN.
YOU STOLE HIS DESIGNS?!
MOTHER RUSSIA DOES NOT STEAL. SHE ACQUIRES.
FAIR ENOUGH. IT LOOKS BIGGER THAN ONE OF HIS MODELS.
BIGGER AND BETTER, WITH OVER TWICE THE LOAD CAPACITY OF HIS BIGGEST AIRSHIP.
IMPRESSIVE.
PLEASE MEET CHRISTIAN AND MIKKEL. THEY WILL BE JOINING OUR MISSION.
HELLO.
GOOD DAY, BEAUTIFUL LADY!
OH MY, A GENTLEMAN.
WHAT'S WITH THE DARK SPECTACLES, MIKKEL?
MIKKEL'S EYES ARE WORSE THAN HIS ENGLISH. THEY ARE SENSITIVE TO THE SUN'S REFRACTION OFF THE METAL HANGAR OUTSIDE. THE DARK SPECTACLES HELP.

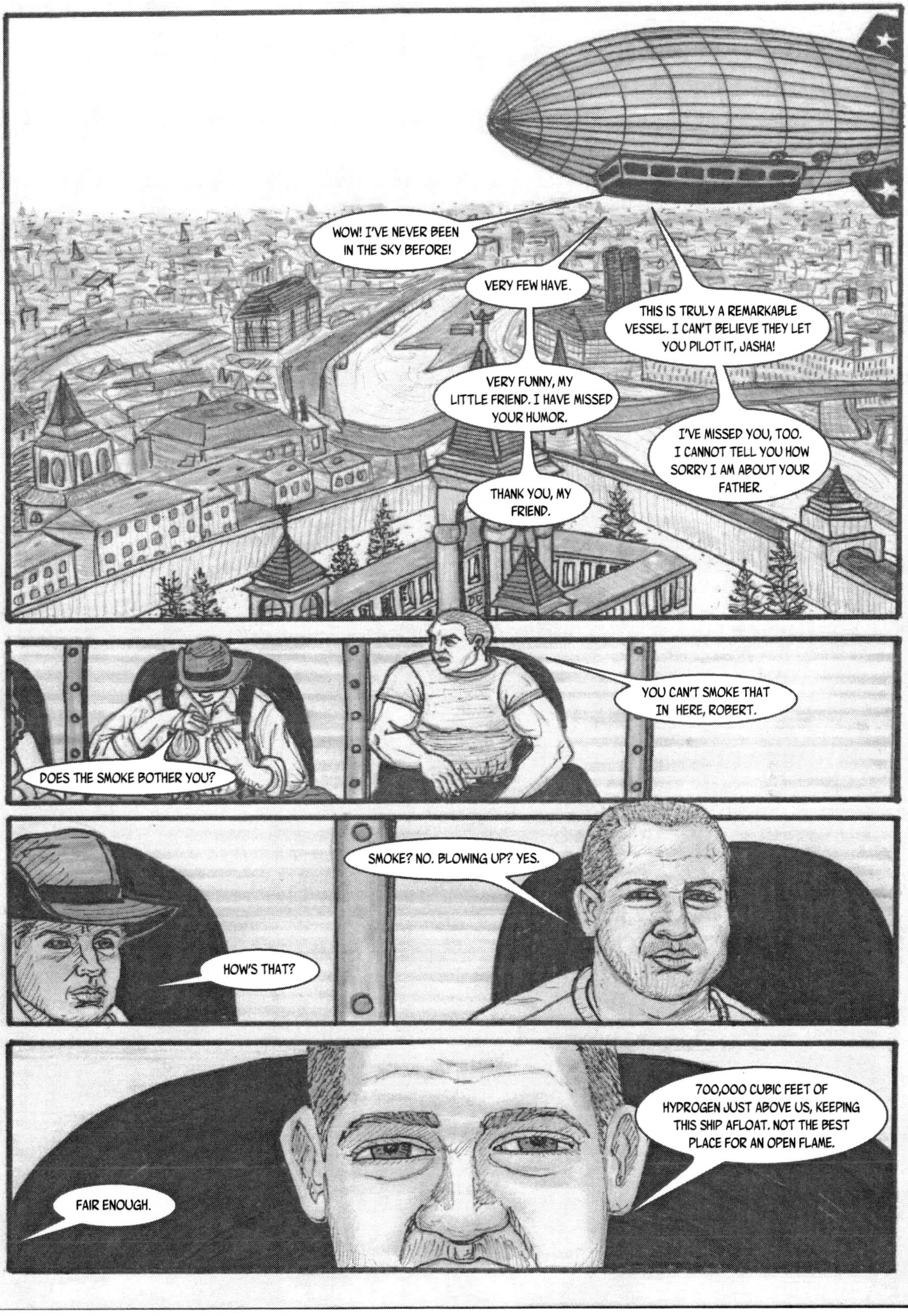
WOW! I'VE NEVER BEEN IN THE SKY BEFORE!
VERY FEW HAVE.
THIS IS TRULY A REMARKABLE VESSEL. I CAN'T BELIEVE THEY LET YOU PILOT IT, JASHA!
VERY FUNNY, MY LITTLE FRIEND. I HAVE MISSED YOUR HUMOR.
I'VE MISSED YOU, TOO. I CANNOT TELL YOU HOW SORRY I AM ABOUT YOUR FATHER.
THANK YOU, MY FRIEND.
DOES THE SMOKE BOTHER YOU?
YOU CAN'T SMOKE THAT IN HERE, ROBERT.
SMOKE? NO. BLOWING UP? YES.
HOW'S THAT?
700,000 CUBIC FEET OF HYDROGEN JUST ABOVE US, KEEPING THIS SHIP AFLOAT. NOT THE BEST PLACE FOR AN OPEN FLAME.
FAIR ENOUGH.

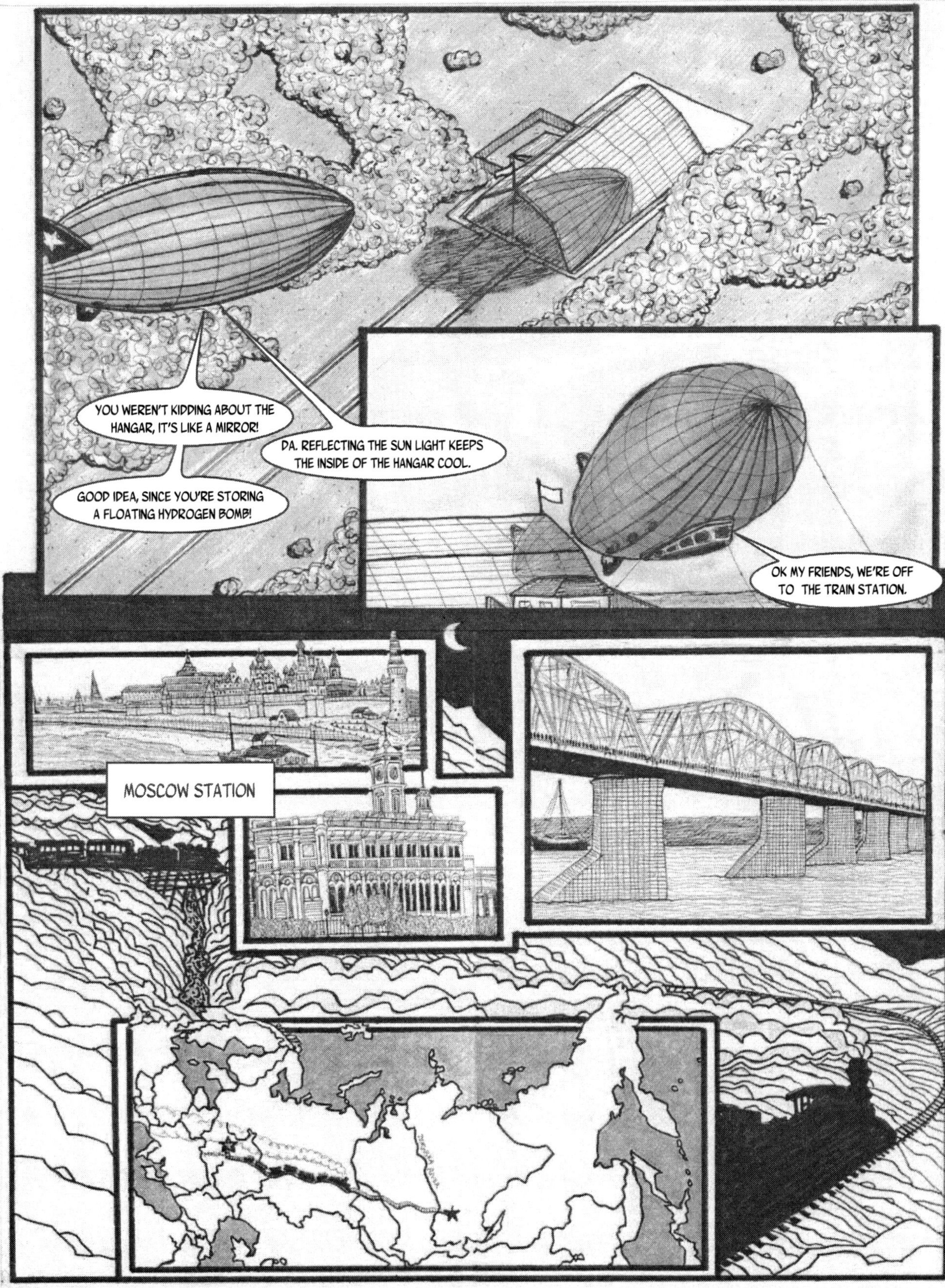
YOU WEREN'T KIDDING ABOUT THE HANGAR, IT'S LIKE A MIRROR!
DA. REFLECTING THE SUN LIGHT KEEPS THE INSIDE OF THE HANGAR COOL.
GOOD IDEA, SINCE YOU'RE STORING A FLOATING HYDROGEN BOMB!
OK MY FRIENDS, WE'RE OFF TO THE TRAIN STATION.
MOSCOW STATION

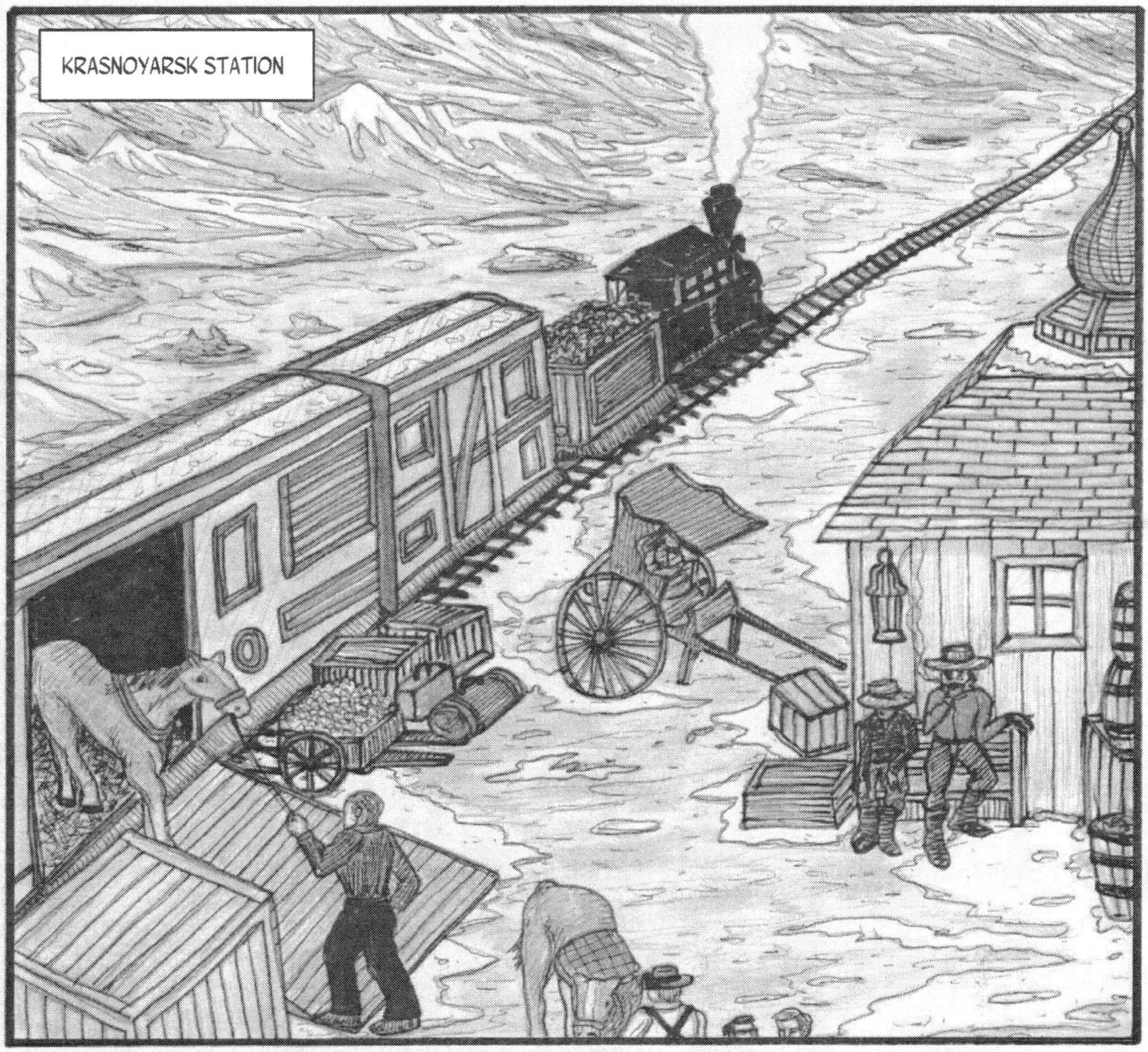
KRASNOYARSK STATION

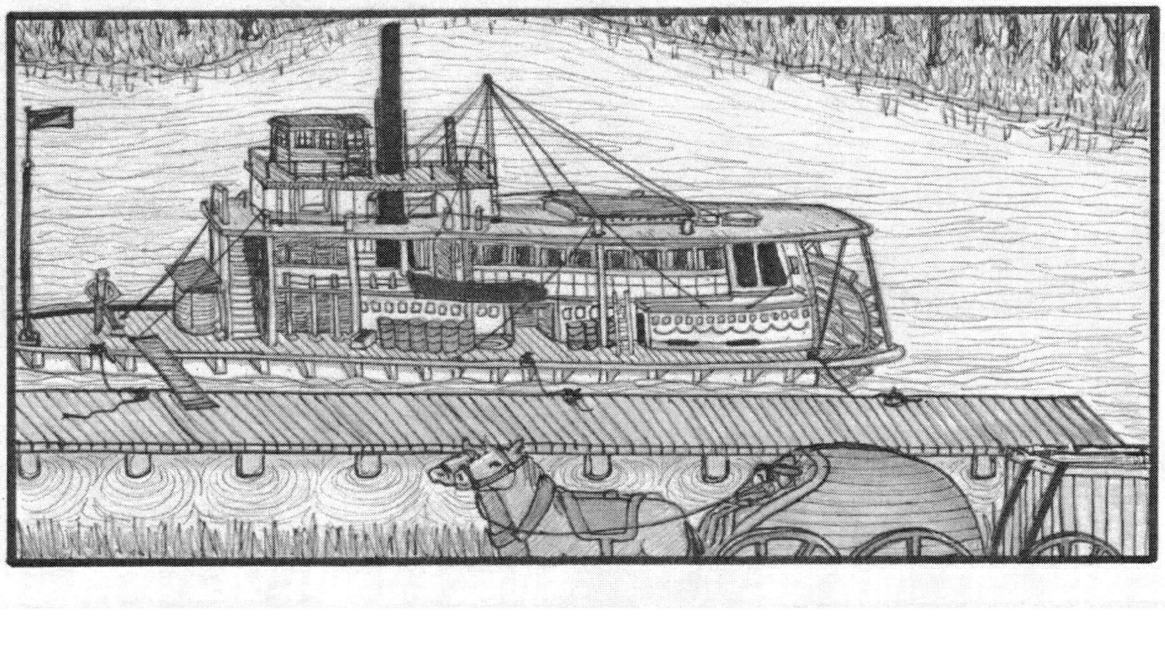

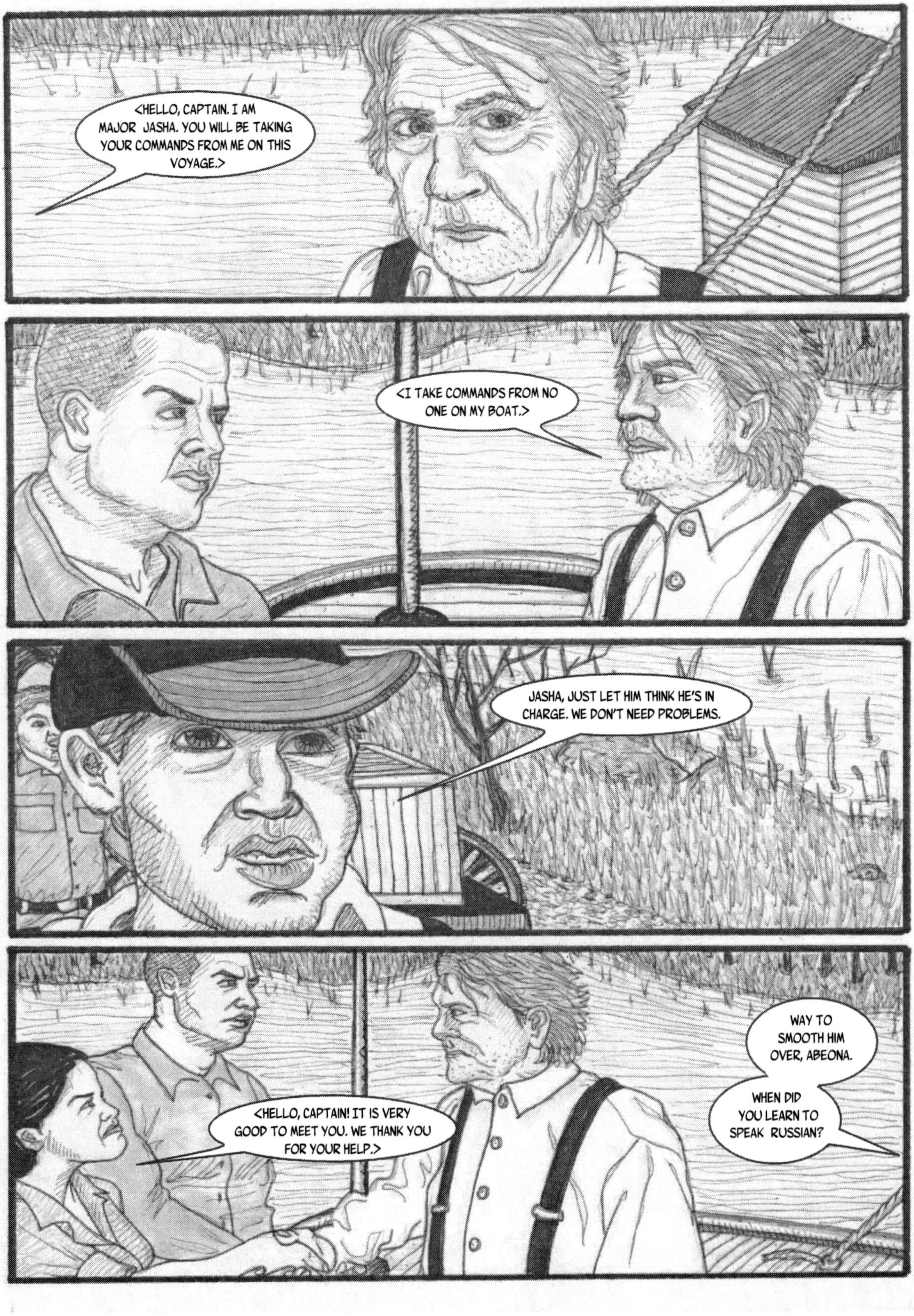
<HELLO, CAPTAIN. I AM MAJOR JASHA. YOU WILL BE TAKING YOUR COMMANDS FROM ME ON THIS VOYAGE.>
<I TAKE COMMANDS FROM NO ONE ON MY BOAT.>
JASHA, JUST LET HIM THINK HE'S IN CHARGE. WE DON'T NEED PROBLEMS.
<HELLO, CAPTAIN! IT IS VERY GOOD TO MEET YOU. WE THANK YOU FOR YOUR HELP.>
WAY TO SMOOTH HIM OVER, ABEONA.
WHEN DID YOU LEARN TO SPEAK RUSSIAN?

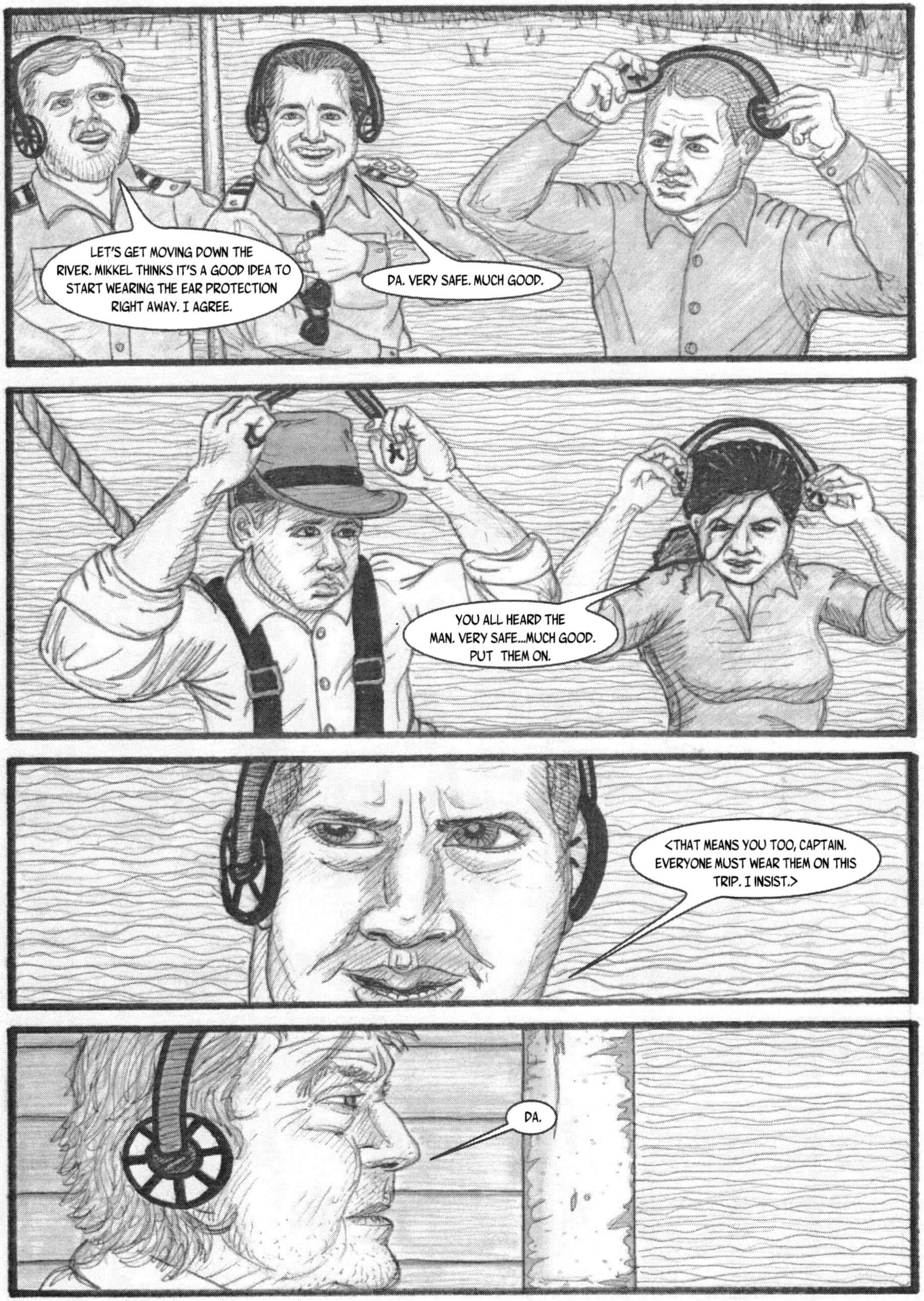
LET'S GET MOVING DOWN THE RIVER. MIKKEL THINKS IT'S A GOOD IDEA TO START WEARING THE EAR PROTECTION RIGHT AWAY. I AGREE.
DA. VERY SAFE. MUCH GOOD.
YOU ALL HEARD THE MAN. VERY SAFE...MUCH GOOD. PUT THEM ON.
<THAT MEANS YOU TOO, CAPTAIN. EVERYONE MUST WEAR THEM ON THIS TRIP. I INSIST.>
DA.

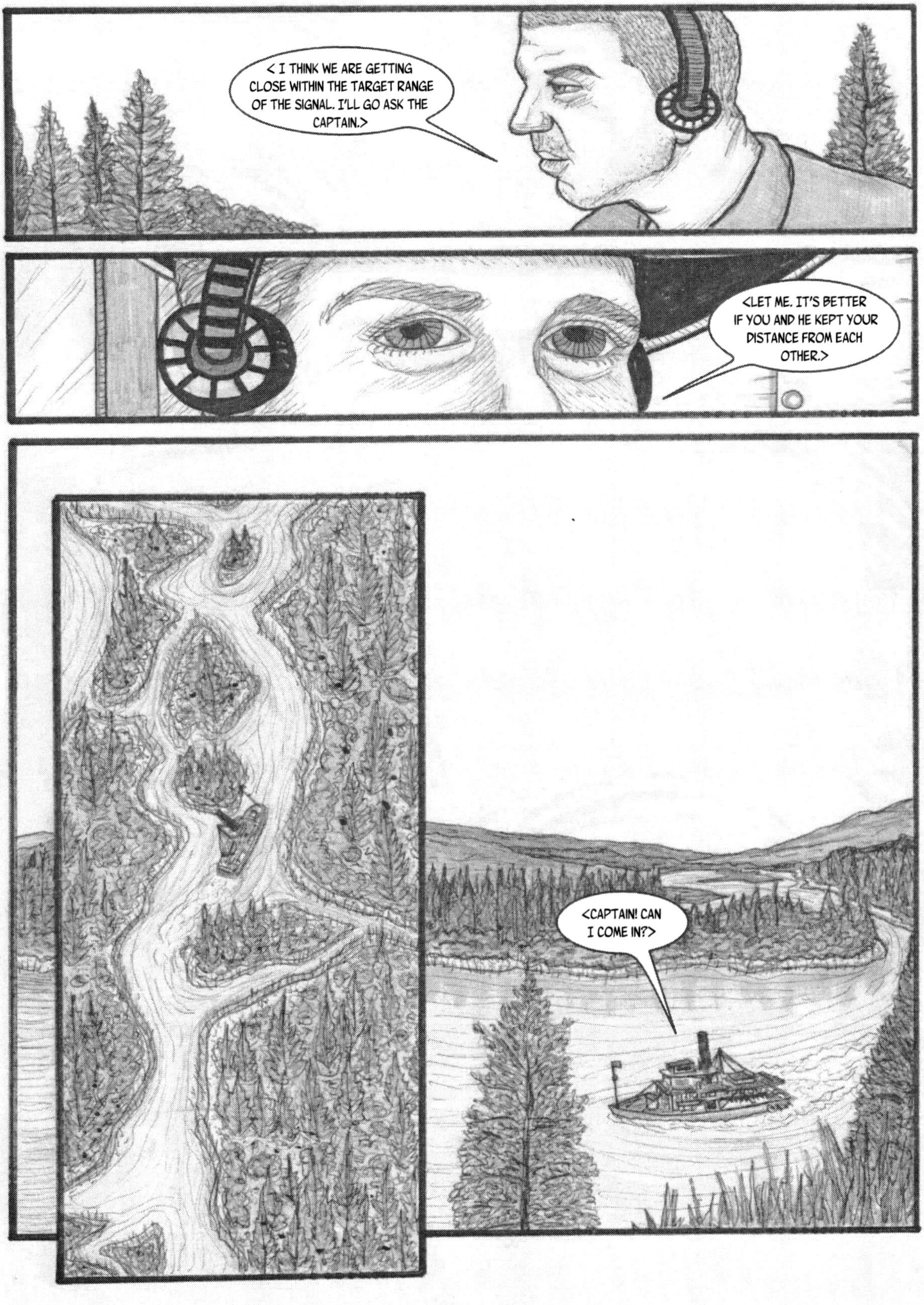
< I THINK WE ARE GETTING CLOSE WITHIN THE TARGET RANGE OF THE SIGNAL. I'LL GO ASK THE CAPTAIN.>
<LET ME. IT'S BETTER IF YOU AND HE KEPT YOUR DISTANCE FROM EACH OTHER.>
<CAPTAIN! CAN I COME IN?>

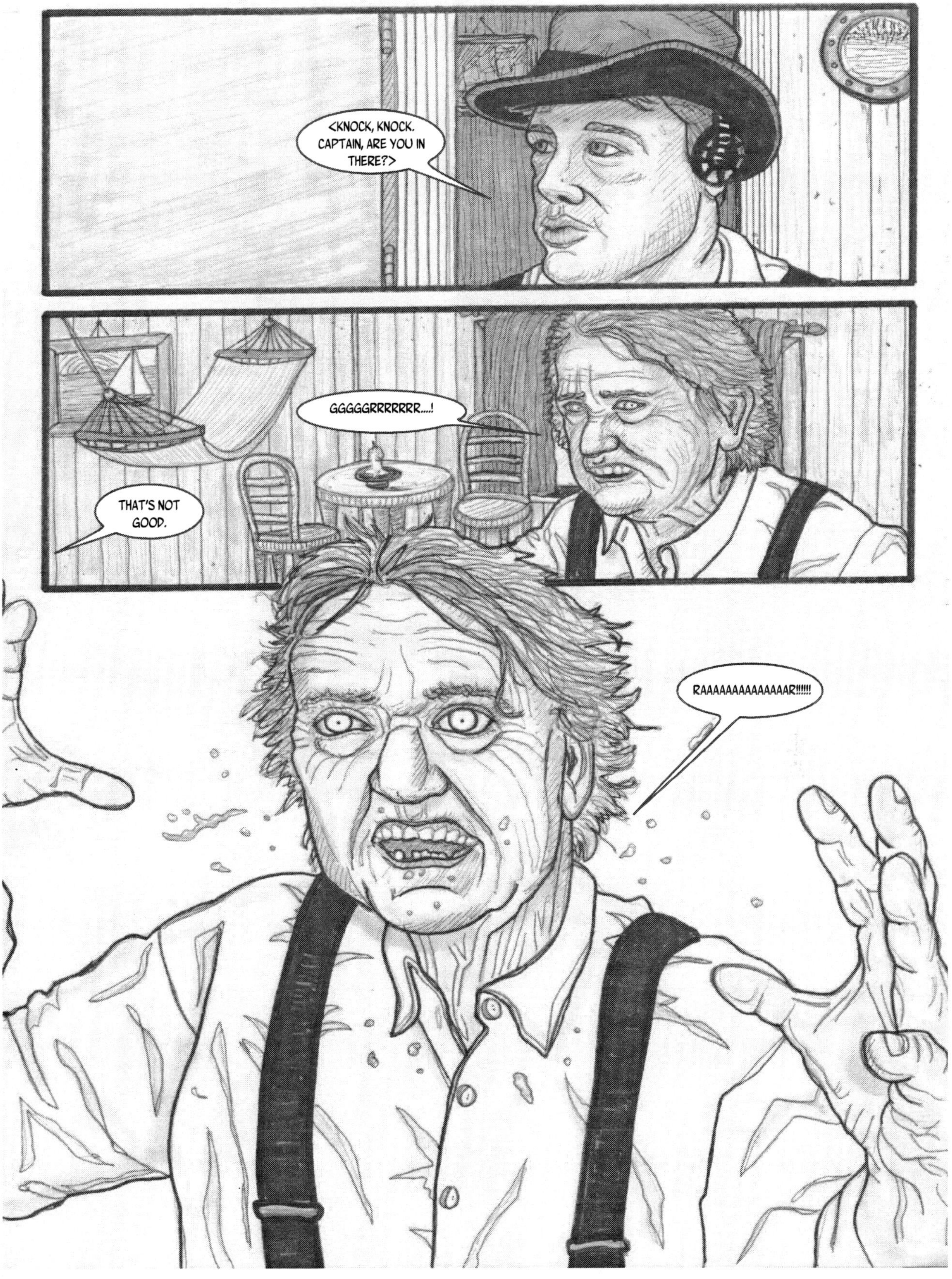
<KNOCK, KNOCK. CAPTAIN, ARE YOU IN THERE?>
GGGGGRRRRRRR....!
THAT'S NOT GOOD.
RAAAAAAAAAAAAAAR!!!!!!

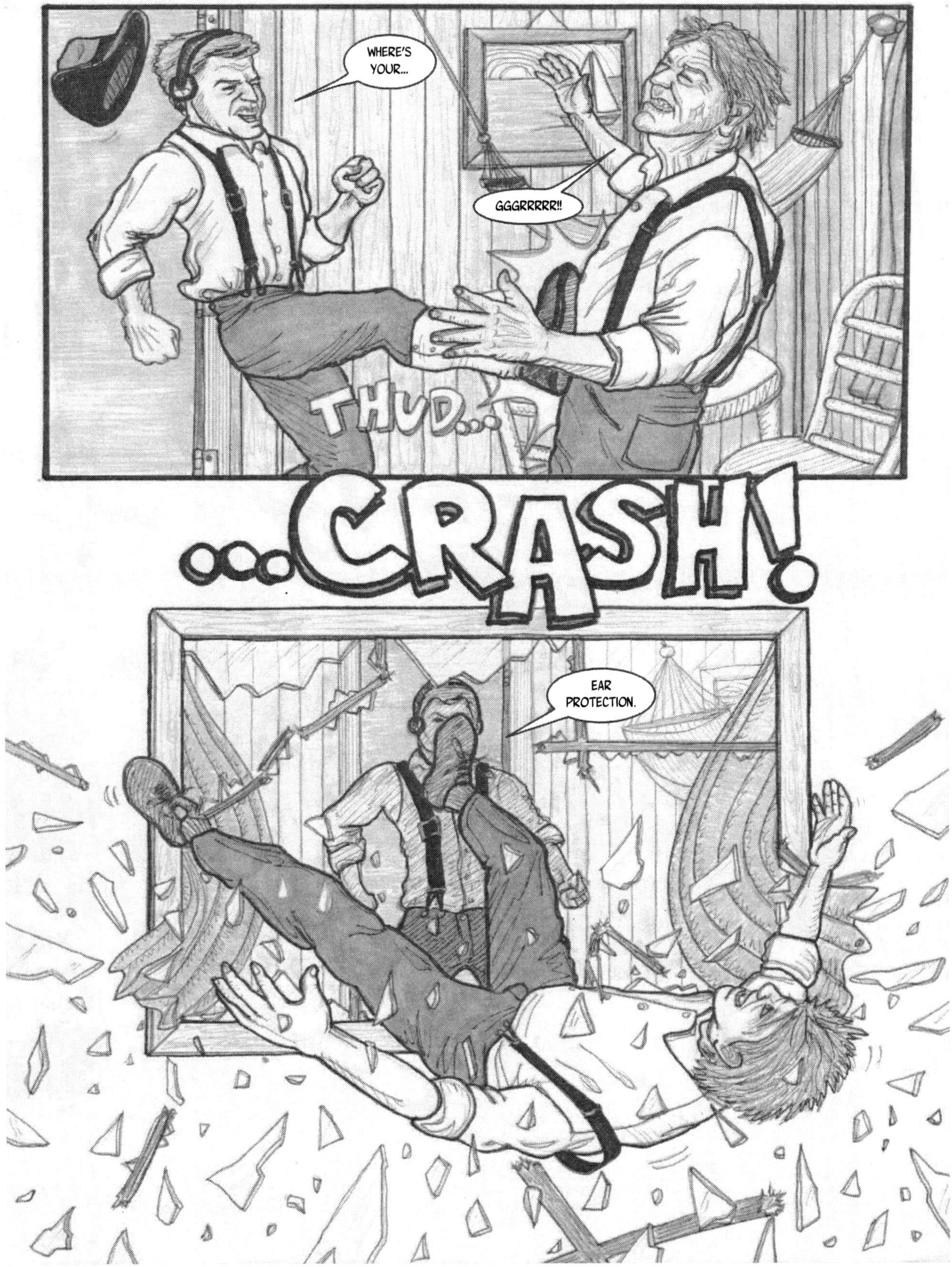
WHERE'S YOUR...
GGGRRRRR!!
THUD...
...CRASH!
EAR PROTECTION.

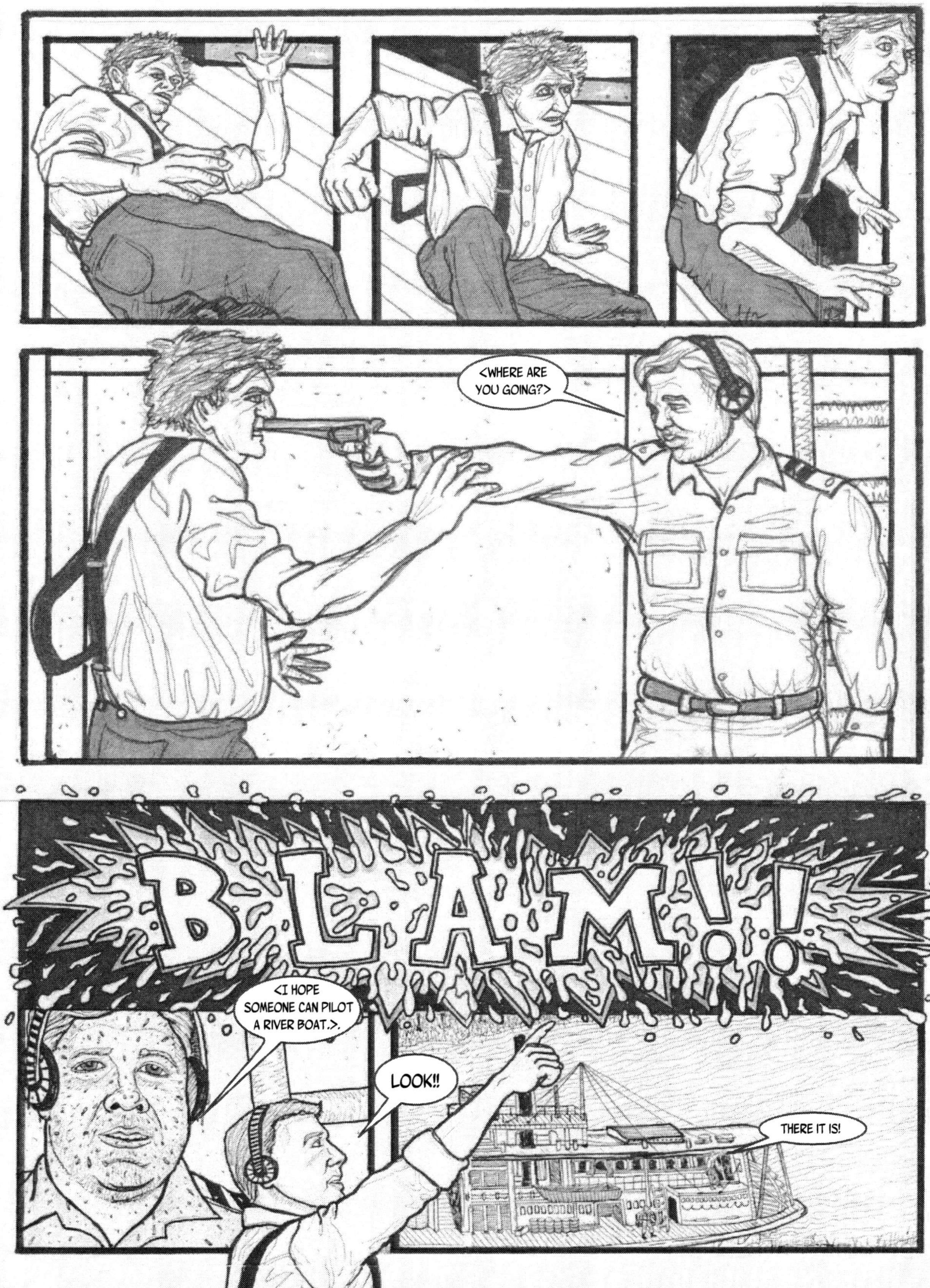
<WHERE ARE YOU GOING?>
BLAM!!
<I HOPE SOMEONE CAN PILOT A RIVER BOAT.>.
LOOK!!
THERE IT IS!

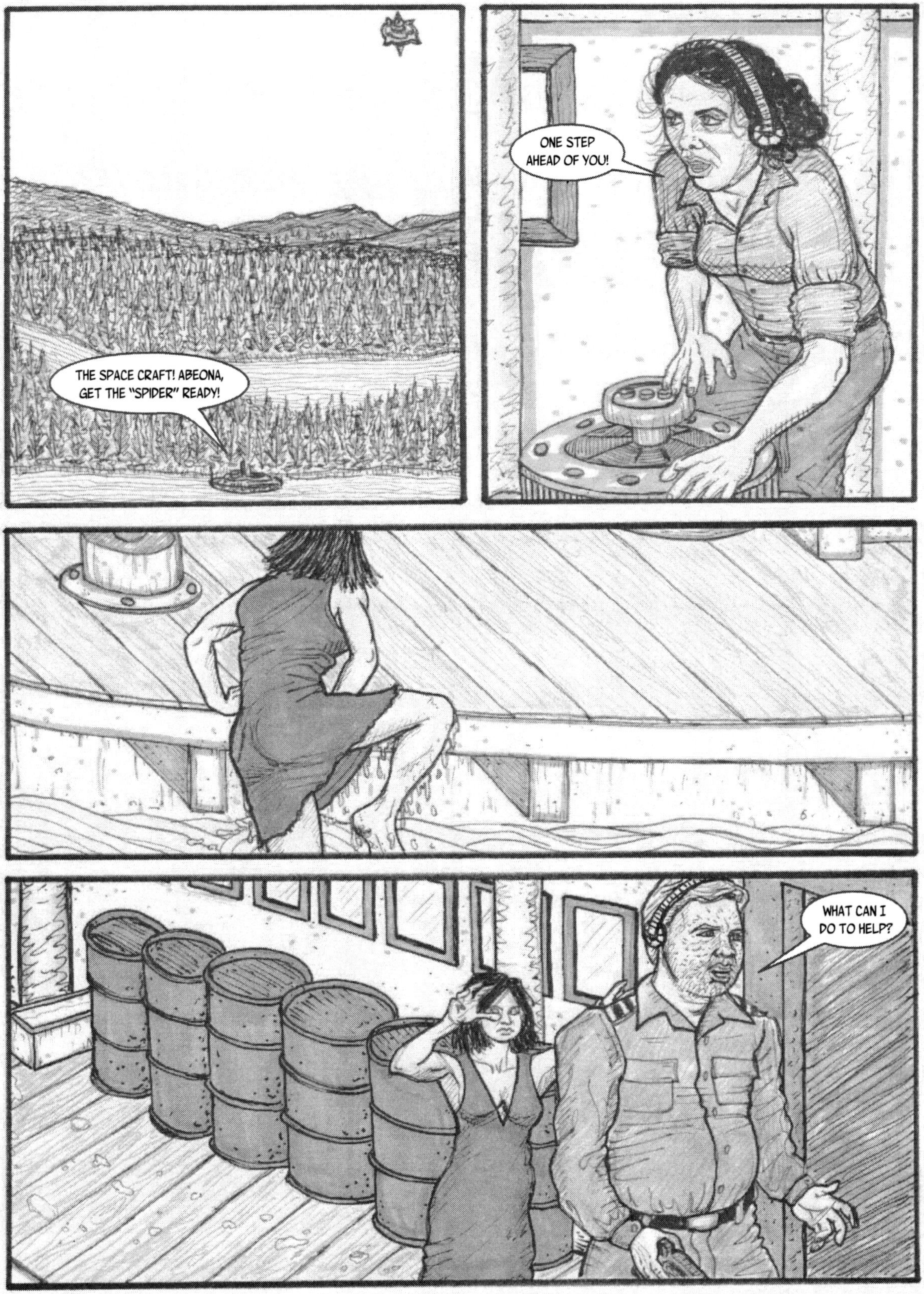
THE SPACE CRAFT! ABEONA, GET THE "SPIDER" READY!
ONE STEP AHEAD OF YOU!
WHAT CAN I DO TO HELP?

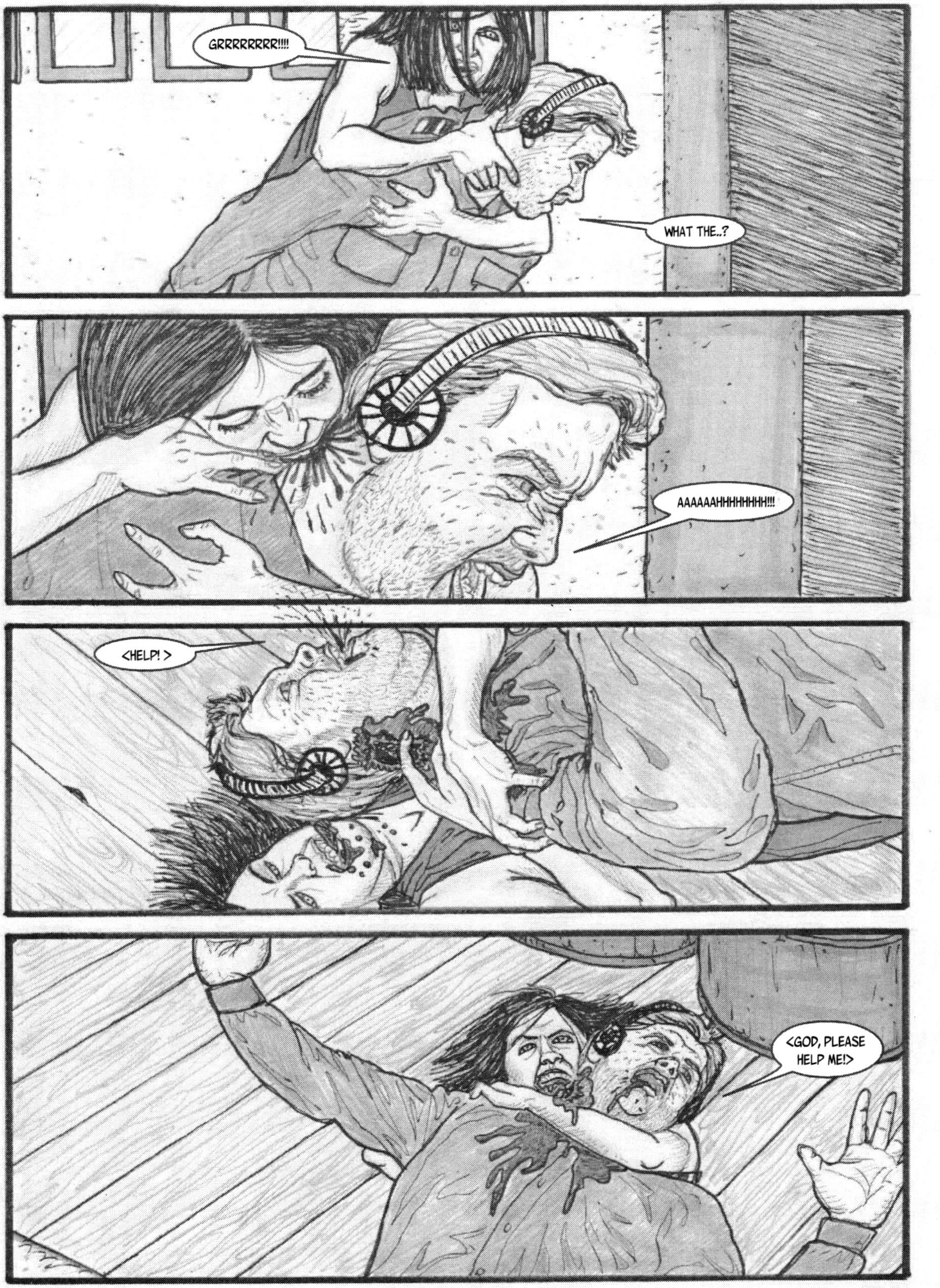
GRRRRRRRR!!!!
WHAT THE..?
AAAAAAHHHHHHHH!!!
<HELP! >
<GOD, PLEASE
HELP ME!>

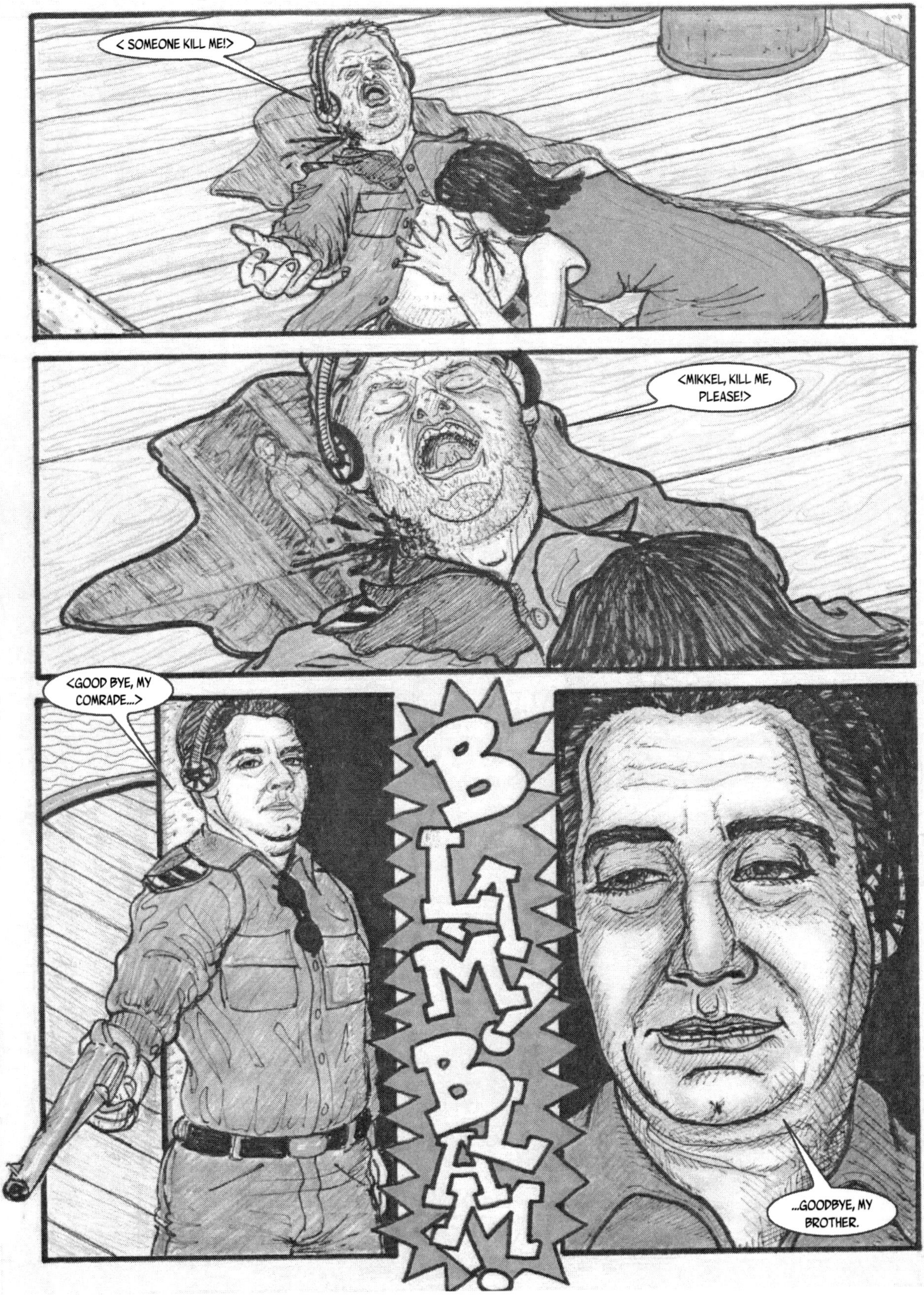
< SOMEONE KILL ME!>
<MIKKEL, KILL ME, PLEASE!>
<GOOD BYE, MY COMRADE...>
BLAM! BLAM!
...GOODBYE, MY BROTHER.

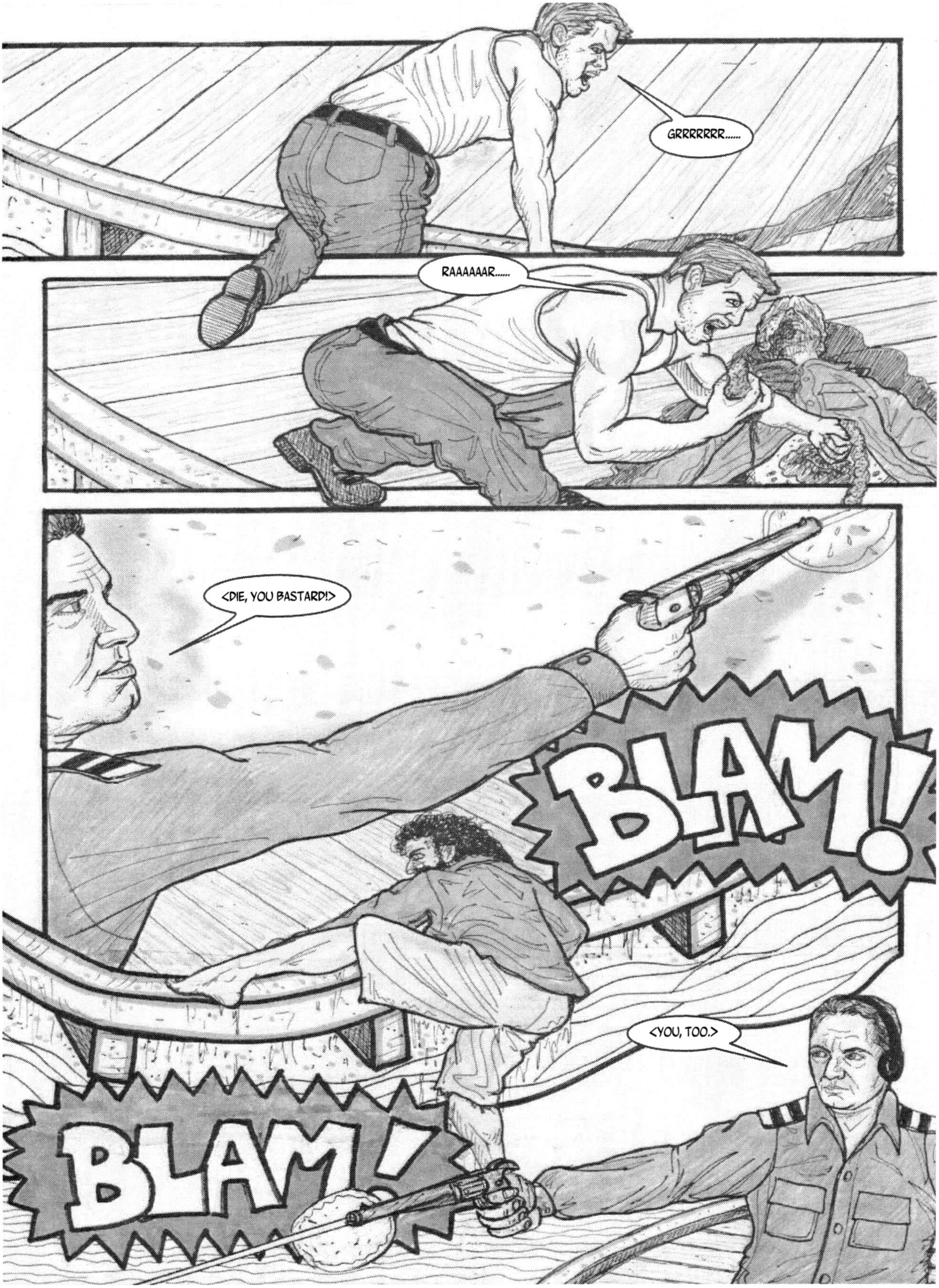
GRRRRRRR......
RAAAAAAR......
<DIE, YOU BASTARD!>
BLAM!
<YOU, TOO.>
BLAM!

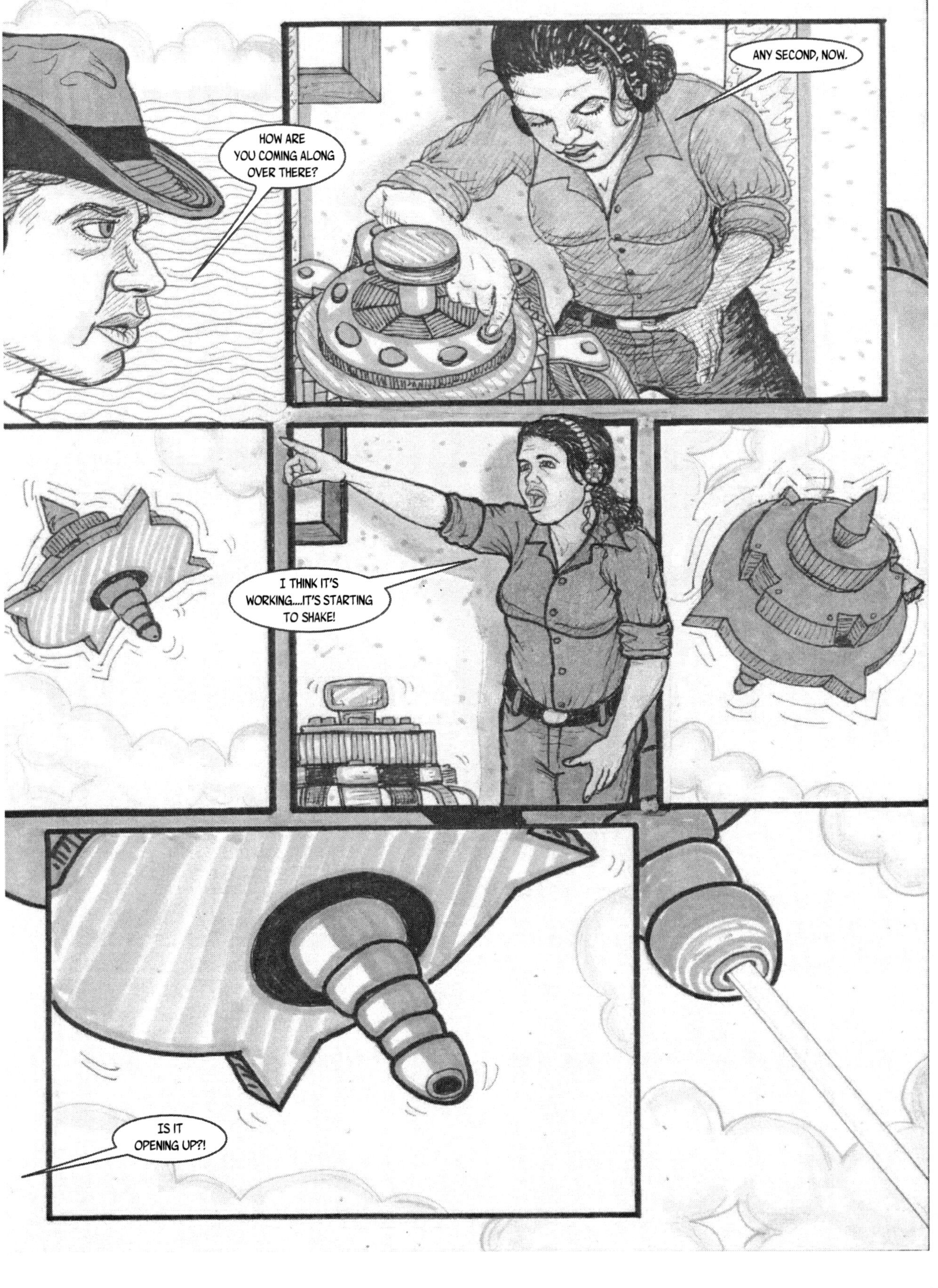
HOW ARE YOU COMING ALONG OVER THERE?
ANY SECOND, NOW.
I THINK IT'S WORKING....IT'S STARTING TO SHAKE!
IS IT OPENING UP?!

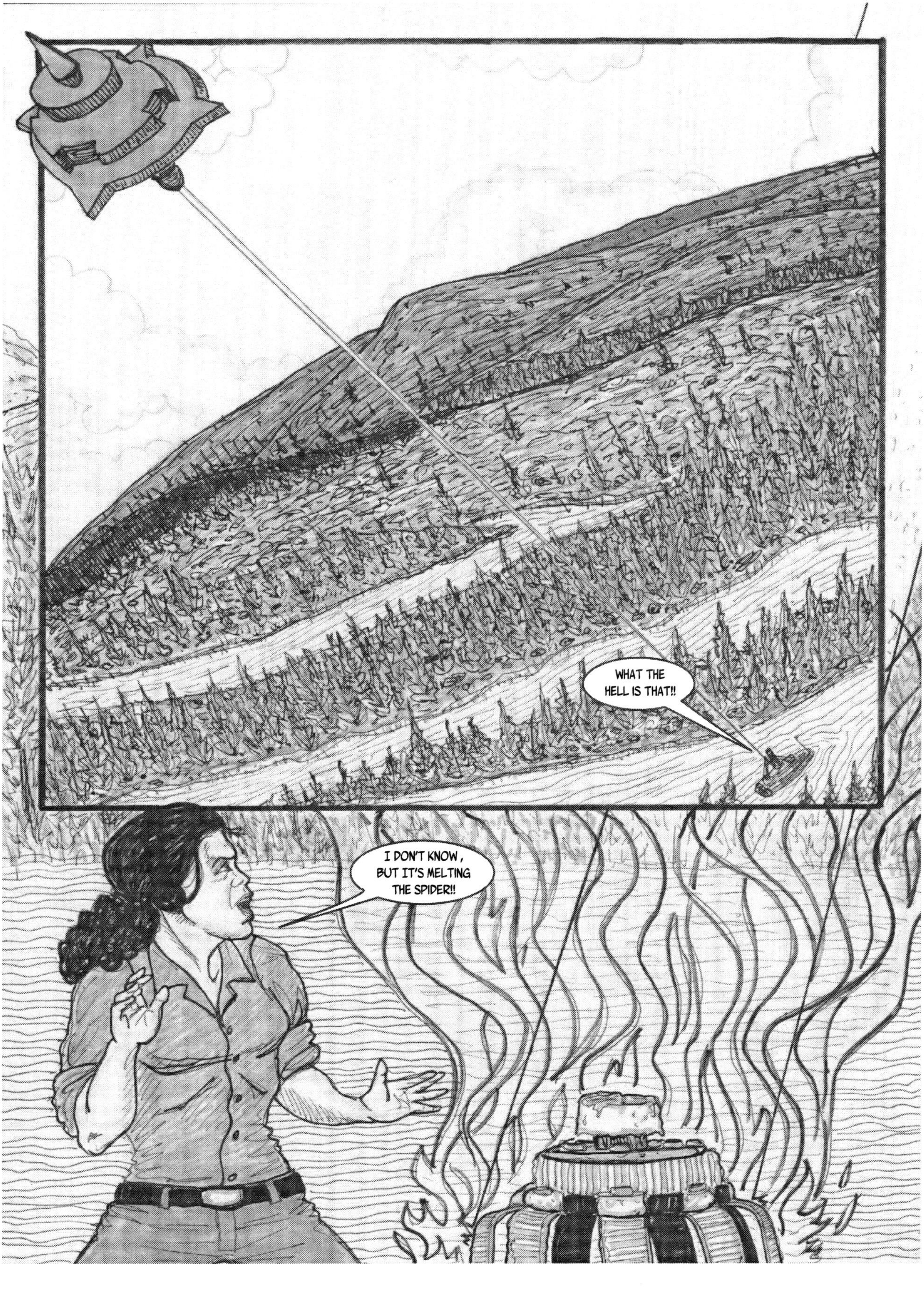
WHAT THE HELL IS THAT!!
I DON'T KNOW , BUT IT'S MELTING THE SPIDER!!

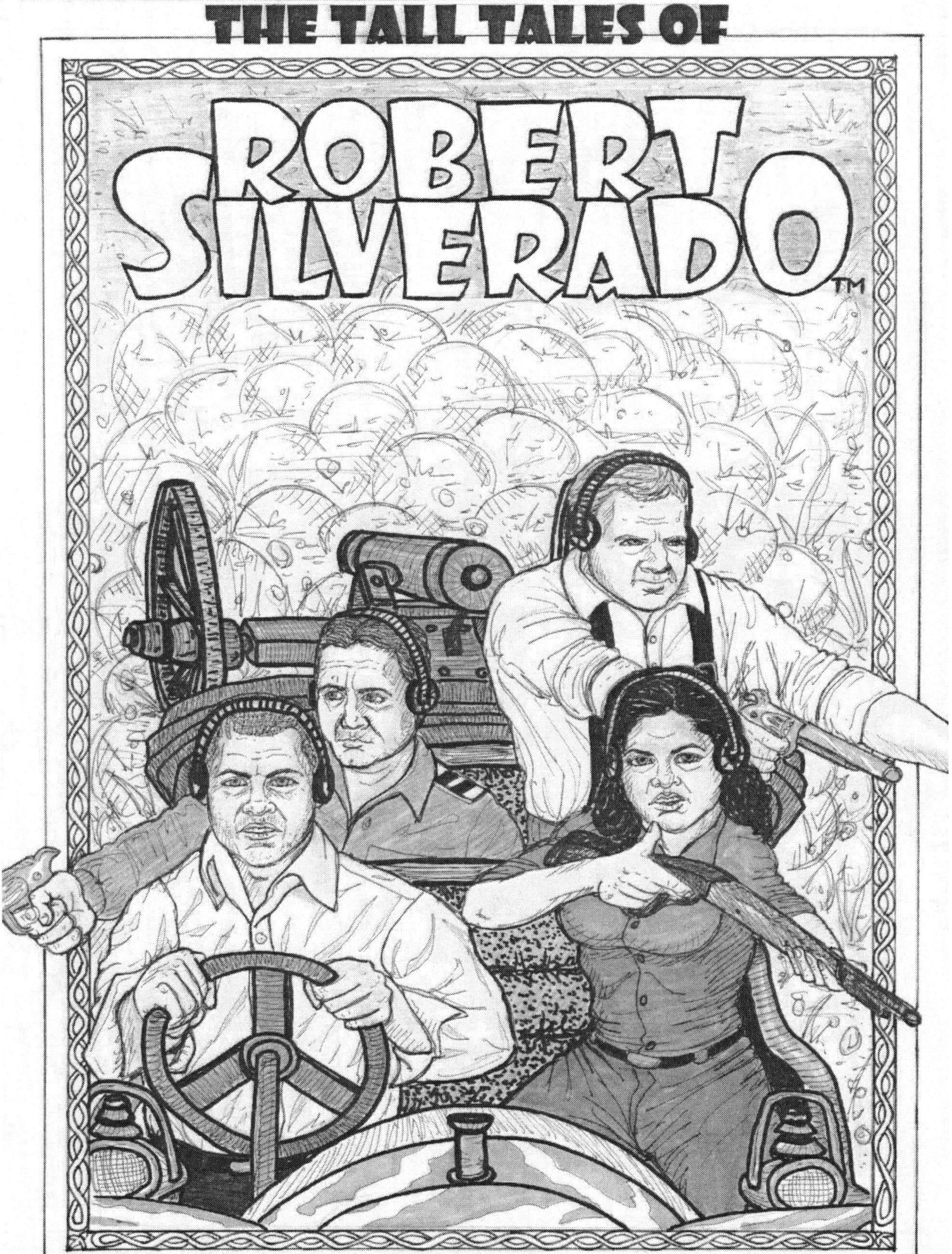
THE TALL TALES OF
ROBERT SILVERADO
TM

THE TALL TALES OF ROBERT SILVERADO

SIBERIAN INVASION

CHAPTER FOUR

WE JOIN SPECIAL AGENT ROBERT SILVERADO AND HIS TEAM AS THEY CULMINATE IN THE THICK OF BATTLE. AFTER A FAILED ATTEMPT TO REPEL THE DEADLY RADIO SIGNAL (THAT AN ALIEN SATELLITE IS SPREADING IN A DEADLY CIRCUMFERENCE... POSSESSING ALL IN ITS PATH) THEY MAKE A DESPERATE ATTEMPT TO ESCAPE BOTH THE SATELLITE'S DEADLY LIGHT BEAM, AS WELL AS THE CRAZED CANNIBALS IT HAS UNDER ITS CONTROL. "PLAN A" HAS HOPELESSLY FAILED IN THEIR ATTEMPT TO SAVE THE WORLD FROM THIS GROWING PLIGHT, BUT NEVER COUNT ROBERT OUT OF THE FIGHT! "PLAN B" IS USUALLY UP HIS SLEEVE, WITH A "PLAN C" UNDER HIS HAT, TO BOOT!

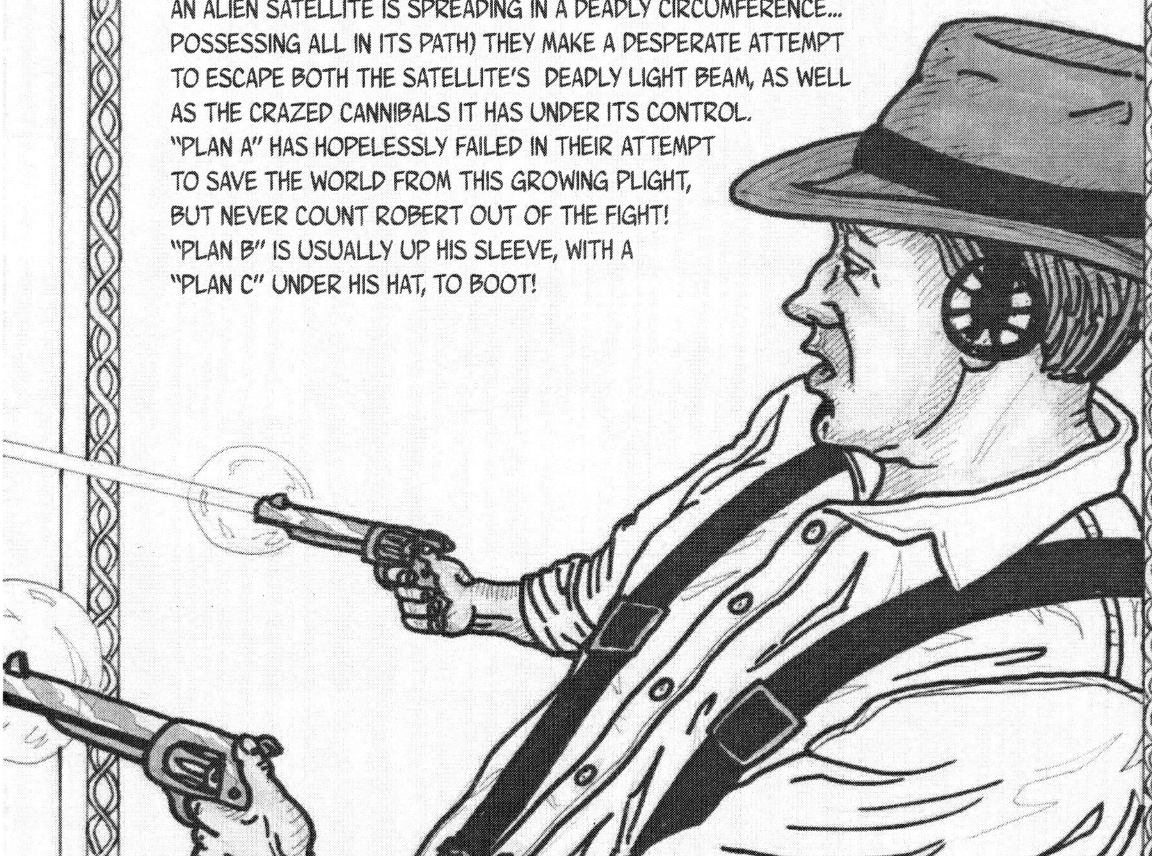

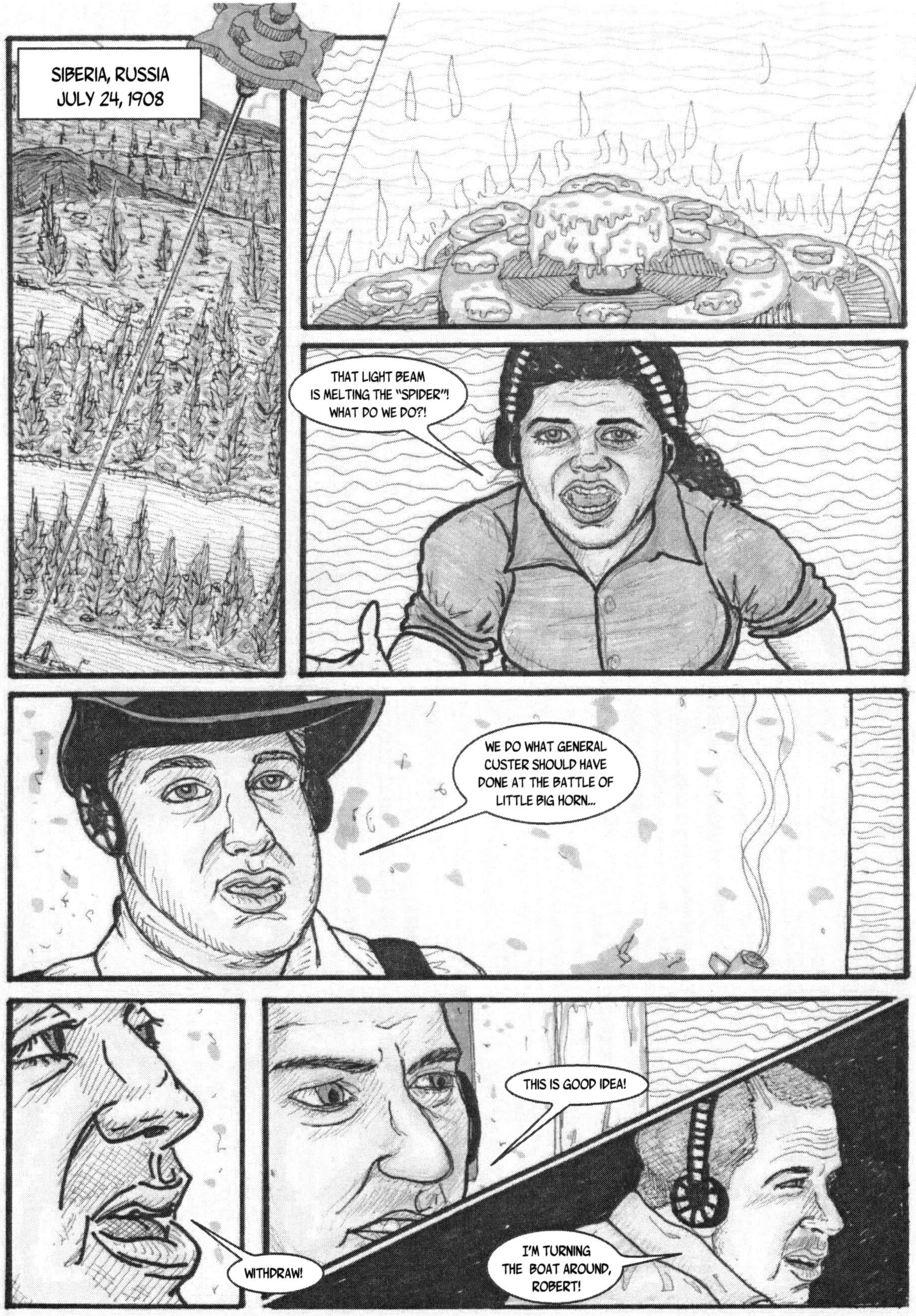
SIBERIA, RUSSIA
JULY 24, 1908
THAT LIGHT BEAM IS MELTING THE "SPIDER"! WHAT DO WE DO?!
WE DO WHAT GENERAL CUSTER SHOULD HAVE DONE AT THE BATTLE OF LITTLE BIG HORN...
WITHDRAW!
THIS IS GOOD IDEA!
I'M TURNING THE BOAT AROUND, ROBERT!

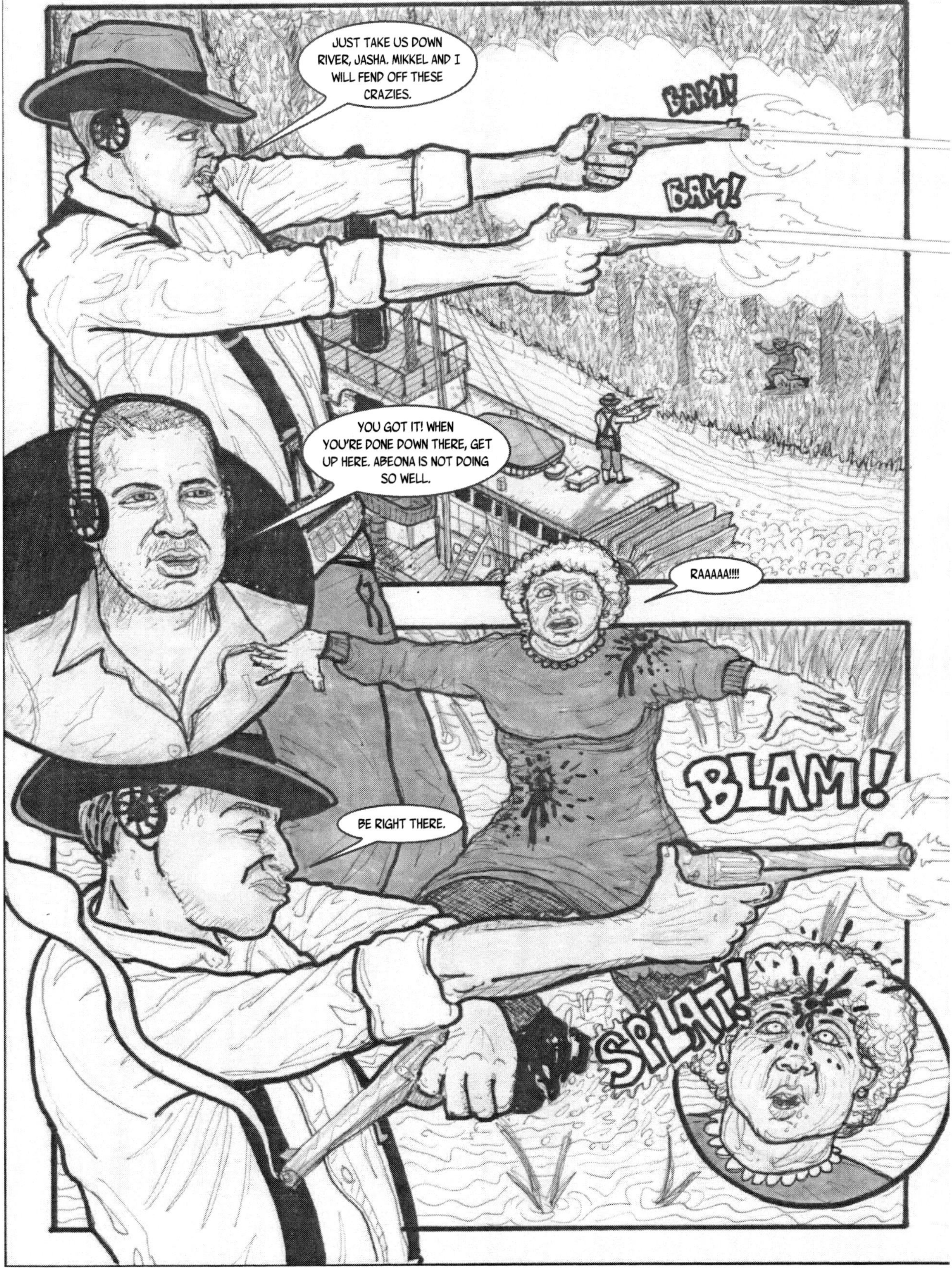
JUST TAKE US DOWN RIVER, JASHA. MIKKEL AND I WILL FEND OFF THESE CRAZIES.
BAM!
BAM!
YOU GOT IT! WHEN YOU'RE DONE DOWN THERE, GET UP HERE. ABEONA IS NOT DOING SO WELL.
RAAAAA!!!!
BLAM!
BE RIGHT THERE.
SPLAT!

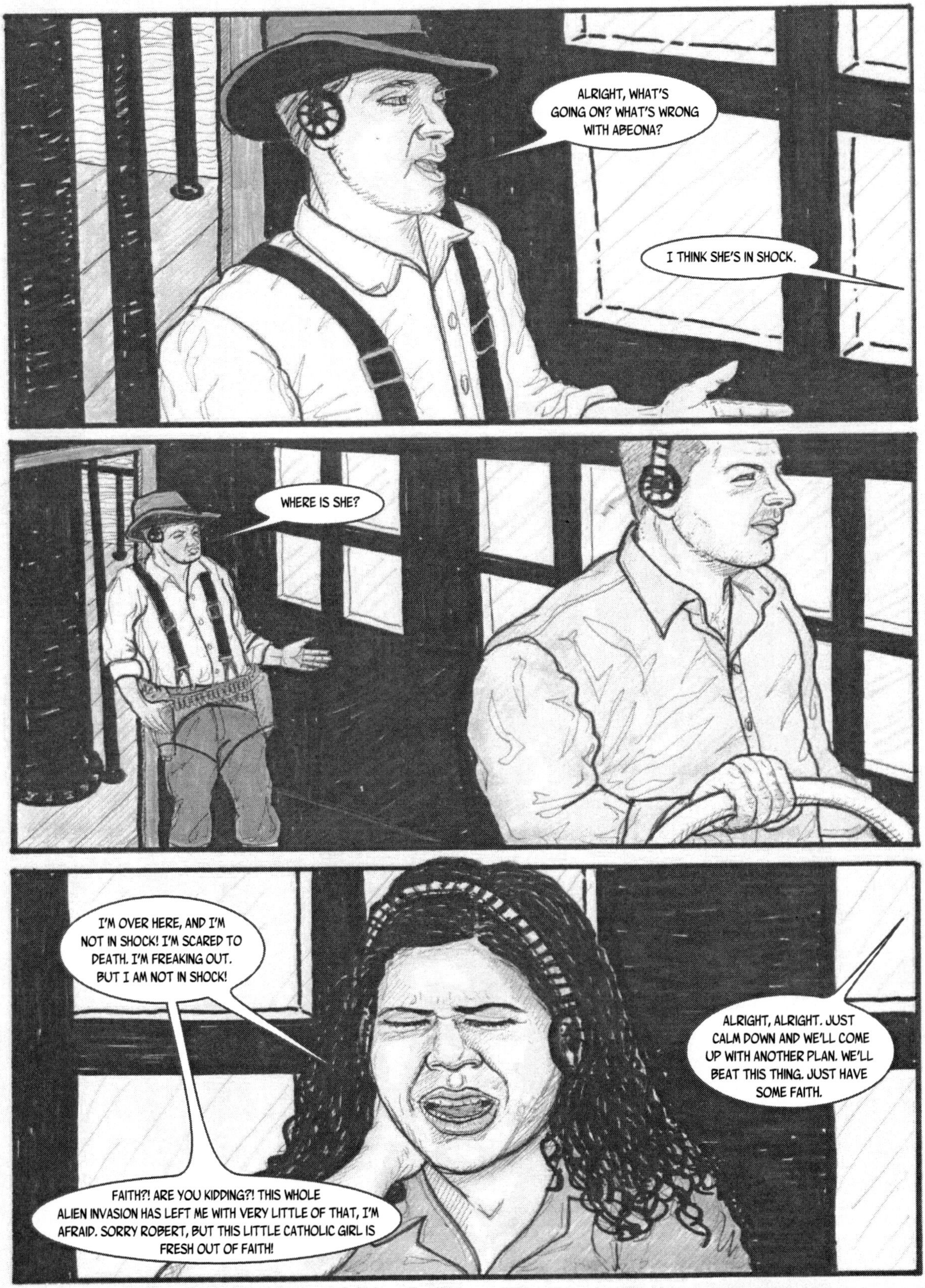
ALRIGHT, WHAT'S GOING ON? WHAT'S WRONG WITH ABEONA?
I THINK SHE'S IN SHOCK.
WHERE IS SHE?
I'M OVER HERE, AND I'M NOT IN SHOCK! I'M SCARED TO DEATH. I'M FREAKING OUT. BUT I AM NOT IN SHOCK!
ALRIGHT, ALRIGHT. JUST CALM DOWN AND WE'LL COME UP WITH ANOTHER PLAN. WE'LL BEAT THIS THING. JUST HAVE SOME FAITH.
FAITH?! ARE YOU KIDDING?! THIS WHOLE ALIEN INVASION HAS LEFT ME WITH VERY LITTLE OF THAT, I'M AFRAID. SORRY ROBERT, BUT THIS LITTLE CATHOLIC GIRL IS FRESH OUT OF FAITH!

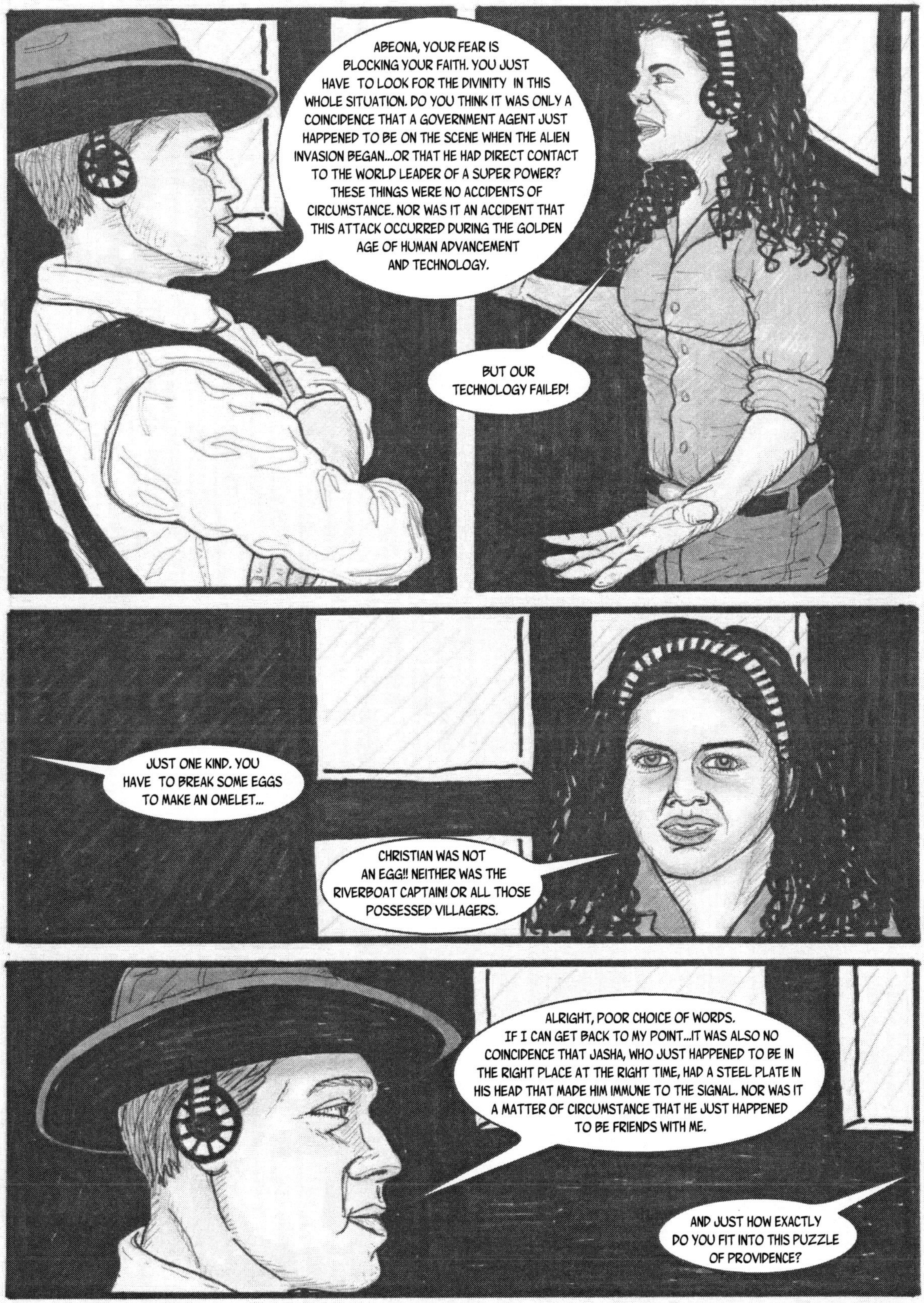
ABEONA, YOUR FEAR IS BLOCKING YOUR FAITH. YOU JUST HAVE TO LOOK FOR THE DIVINITY IN THIS WHOLE SITUATION. DO YOU THINK IT WAS ONLY A COINCIDENCE THAT A GOVERNMENT AGENT JUST HAPPENED TO BE ON THE SCENE WHEN THE ALIEN INVASION BEGAN...OR THAT HE HAD DIRECT CONTACT TO THE WORLD LEADER OF A SUPER POWER? THESE THINGS WERE NO ACCIDENTS OF CIRCUMSTANCE. NOR WAS IT AN ACCIDENT THAT THIS ATTACK OCCURRED DURING THE GOLDEN AGE OF HUMAN ADVANCEMENT AND TECHNOLOGY.
BUT OUR TECHNOLOGY FAILED!
JUST ONE KIND. YOU HAVE TO BREAK SOME EGGS TO MAKE AN OMELET...
CHRISTIAN WAS NOT AN EGG!! NEITHER WAS THE RIVERBOAT CAPTAIN! OR ALL THOSE POSSESSED VILLAGERS.
ALRIGHT, POOR CHOICE OF WORDS. IF I CAN GET BACK TO MY POINT...IT WAS ALSO NO COINCIDENCE THAT JASHA, WHO JUST HAPPENED TO BE IN THE RIGHT PLACE AT THE RIGHT TIME, HAD A STEEL PLATE IN HIS HEAD THAT MADE HIM IMMUNE TO THE SIGNAL. NOR WAS IT A MATTER OF CIRCUMSTANCE THAT HE JUST HAPPENED TO BE FRIENDS WITH ME.
AND JUST HOW EXACTLY DO YOU FIT INTO THIS PUZZLE OF PROVIDENCE?

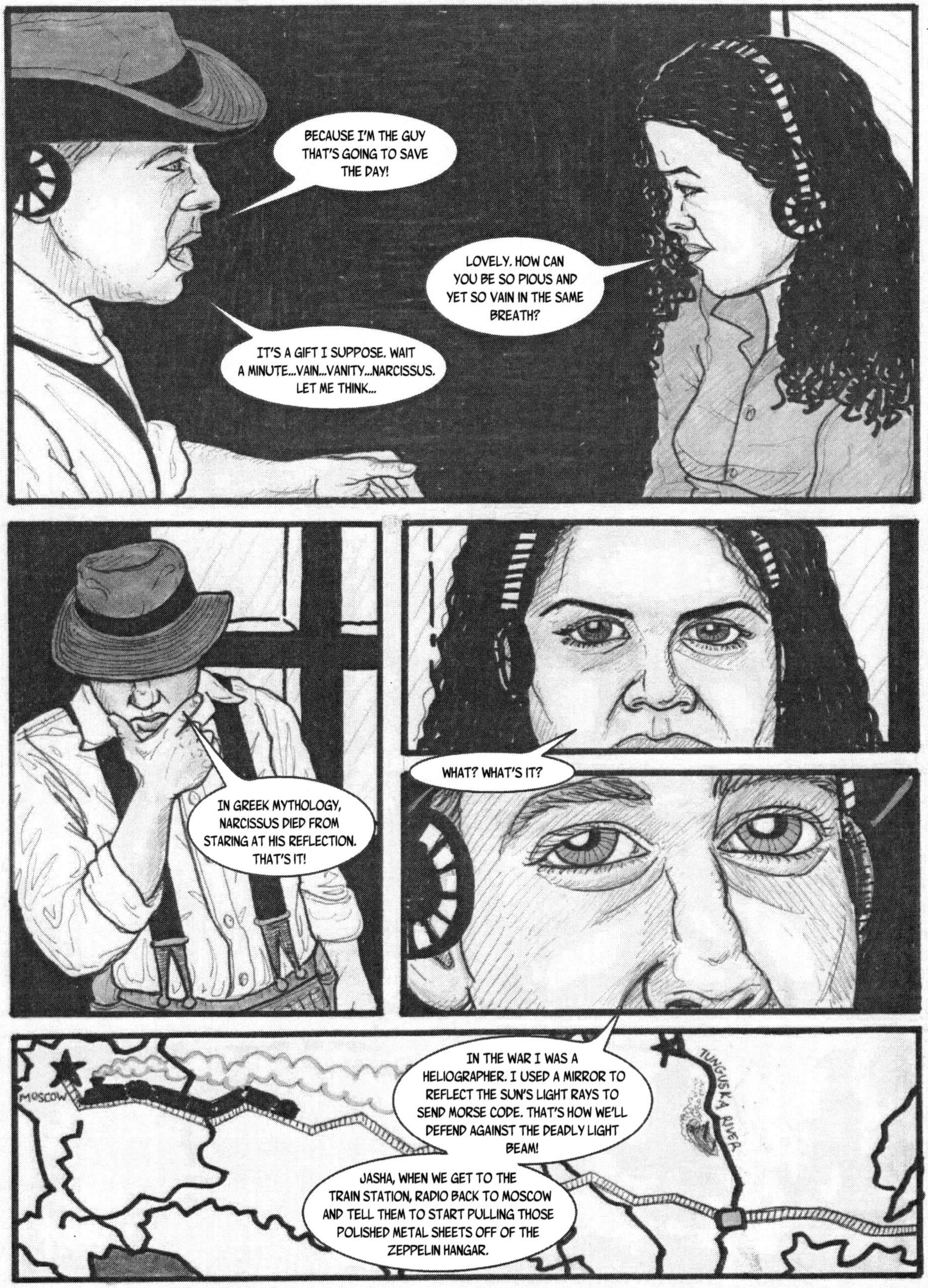
BECAUSE I'M THE GUY THAT'S GOING TO SAVE THE DAY!
LOVELY. HOW CAN YOU BE SO PIOUS AND YET SO VAIN IN THE SAME BREATH?
IT'S A GIFT I SUPPOSE. WAIT A MINUTE...VAIN...VANITY...NARCISSUS. LET ME THINK...
IN GREEK MYTHOLOGY, NARCISSUS DIED FROM STARING AT HIS REFLECTION. THAT'S IT!
WHAT? WHAT'S IT?
MOSCOW
TUNGUSKA RIVER
IN THE WAR I WAS A HELIOGRAPHER. I USED A MIRROR TO REFLECT THE SUN'S LIGHT RAYS TO SEND MORSE CODE. THAT'S HOW WE'LL DEFEND AGAINST THE DEADLY LIGHT BEAM!
JASHA, WHEN WE GET TO THE TRAIN STATION, RADIO BACK TO MOSCOW AND TELL THEM TO START PULLING THOSE POLISHED METAL SHEETS OFF OF THE ZEPPELIN HANGAR.

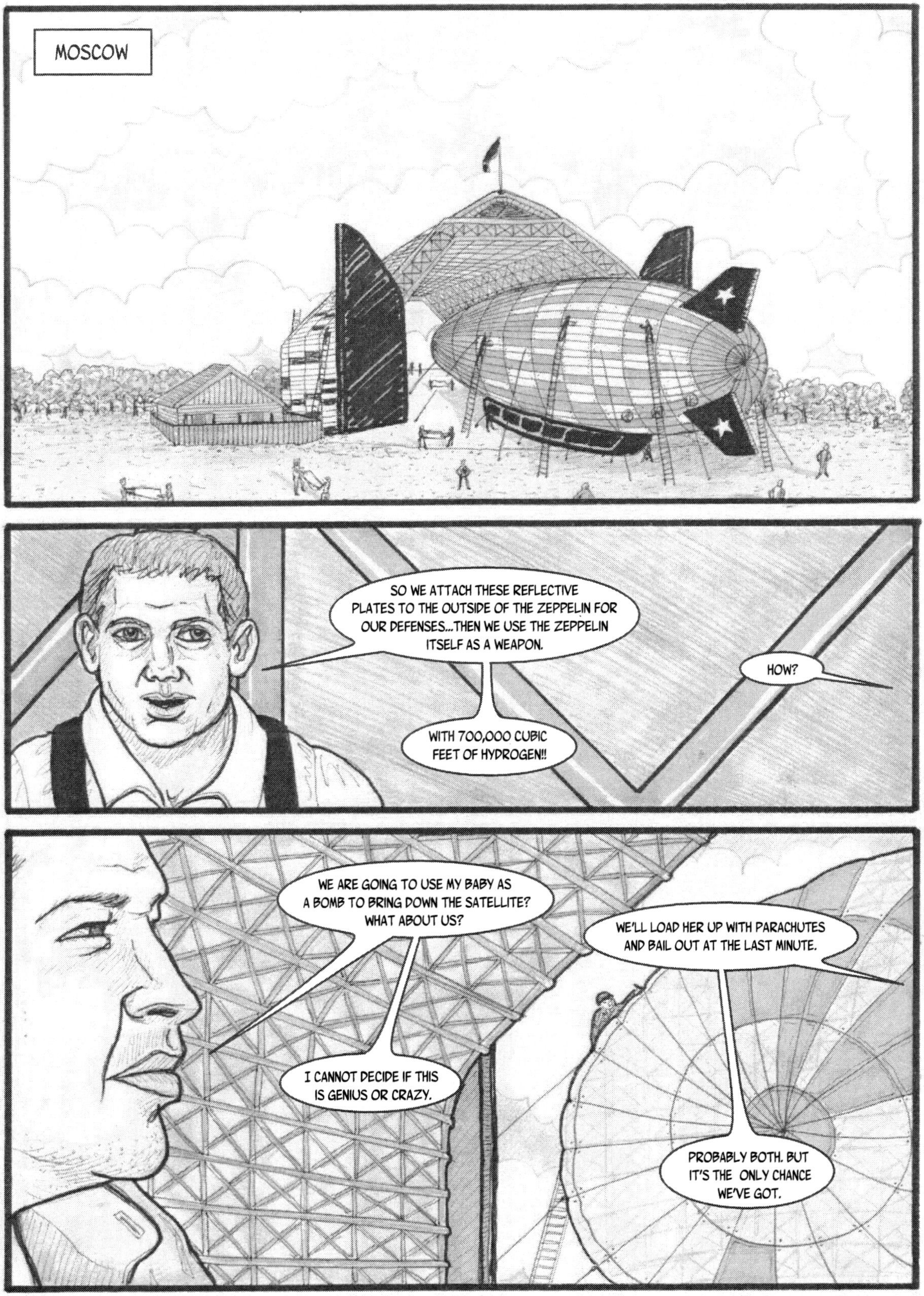
MOSCOW
SO WE ATTACH THESE REFLECTIVE PLATES TO THE OUTSIDE OF THE ZEPPELIN FOR OUR DEFENSES...THEN WE USE THE ZEPPELIN ITSELF AS A WEAPON.
HOW?
WITH 700,000 CUBIC FEET OF HYDROGEN!!
WE ARE GOING TO USE MY BABY AS A BOMB TO BRING DOWN THE SATELLITE? WHAT ABOUT US?
WE'LL LOAD HER UP WITH PARACHUTES AND BAIL OUT AT THE LAST MINUTE.
I CANNOT DECIDE IF THIS IS GENIUS OR CRAZY.
PROBABLY BOTH. BUT IT'S THE ONLY CHANCE WE'VE GOT.

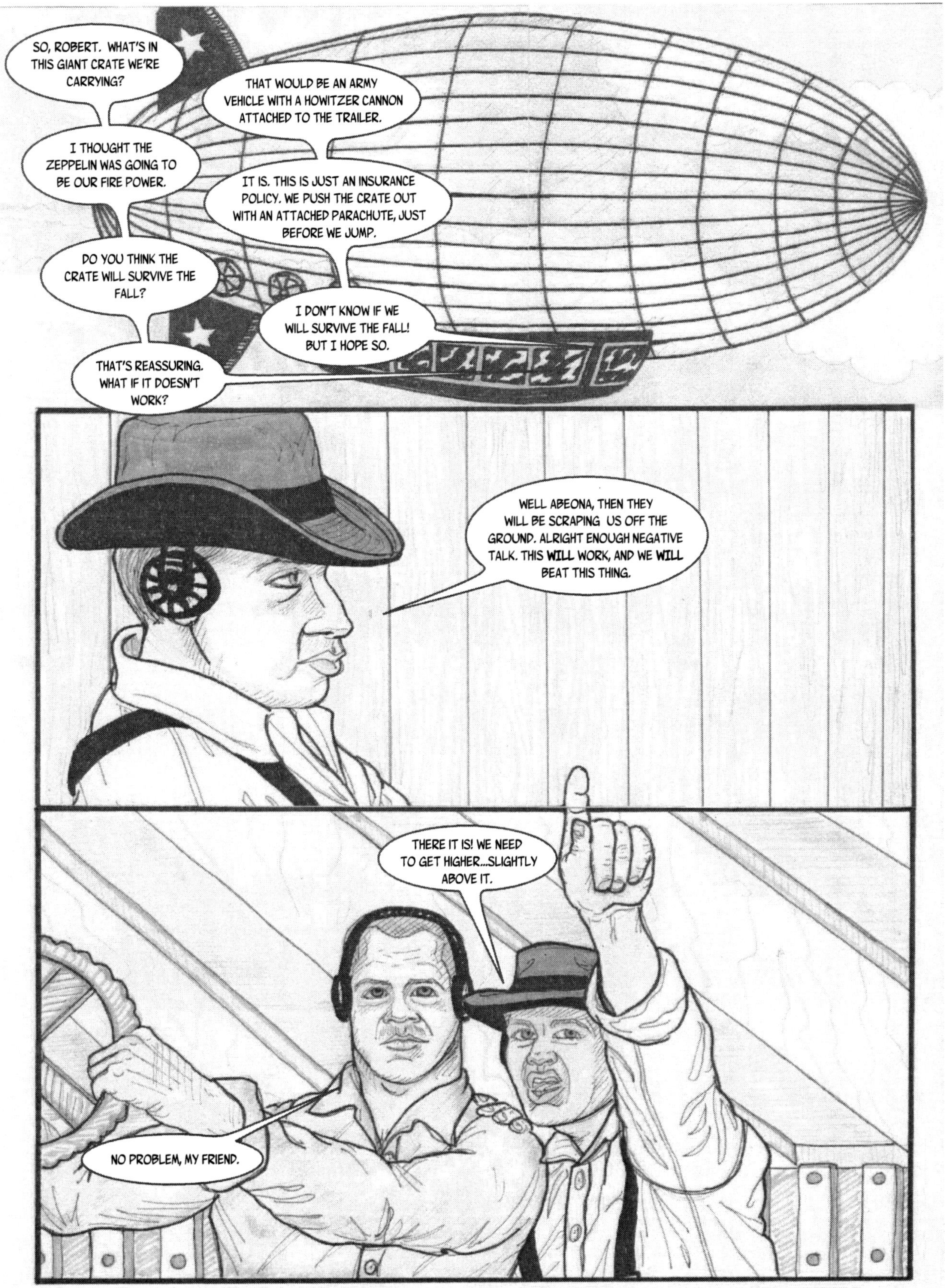
SO, ROBERT. WHAT'S IN THIS GIANT CRATE WE'RE CARRYING?
THAT WOULD BE AN ARMY VEHICLE WITH A HOWITZER CANNON ATTACHED TO THE TRAILER.
I THOUGHT THE ZEPPELIN WAS GOING TO BE OUR FIRE POWER.
IT IS. THIS IS JUST AN INSURANCE POLICY. WE PUSH THE CRATE OUT WITH AN ATTACHED PARACHUTE, JUST BEFORE WE JUMP.
DO YOU THINK THE CRATE WILL SURVIVE THE FALL?
I DON'T KNOW IF WE WILL SURVIVE THE FALL! BUT I HOPE SO.
THAT'S REASSURING. WHAT IF IT DOESN'T WORK?
WELL ABEONA, THEN THEY WILL BE SCRAPING US OFF THE GROUND. ALRIGHT ENOUGH NEGATIVE TALK. THIS **WILL** WORK, AND WE **WILL** BEAT THIS THING.
THERE IT IS! WE NEED TO GET HIGHER...SLIGHTLY ABOVE IT.
NO PROBLEM, MY FRIEND.

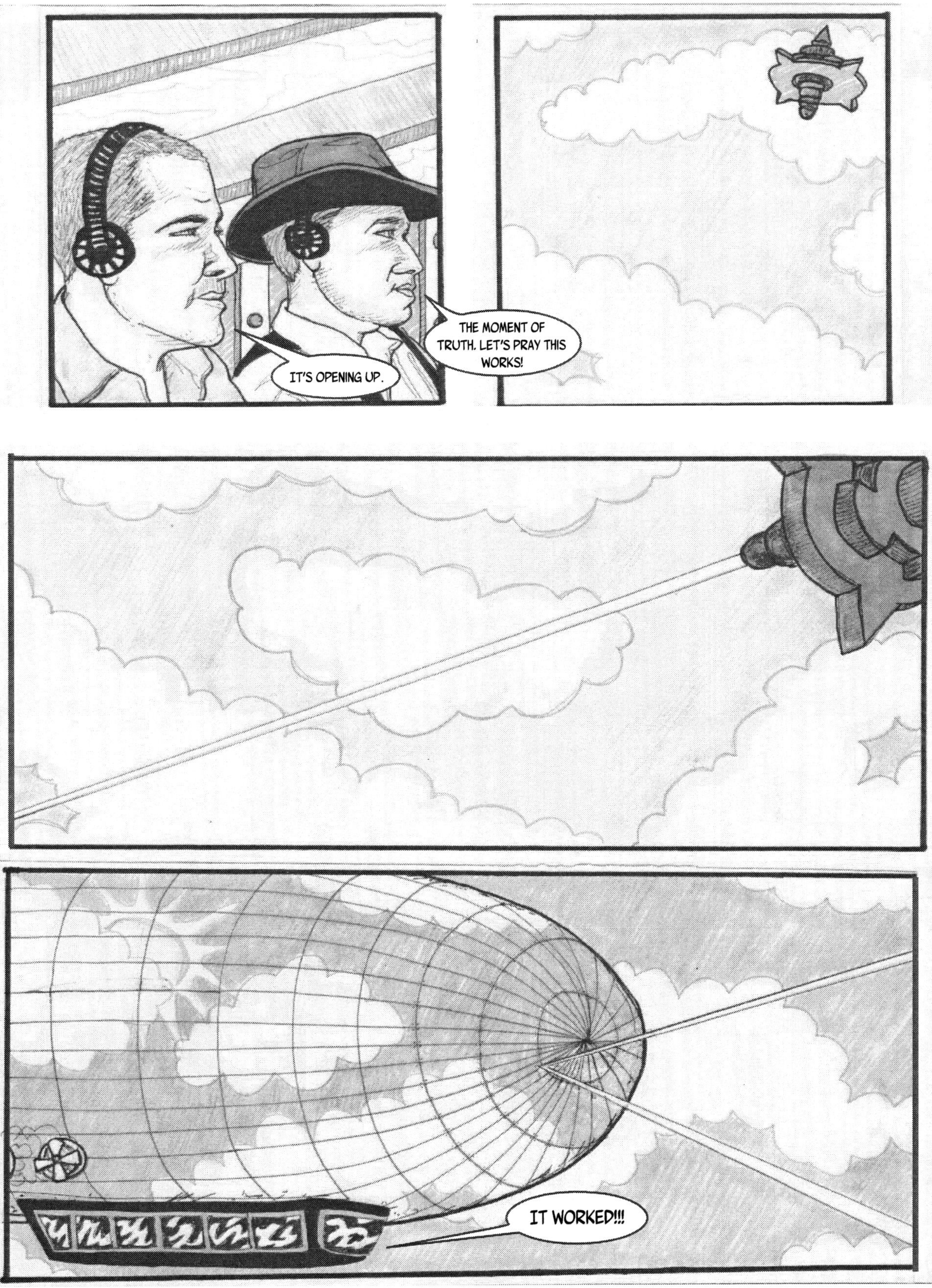
IT'S OPENING UP.
THE MOMENT OF TRUTH. LET'S PRAY THIS WORKS!
IT WORKED!!!

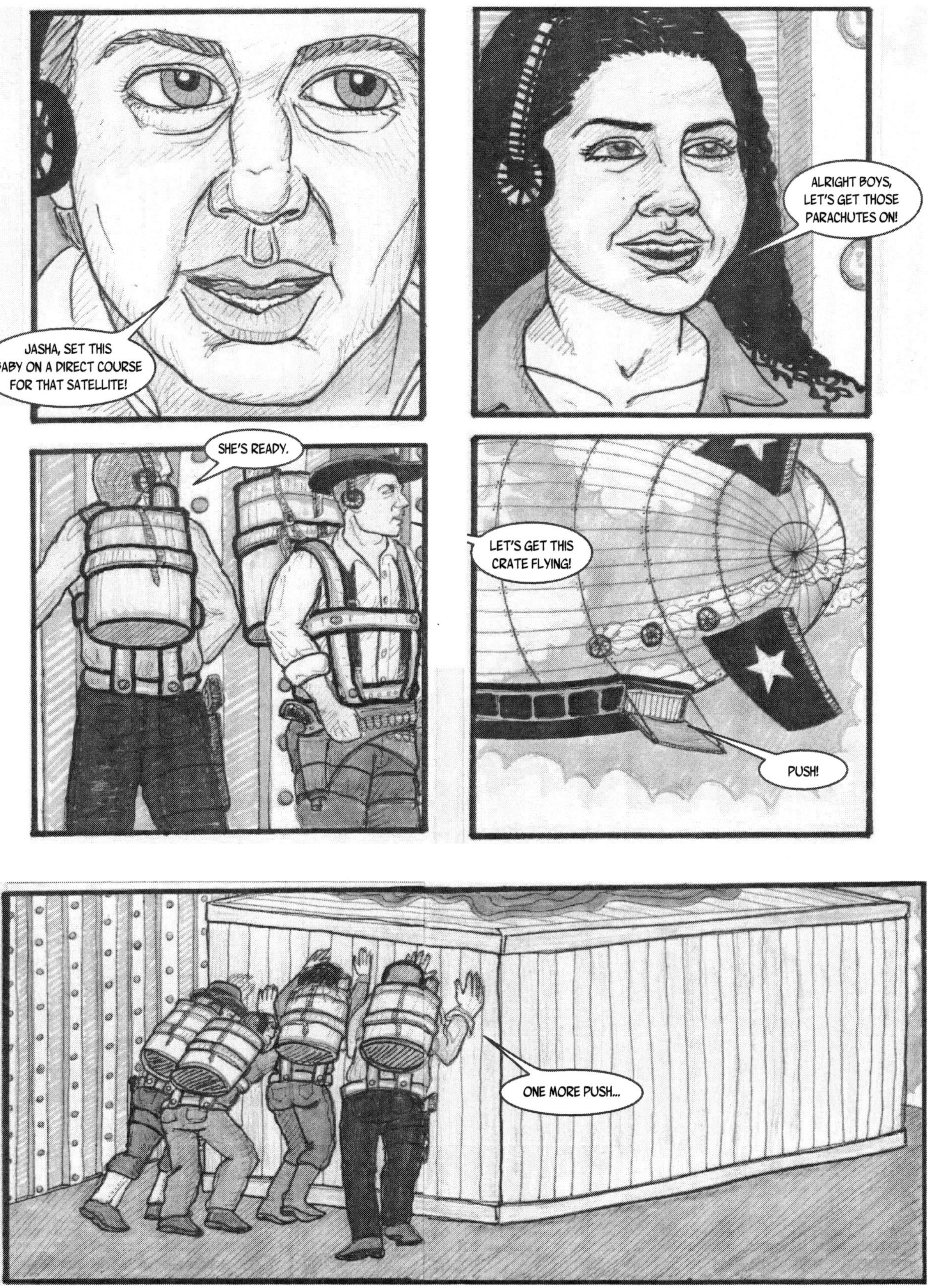
JASHA, SET THIS BABY ON A DIRECT COURSE FOR THAT SATELLITE!
ALRIGHT BOYS, LET'S GET THOSE PARACHUTES ON!
SHE'S READY.
LET'S GET THIS CRATE FLYING!
PUSH!
ONE MORE PUSH...

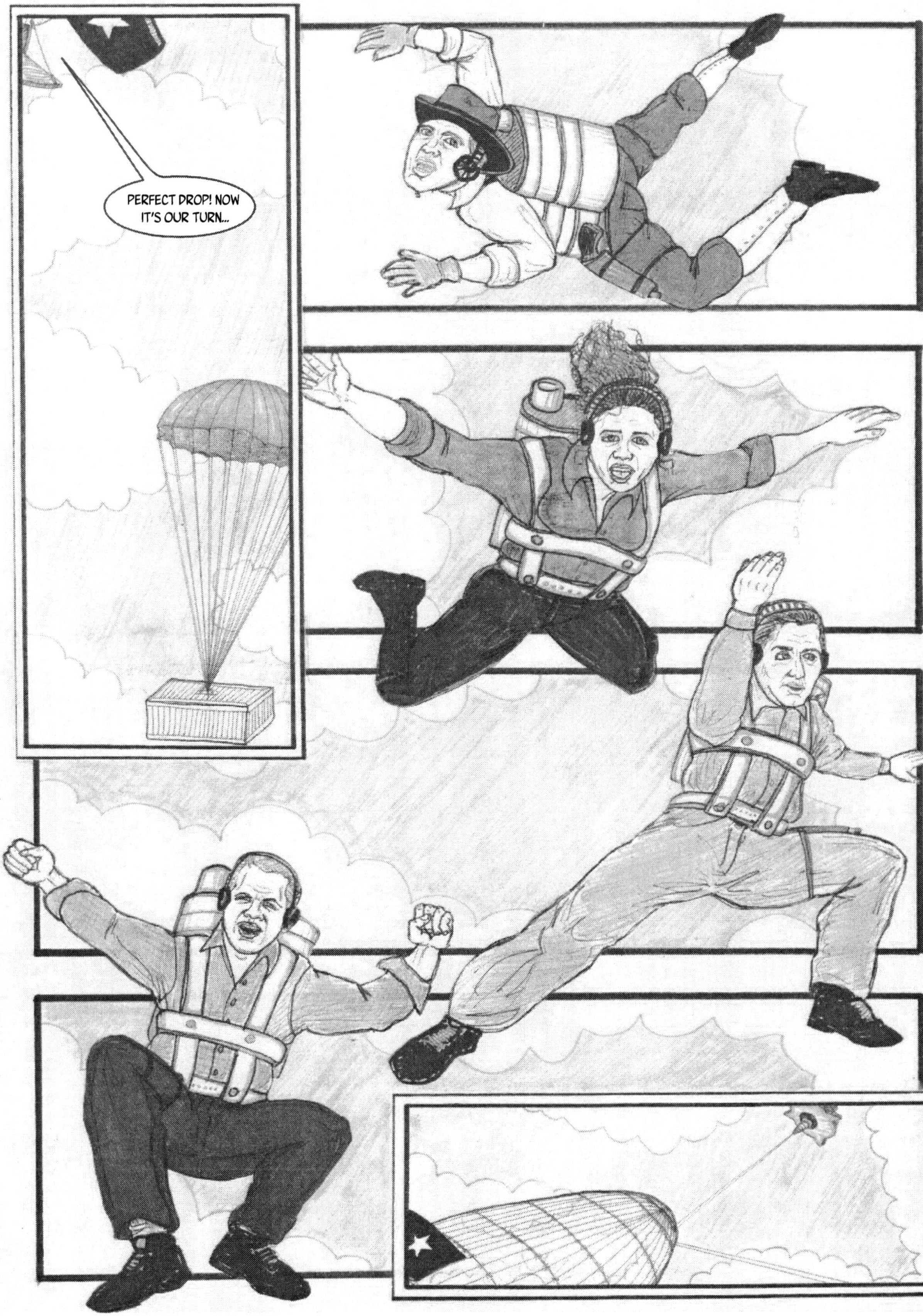
PERFECT DROP! NOW IT'S OUR TURN...

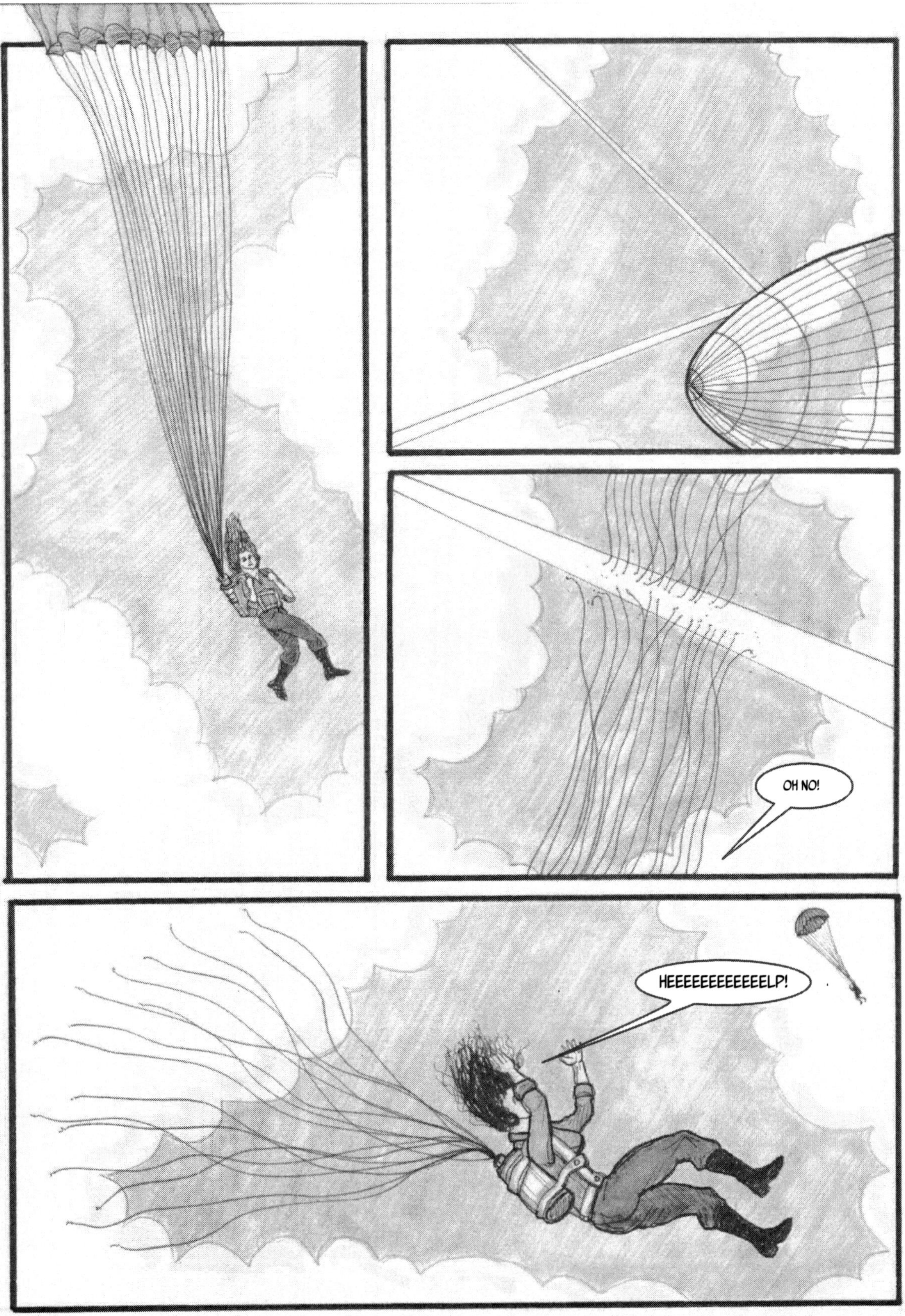
OH NO!
HEEEEEEEEEEEEELP!

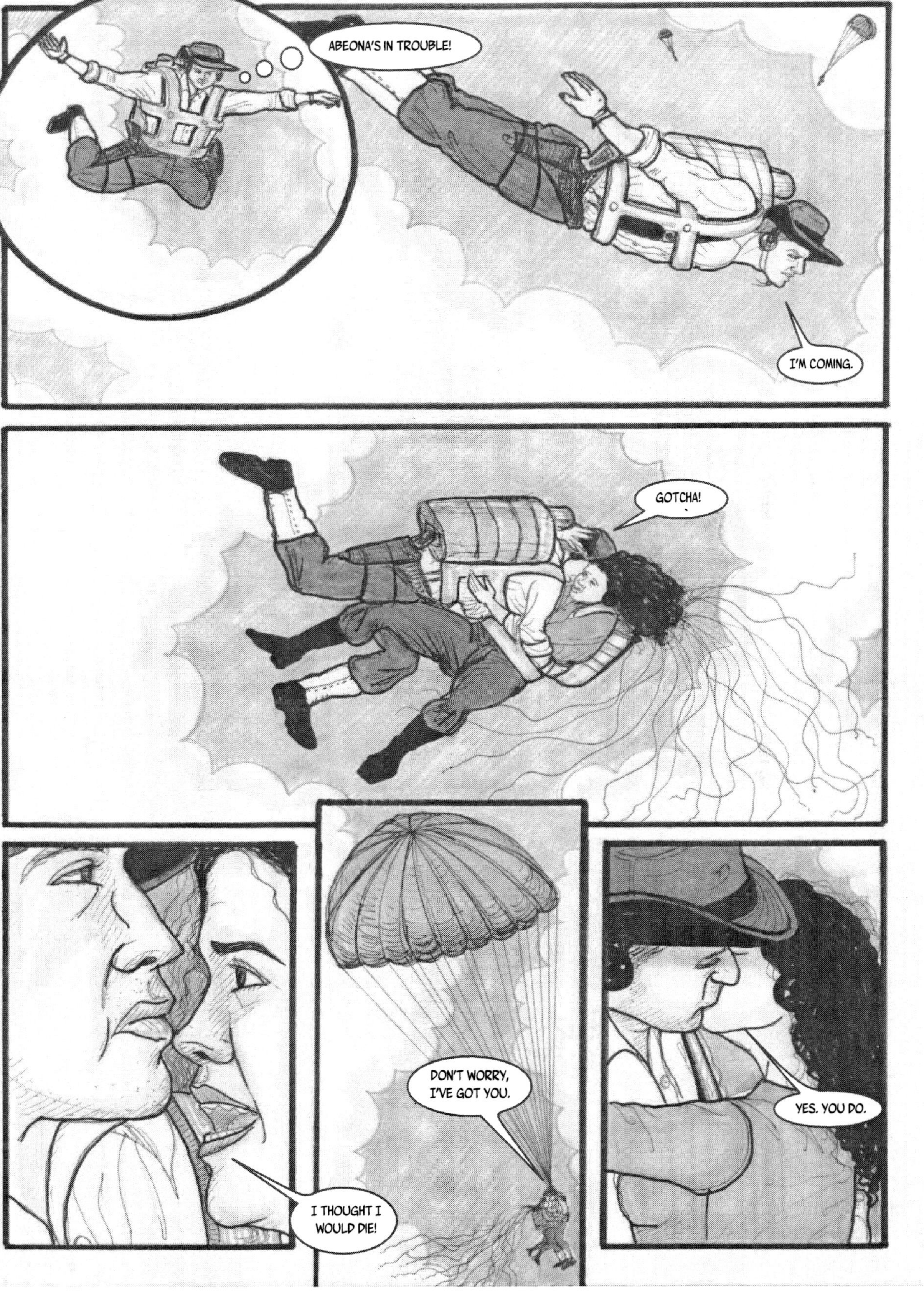
ABEONA'S IN TROUBLE!
I'M COMING.
GOTCHA!
I THOUGHT I WOULD DIE!
DON'T WORRY, I'VE GOT YOU.
YES. YOU DO.

IT BROUGHT IT DOWN!
IT BROUGHT DOWN THE ZEPPELIN, BUT NOT THE VILLAGERS!

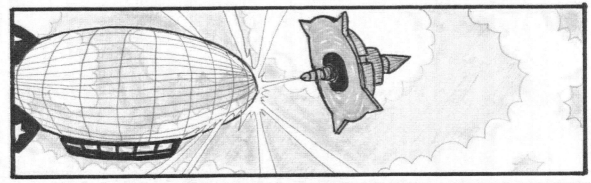

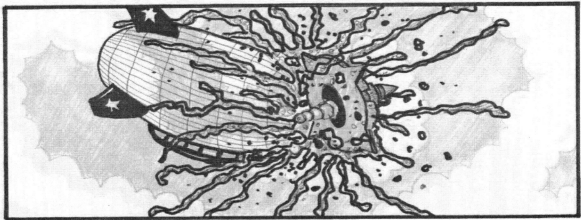

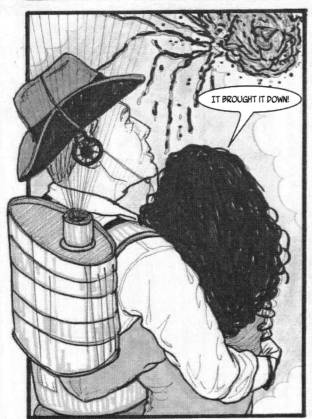

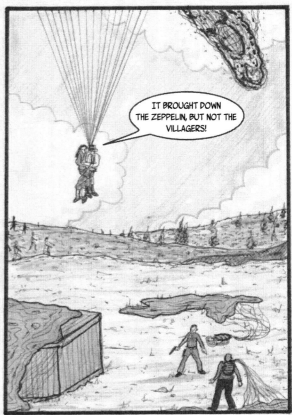

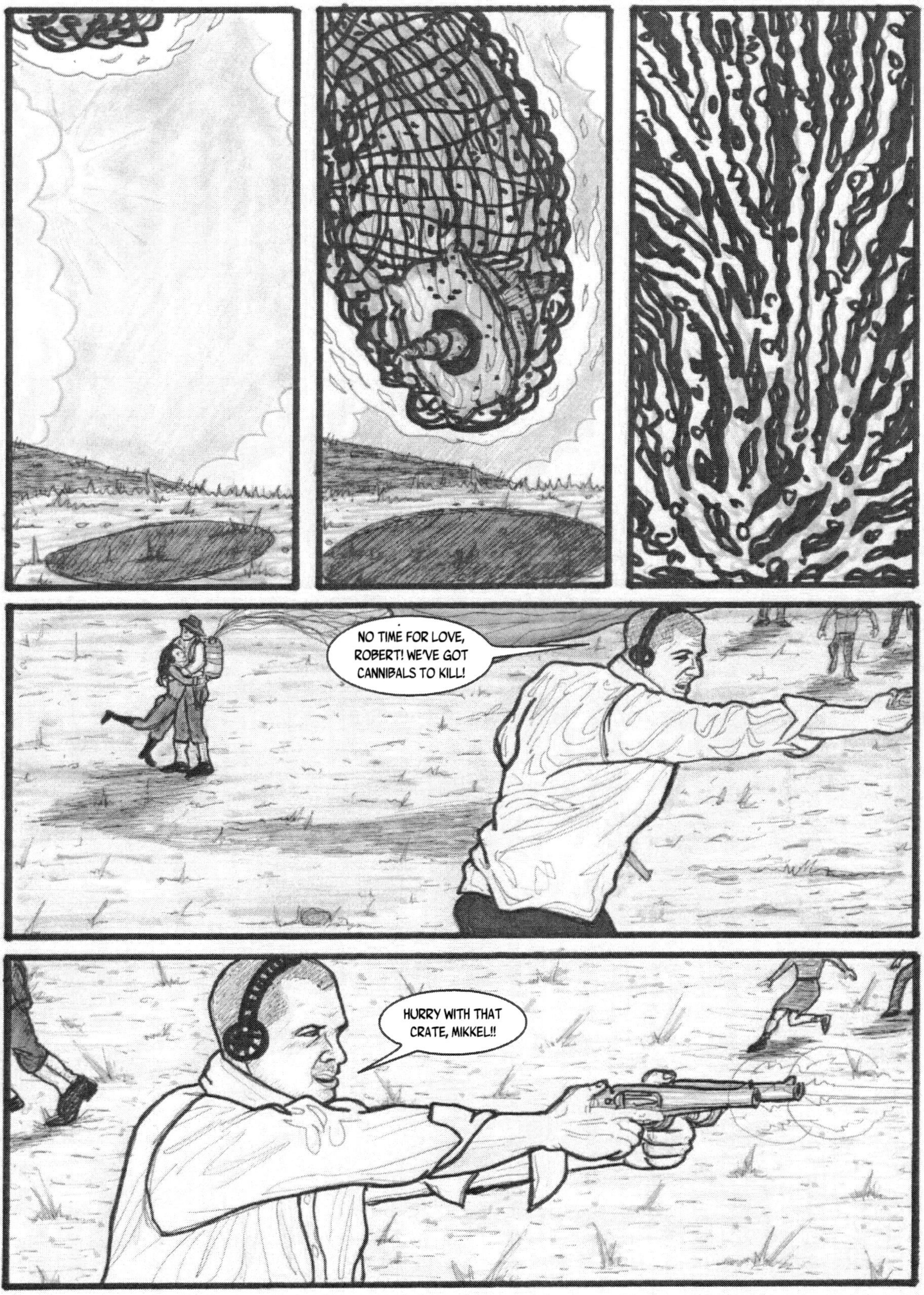
NO TIME FOR LOVE, ROBERT! WE'VE GOT CANNIBALS TO KILL!
HURRY WITH THAT CRATE, MIKKEL!!

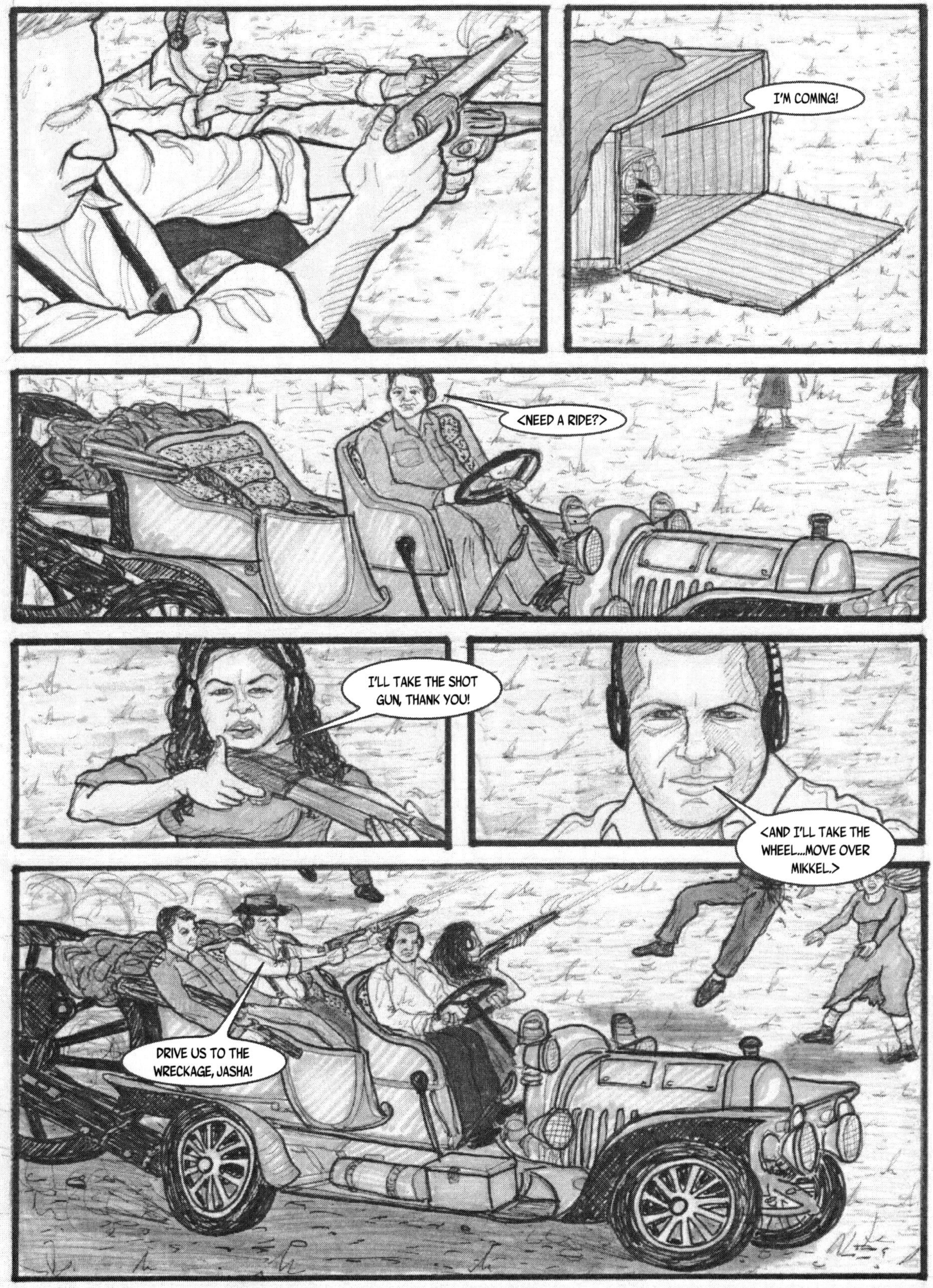
I'M COMING!
<NEED A RIDE?>
I'LL TAKE THE SHOT GUN, THANK YOU!
<AND I'LL TAKE THE WHEEL...MOVE OVER MIKKEL.>
DRIVE US TO THE WRECKAGE, JASHA!

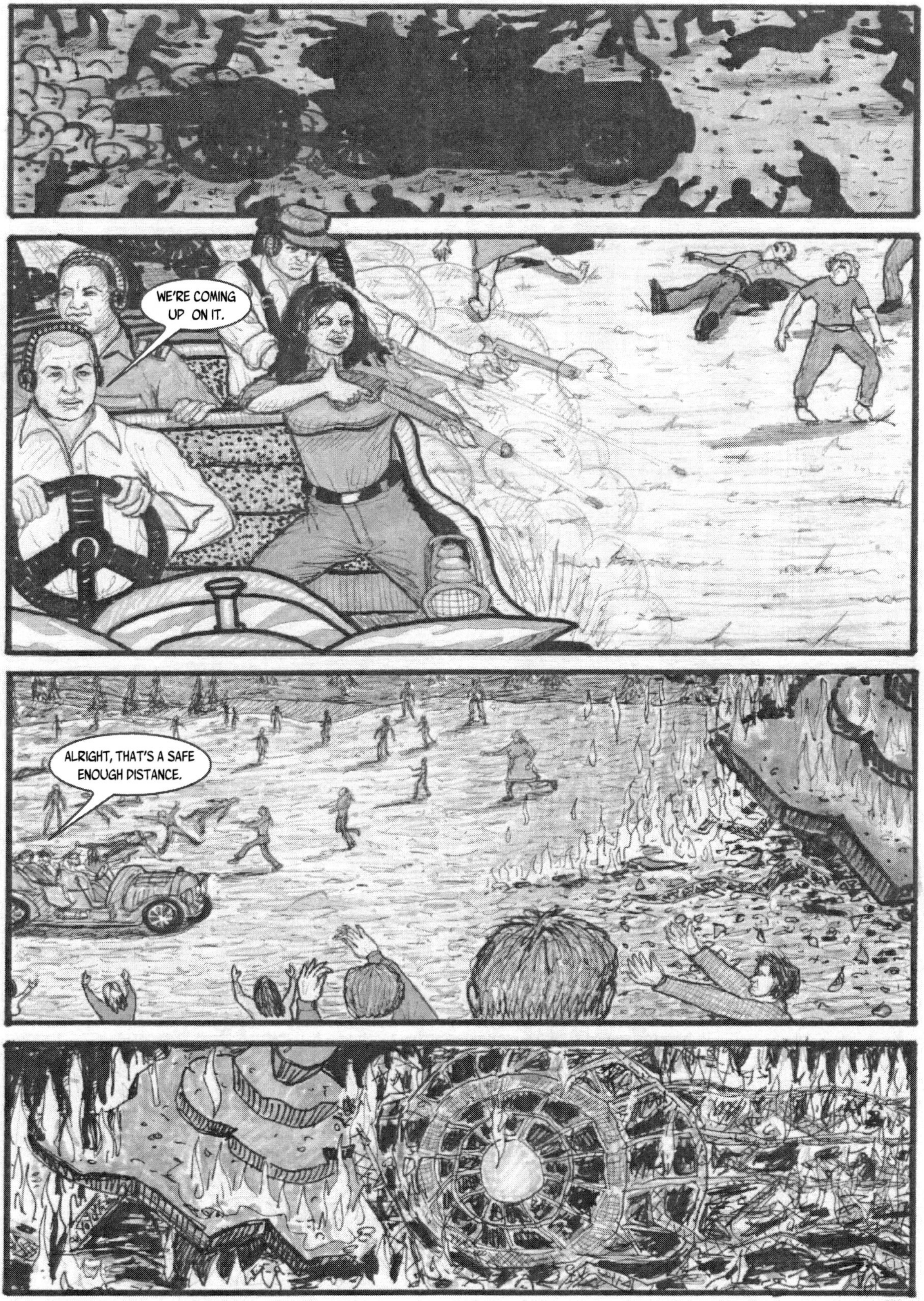
WE'RE COMING UP ON IT.
ALRIGHT, THAT'S A SAFE ENOUGH DISTANCE.

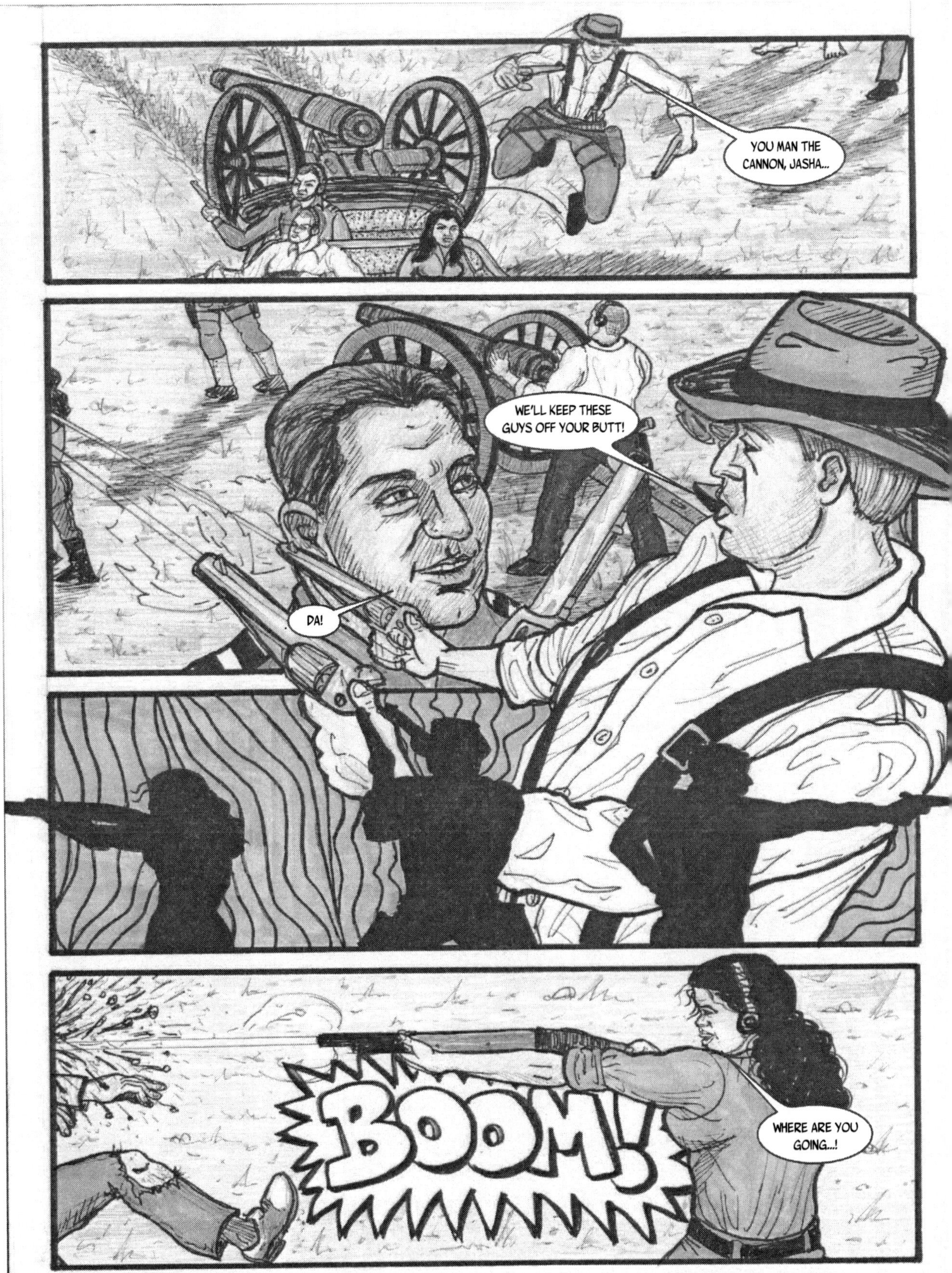
YOU MAN THE CANNON, JASHA...
WE'LL KEEP THESE GUYS OFF YOUR BUTT!
DA!
BOOM!
WHERE ARE YOU GOING...!

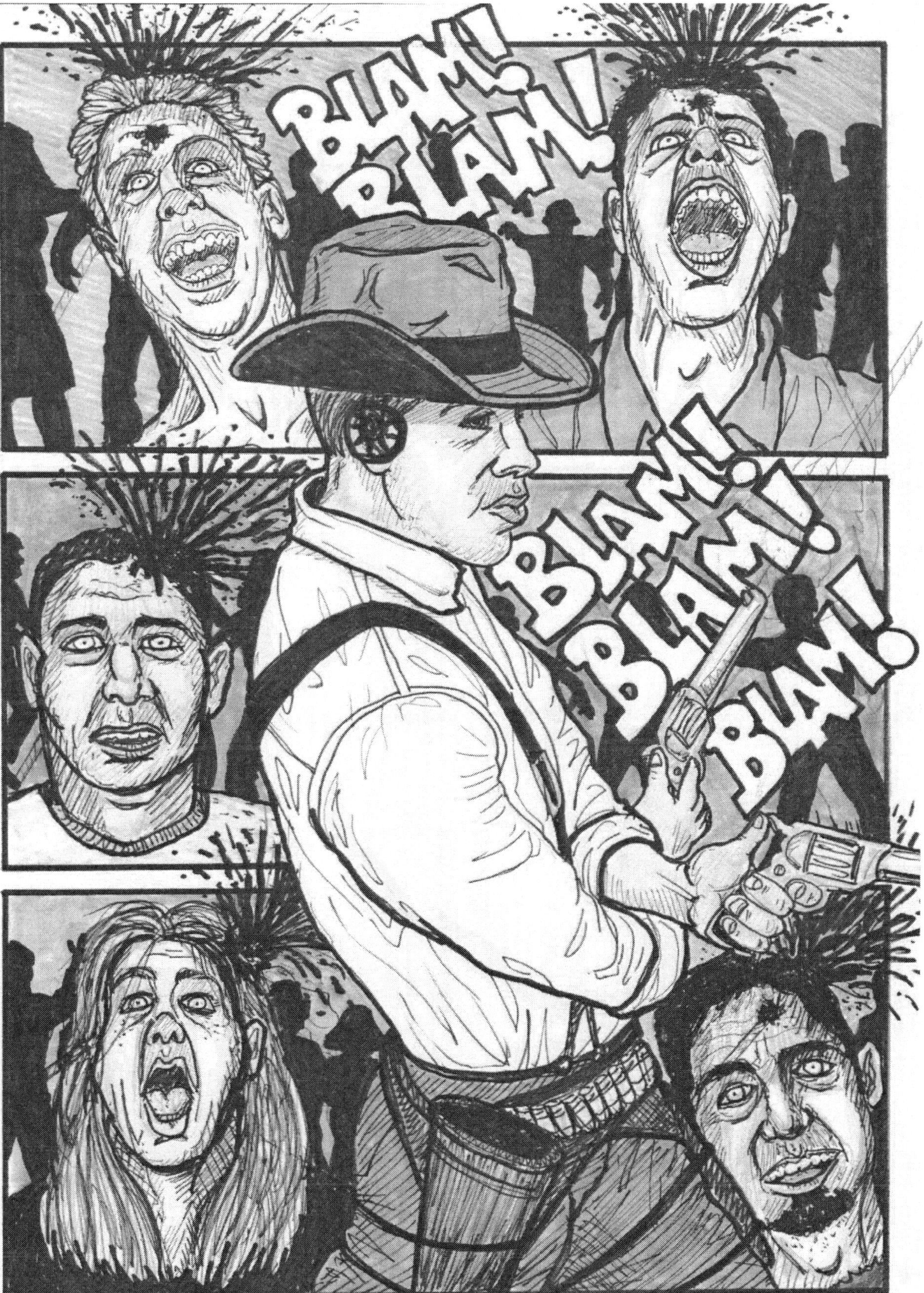
BLAM! BLAM!
BLAM! BLAM! BLAM!

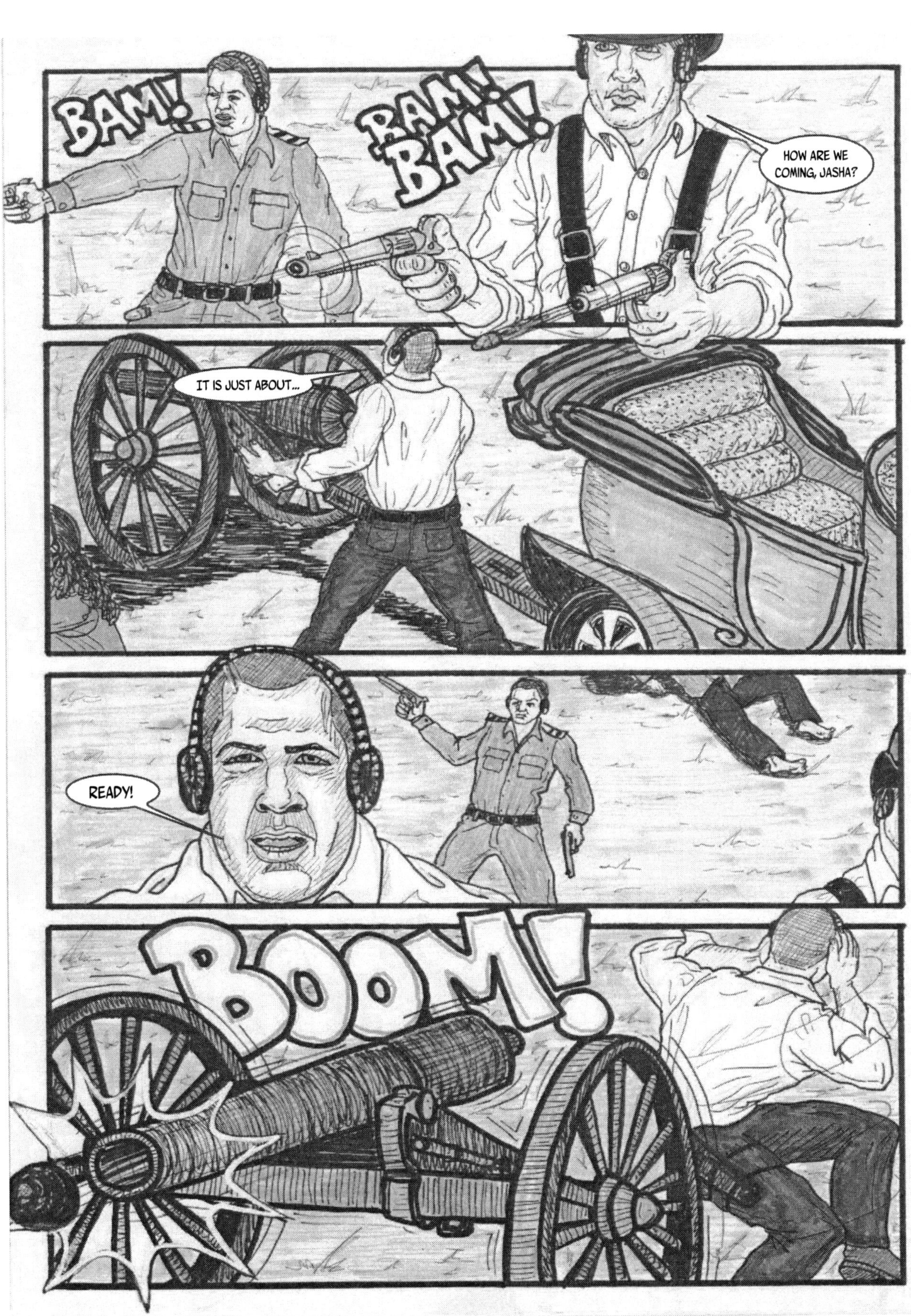
BAM!
RAM! BAM!
HOW ARE WE COMING, JASHA?
IT IS JUST ABOUT...
READY!
BOOM!

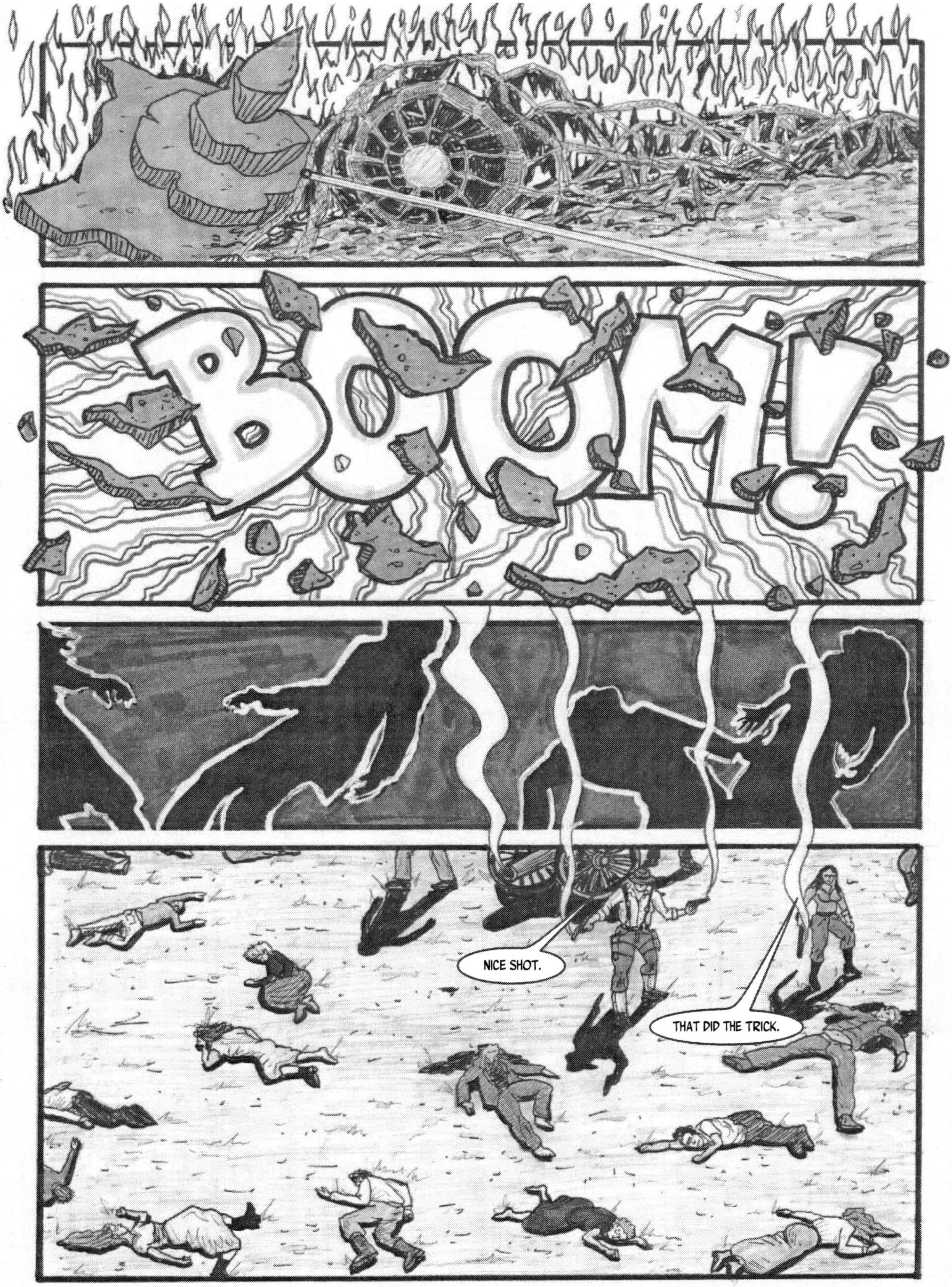
BOOM!
NICE SHOT.
THAT DID THE TRICK.

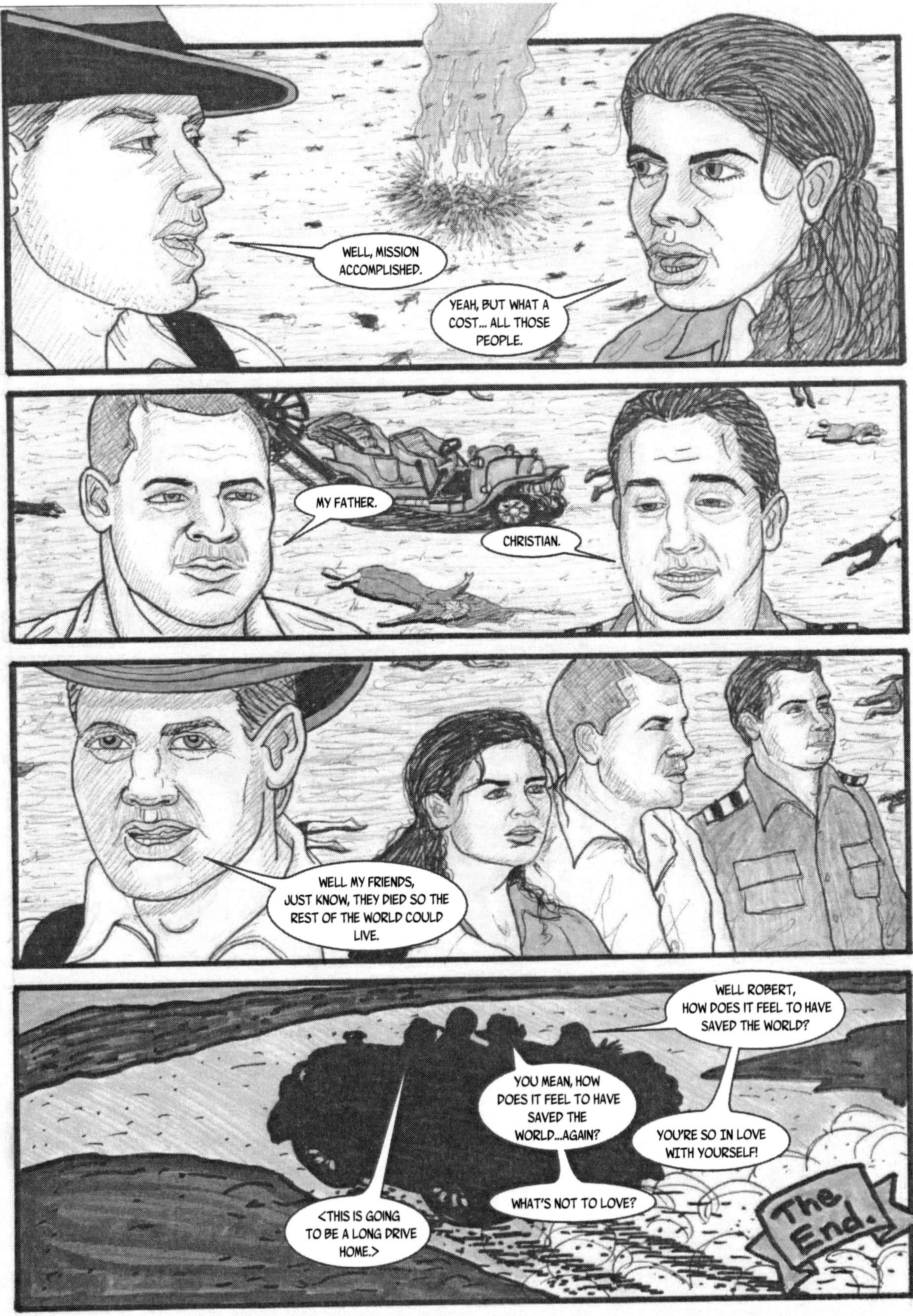
WELL, MISSION ACCOMPLISHED.
YEAH, BUT WHAT A COST... ALL THOSE PEOPLE.
MY FATHER.
CHRISTIAN.
WELL MY FRIENDS, JUST KNOW, THEY DIED SO THE REST OF THE WORLD COULD LIVE.
WELL ROBERT, HOW DOES IT FEEL TO HAVE SAVED THE WORLD?
YOU MEAN, HOW DOES IT FEEL TO HAVE SAVED THE WORLD...AGAIN?
YOU'RE SO IN LOVE WITH YOURSELF!
WHAT'S NOT TO LOVE?
<THIS IS GOING TO BE A LONG DRIVE HOME.>
The End.

FACT FROM FICTION

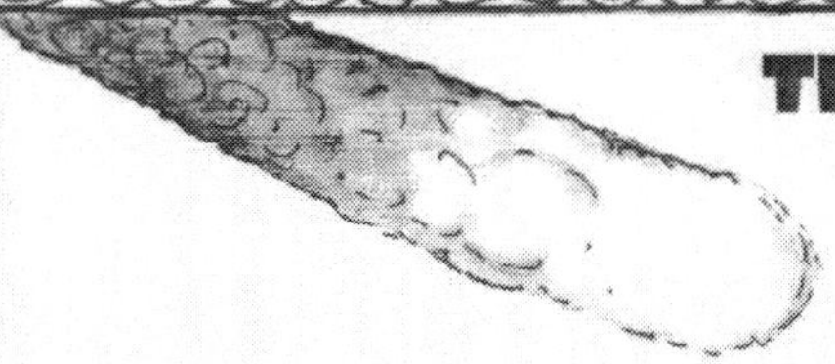

THE TUNGUSKA EVENT

ON JUNE 30TH, 1908, A LARGE COMET OR METEOR EXPLODED BETWEEN 3-6 MILES ABOVE THE EARTH'S SURFACE IN THE TUNGUSKA REGION OF SIBERIA. THE EXPLOSION WAS OVER 1,000 TIMES MORE POWERFUL THAN THE ATOM BOMB DROPPED ON HIROSHIMA AND KNOCKED OVER AN ESTIMATED 80 MILLION TREES THAT COVERED OVER 830 SQUARE MILES. THE BLAST WOULD HAVE MEASURED A 5 ON THE RICHTER SCALE. THE FIRST RECORDED EXPEDITION TO THE SITE OF IMPACT WAS MORE THAN A DECADE LATER, WHERE THERE WAS STILL A FIVE MILE PERIMETER OF SCORCHED, KNOCKED DOWN TREES.

TWO BILL'S WILD WEST SHOW

WILLIAM FREDERICK "BUFFALO BILL" CODY AND GORDON WILLIAM "PAWNEE BILL" LILLIE WERE FAMOUS FRONTIERSMEN AND SHOWMEN WHO PERFORMED IN A VARIETY OF THEIR OWN WILD WEST SHOWS IN THE LATE 19TH AND EARLY 20TH CENTURY. WILD WEST SHOWS WERE VERY POPULAR AT THAT TIME AND A GREAT SOURCE OF ENTERTAINMENT ACROSS THE AMERICAN FRONTIER. IN 1908, THE TWO JOINED FORCES TO CREATE THE "TWO BILL'S WILD WEST SHOW". ALTHOUGH THE SHOW EVENTUALLY WAS FORECLOSED ON WHILE IN DENVER, COLORADO. BOTH MEN WENT ON TO LIVE LONG AND PRODUCTIVE LIVES.

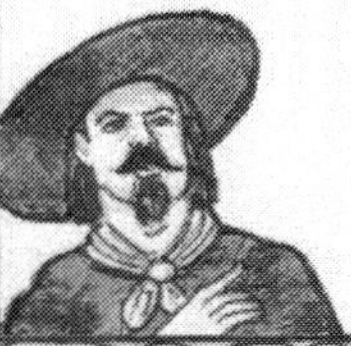

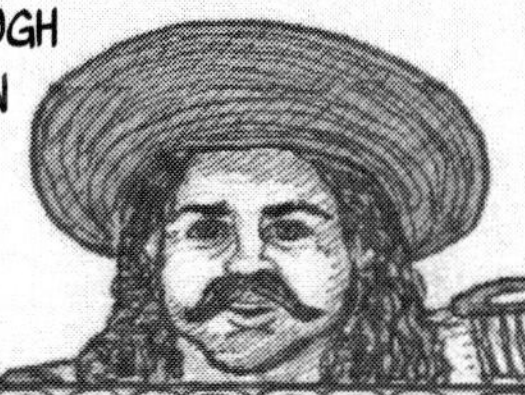

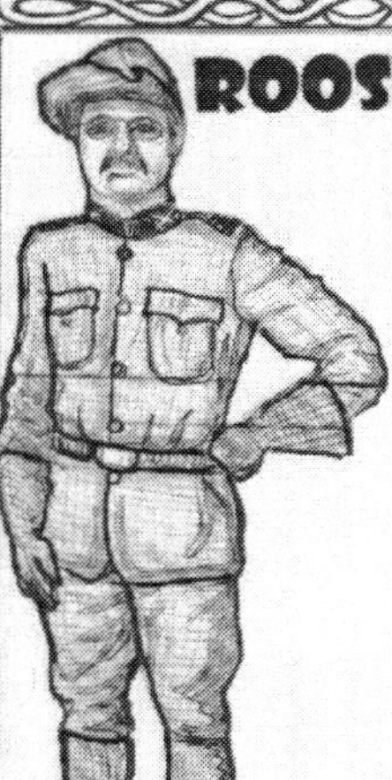

ROOSEVELT'S ROUGH RIDERS

IN 1898, THEODORE ROOSEVELT RESIGNED FROM THE NAVY DEPARTMENT TO FORM THE FIRST U.S. VOLUNTEER CAVALRY REGIMENT, NICKNAMED "THE ROUGH RIDERS". FROM THE EASTERN IVY LEAGUES OF GREAT WEALTH TO THE POOREST OF COWBOYS FROM THE WESTERN TERRITORIES, VOLUNTEERS FROM ALL OVER SIGNED UP TO FOLLOW TEDDY AND U.S. ARMY COLONEL LEONARD WOOD INTO BATTLE. THESE BRAVE MEN FACED SPANISH SOLDIERS AT BOTH KETTLE HILL AND SAN JUAN HILL AND HELPED TO WIN THE SPANISH-AMERICAN WAR. ROOSELVELT WENT ON TO BECOME OUR 26TH PRESIDENT!

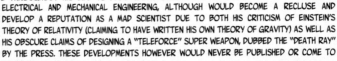

NIKOLA TESLA

NIKOLA TESLA WAS A FAMOUS (AND SOMETIMES INFAMOUS) LATE 19TH AND EARLY 20TH CENTURY INVENTOR. BEST KNOWN FOR DEVELOPING THE MODERN ALTERNATING CURRENT (AC) ELECTRICAL SUPPLY SYSTEM. HE WAS ALSO A PIONEER IN THE FIELDS OF ELECTROMAGNETISM AND RADIO CURRENTS.

EARLY IN TESLA'S CAREER, HE WORKED FOR THOMAS EDISON AND COMPLETELY REDESIGNED THE COMPANY'S DIRECT CURRENT GENERATORS. TESLA EVENTUALLY RESIGNED AFTER A FINANCIAL DISPUTE. EDISON AND TESLA WOULD GO ON TO BECOME ADVERSARIES IN THE "WAR OF CURRENTS" (AC VS. DC), WHICH TESLA'S MUCH SAFER AND EFFICIENT AC WOULD WIN, ALMOST BANKRUPTING EDISON.

TESLA WOULD CONTINUE THROUGHOUT HIS LIFE TO MAKE GREAT STRIDES AND DEVELOPMENTS IN THE FIELDS OF ELECTRICAL AND MECHANICAL ENGINEERING, ALTHOUGH WOULD BECOME A RECLUSE AND DEVELOP A REPUTATION AS A MAD SCIENTIST DUE TO BOTH HIS CRITICISM OF EINSTEIN'S THEORY OF RELATIVITY (CLAIMING TO HAVE WRITTEN HIS OWN THEORY OF GRAVITY) AS WELL AS HIS OBSCURE CLAIMS OF DESIGNING A "TELEFORCE" SUPER WEAPON, DUBBED THE "DEATH RAY" BY THE PRESS. THESE DEVELOPMENTS HOWEVER WOULD NEVER BE PUBLISHED OR COME TO FRUITION.

TESLA DIED IN 1943 AT THE AGE OF 86 FROM HEART THROMBUS, WHILE LIVING ALONE AND BROKE IN AT A HOTEL IN NEW YORK. IT WOULD NOT BE UNTIL AFTER HIS DEATH THAT TESLA WOULD GET THE HONOR AND ACCLAIM THAT HE TRULY DESERVED FOR ALL HIS CONTRIBUTIONS TO TODAY'S MODERN SOCIETY.

TRANSATLANTIC CROSSING

FOR CENTURIES, BRAVE AND ADVENTUROUS SAILORS HAVE BEEN CROSSING THE ATLANTIC OCEAN, TRAVELING FROM EUROPE TO THE AMERICAS AND BACK, SOMETIMES AT A GREAT PRICE AND OTHER TIMES NEVER COMPLETING THEIR PERILOUS QUEST AT ALL. THE HISTORY OF TRAVEL WOULD CHANGE HOWEVER IN THE 19TH CENTURY. WITH THE INVENTION OF STEAMBOATS WHAT WAS ONCE A DANGEROUS AND EPIC JOURNEY BY SAILBOAT HAD BECOME A MUCH SAFER AND TIME EFFICIENT UNDERTAKING.

THE GREAT NATIONS OF THE 19TH CENTURY AND POWERED OCEAN LINERS

THE UNITED STATES AND THE UNITED KINGDOM, AS WELL AS FRANCE, GERMANY AND ITALY, WOULD SPEND MOST OF THE BEGINNING OF THE 20TH CENTURY RACING TO SEE WHO COULD BUILD THE BIGGEST AND THE FASTEST STEAM TO CUT THROUGH THESE TREACHEROUS WATERS, TURNING MONTH LONG JOURNEYS INTO SOMETIMES ONE WEEK LONG VACATIONS.

SOME OF THE MORE FAMOUS OCEAN LINERS OF THIS ERA WERE THE *SS SAVANNAH* (A HYBRID STEAM AND SAIL SHIP AND THE FIRST TO MAKE THE CROSSING IN 1819); THE *RMS MAURETANIA* (A BRITISH LINER THAT WAS SISTER TO THE *LUSITANIA*); THE *RMS TITANIC* (THE SUPPOSEDLY UNSINKABLE SHIP AND LARGEST EVER BUILT AT THE TIME, WHICH CRASHED INTO AN ICEBERG AND SANK ON ITS MAIDEN JOURNEY IN 1912); AND THE *RMS LUSITANIA* (WHICH WAS SUNK BY GERMANY IN WWI AND CONSEQUENTLY USED AS THE MODEL FOR THE LINER IN THIS BOOK!).

GUGLIELMO MARCONI

GUGLIELMO MARCONI WAS A NOBEL PRIZE WINNING ITALIAN INVENTOR WHO IS OFTEN CREDITED WITH THE INVENTION OF RADIO. THIS WAS MUCH DISPUTED, HOWEVER, AS HE CLEARLY USED THE DEVELOPMENTS AND TECHNIQUES AND BUILT ON THE WORKS OF NUMEROUS INVENTORS BEFORE HIM, SUCH AS HERTZ, POPOV AND TESLA. UNLIKE THE ABOVE MENTIONED TESLA, HOWEVER, MARCONI WAS A SUCCESSFUL ENTREPRENEUR AND BUSINESSMAN WHO MANAGED TO PARLAY HIS COMMERCIAL ACHIEVEMENTS INTO A FINANCIALLY LUCRATIVE CAREER.

AROUND THE TURN OF THE 20TH CENTURY, MARCONI WAS PREVALENT IN THE DEVELOPMENT AND ESTABLISHMENT OF TRANSATLANTIC TRANSMISSIONS, SENDING RADIO WAVES BACK AND FORTH FROM SHIPS TO EUROPE AND AMERICA, ALLOWING FOR SAFE AND CONVENIENT COMMUNICATIONS. ALTHOUGH THIS ONCE AGAIN LED TO MARCONI BUTTING HEADS

WITH TESLA, WHO CLAIMED THAT "MARCONI WAS USING SEVENTEEN OF MY PATENTS". NEEDLESS TO SAY, MARCONI'S WORK IN THIS TECHNOLOGY WOULD BE CREDITED WITH THE RESCUING OF HUNDREDS OF SURVIVORS FROM THE *RMS TITANIC* THROUGH 72 HOURS OF RADIO COMMUNICATION BETWEEN THE TITANIC'S OPERATOR AND THE RESCUE LINER, THE *RMS CARPATHIA*.

LATER IN LIFE, MARCONI WAS MADE A SENATOR IN THE ITALIAN SENATE AND LATER STILL APPOINTED PRESIDENT OF THE ROYAL ACADEMY OF ITALY BY BENITO MUSSOLINI AND BECAME A MEMBER OF THE FASCIST GRAND COUNCIL. HE DIED IN 1937 AT THE AGE OF 63 OF A HEART ATTACK WHILE RESIDING IN ROME, ITALY.

FACT FROM FICTION

TSAR NICHOLAS II

IN 1896, TSAR NICHOLAS II OF RUSSIA RECEIVED HIS CORONATION, REPLACING ALEXANDER III AS THE NEW EMPEROR AND AUTOCRAT OF ALL RUSSIA. LITTLE DID HE OR ANYONE REALIZE, HOWEVER, IS THAT HE WOULD ALSO BE THE LAST.

UNDER NICHOLAS' RULE, RUSSIA WENT FROM BEING ONE OF THE WORLD'S MOST PROMINENT SUPERPOWERS TO NEAR ECONOMIC AND MILITARY COLLAPSE, DUE TO A COMBINATION OF BOTH UNFORTUNATE CIRCUMSTANCES AND POOR DECISION MAKING ON HIS PART. HE LED HIS MILITARY INTO TWO DETRIMENTAL WARS. THE FIRST WAR WAS WITH JAPAN, IN WHICH THEY LOST NEARLY THE ENTIRE RUSSIAN FLEET. THE SECOND WAS AGAINST THE CENTRAL POWERS IN WORLD WAR I, KILLING NEARLY 3.3 MILLION RUSSIANS AND BRINGING THE COUNTRY TO THE BRINK OF STARVATION.

ULTIMATELY, THE POLICIES AND DECISIONS MADE DURING NICHOLAS' REIGN LED TO THE FALL OF THE ROMANOV DYNASTY AND THE RISE OF THE SOVIET UNION (U.S.S.R.). ALTHOUGH NICHOLAS ABDICATED HIS THRONE AFTER THE FEBRUARY REVOLUTION IN 1917, RELINQUISHING HIS POWER TO THE BOLSHEVIKS, HE AND HIS FAMILY WERE NEVER THE LESS IMPRISONED AND LATER EXECUTED ON THE NIGHT OF JULY 16, 1918, TO ENSURE THE END OF ROMANOV DYNASTY.

NICHOLAS WOULD NOT BE REMEMBERED IN HISTORY FOR HIS GREATNESS AS SOME FORMER RUSSIAN TSARS, NOR, HOWEVER WOULD BECOME INFAMOUS FOR TERRIBLE CRUELTIES LIKE OTHERS. HE WOULD BE REMEMBERED FOR HIS ULTIMATE SACRIFICE, MOST ESPECIALLY BY THE RUSSIAN ORTHODOX CHURCH, WHO WOULD GO ON TO CANONIZE HIM AND RECOGNIZE THE ENTIRE FAMILY AS MARTYRS. HE IS OFTEN REFERRED TO AS SAINT NICHOLS THE PASSION-BEARER.

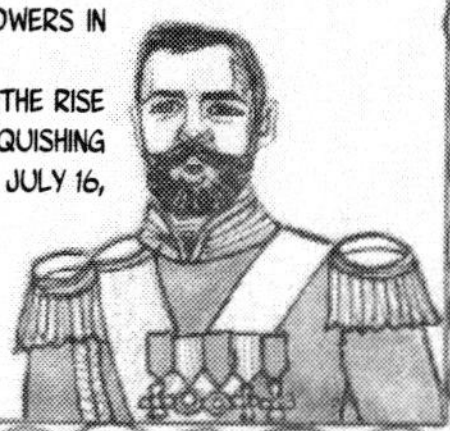

TRANS-SIBERIAN RAILWAY

AT THE END OF HIS WORLD TOUR, THE SOON-TO -BE TSAR NICHOLAS II INAUGURATED THE START OF CONSTRUCTION ON THE TRANS-SIBERIAN RAILWAY, IN 1890. FROM THEN UNTIL 1916, CONSTRUCTION WOULD CONTINUE ON THE LARGEST (AND LONGEST) NATIONAL PROJECT THAT RUSSIA HAD EVER UNDERTAKEN. THE ROUTE WOULD STRETCH ALL THE WAY FROM MOSCOW TO THE FAR EAST, AND EVENTUALLY WOULD ALSO ADD ROUTES TO MONGOLIA AND CHINA.

THE RAILWAY WAS THE LONGEST IN THE WORLD AT THE TIME, SPANNING OVER 5,753 MILES FROM MOSCOW TO VLADIVOSTOK ON THE EAST COAST OF ASIA. ALTHOUGH THE RAILWAY WOULD BRING GREAT ADVANTAGES TO THE NATION AS A WHOLE, THE FACT THAT THERE WAS ONLY ONE TRACK THAT WOULD ONLY ALLOW TRAVEL IN ONE DIRECTION WAS A HUGE HINDRANCE TO THE ARMY DURING THE RUSSO-JAPANESE WAR. MANY THOUGH THAT THIS WAS A LARGE CONTRIBUTOR TO THE RUSSIAN'S MANY DEFEATS IN THE WAR.

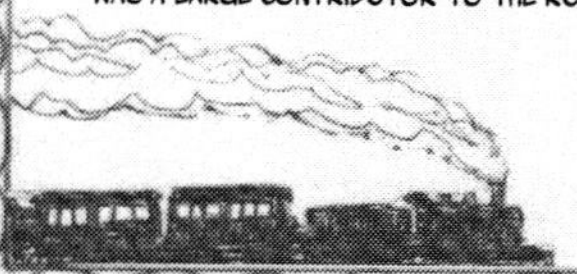

EVENTUALLY A SECOND TRACK WOULD BE ADDED, ALLOWING TRAVEL IN BOTH DIRECTIONS AT THE SAME TIME. IN 1929, THEY WOULD BEGIN ELECTRIFYING THE TRACKS ALLOWING FOR TWICE AS MUCH WEIGHT TO BE SHIPPED FROM ONE SIDE OF THE WORLD'S LARGEST CONTINENT TO THE OTHER.

ZEPPELIN AIRSHIPS

BY THE LATE 1800'S MANY PEOPLE HAD THOUGHT TO DESIGN A RIGID AIRSHIP (OR *DIRIGIBLE)* TO IMPROVE THE QUALITY OF TRAVEL AND TRANSPORT, BY TAKING TO THE SKIES. IT WASN'T UNTIL GERMANY'S OWN COUNT FERDINAND VON ZEPPELIN'S DESIGN OF HIS RIGID AIRSHIP (APPROPRIATE NAMED THE ZEPPELIN) THAT THERE WAS ANY SUCCESS. FROM 1892, CONSTRUCTION WAS UNDERWAY OF THESE BEHEMOTHS OF THE AIR, COMPLETELY REVOLUTIONIZING THE WAY WE TRAVELED.

THE FIRST SUCCESSFULLY FUNCTIONING ZEPPELIN WAS CALLED THE *LZ-1.* AT 420 FEET IN LENGTH AND WEIGHING OVER 13 TONS, IT FLEW ONLY AS HIGH AS 1300 FEET AND LESS THAN 4 MILES IN DISTANCE. HOWEVER, IT WAS PROOF ENOUGH THAT COUNT VON ZEPPELIN WAS ON THE RIGHT TRACK. BY THE 1920'S ZEPPELIN WAS BUILDING MACHINES THAT COULD FLY OVER OCEANS AT INCREDIBLE SPEEDS AND CARRY ALMOST 90 TONS! ORDERS FOR THESE MARVELOUS MACHINES CAME IN FROM ALL OVER THE WORLD, INCLUDING THE US NAVY.

THE USE OF ZEPPELINS CAME TO NEARLY A SCREECHING HALT, HOWEVER, WITH THE INFAMOUS EXPLOSION OF THE *LZ 129 HINDENBURG* IN 1937, KILLING 36 PEOPLE. THE FILMING OF THE CRASH, VIEWED ALL OVER THE WORLD, ALONG WITH THE ADVANCES IN LARGER AND MORE EFFICIENT AIRPLANES, LED TO THE DEPLETE AND EVENTUAL END OF THESE LONG AGO KINGS OF THE SKY.

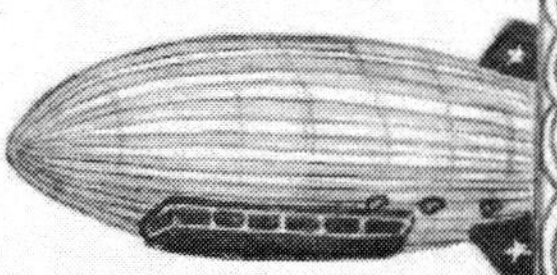

RUSSO-JAPANESE WAR

FROM FEBRUARY 8, 1904 TO SEPTEMBER 5, 1905 THE TWO IMPERIAL EMPIRES OF RUSSIA AND JAPAN WOULD FIGHT FOR CONTROL OVER MANCHURIA AND KOREA, FLEXING THEIR MUSCLES ON THE WORLD STAGE. PRIMARILY A NAVAL WAR, THE ULTIMATE GOAL FOR RUSSIA WAS TO ESTABLISH A WARM WATER PORT ON THE PACIFIC COAST, WHICH COULD STAY OPERATIONAL YEAR ROUND.

DUE TO THE RUSSIANS BEING POORLY ORGANIZED AND THEIR UNDERESTIMATION OF JAPAN (MUCH LIKE THE REST OF THE WESTERN WORD, AT THE TIME), THE JAPANESE WERE ABLE TO WIN A SERIES OF BATTLES ON BOTH LAND AND SEA. TIME AND AGAIN, RUSSIA WAS ROCKED BY DEFEAT AND THE WAR BECAME INCREASINGLY UNPOPULAR AMONG THE PEOPLE.

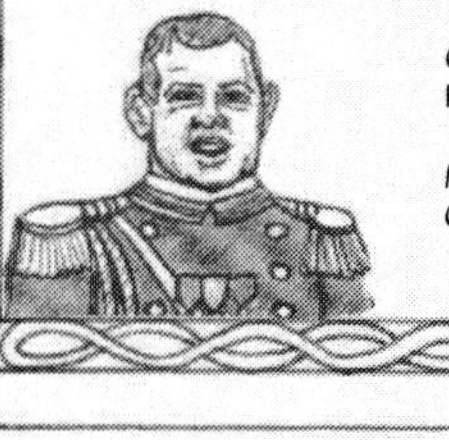

DURING THIS TIME IN RUSSIA, REVOLUTION WAS BREWING AT HOME, AND AFTER THE DISASTER OF BLOODY SUNDAY IN JANUARY OF 1905, THE TSAR DECIDED TO BEGIN NEGOTIATING A PEACE SO HE COULD CONCENTRATE HIS EFFORTS ON THE GROWING INTERNAL PROBLEMS OF THE NATION.

U.S. PRESIDENT THEODORE ROOSEVELT MEDIATED THE PEACE TALKS AT THE PORTSMOUTH NAVAL SHIPYARD IN KITTERY, MAINE. ON SEPTEMBER 5, 1905, THE TREATY OF PORTSMOUTH WAS SIGNED AND THE WAR WAS ENDED. ROOSEVELT WOULD GO ON TO WIN THE NOBEL PEACE PRIZE FOR HIS ROLE.

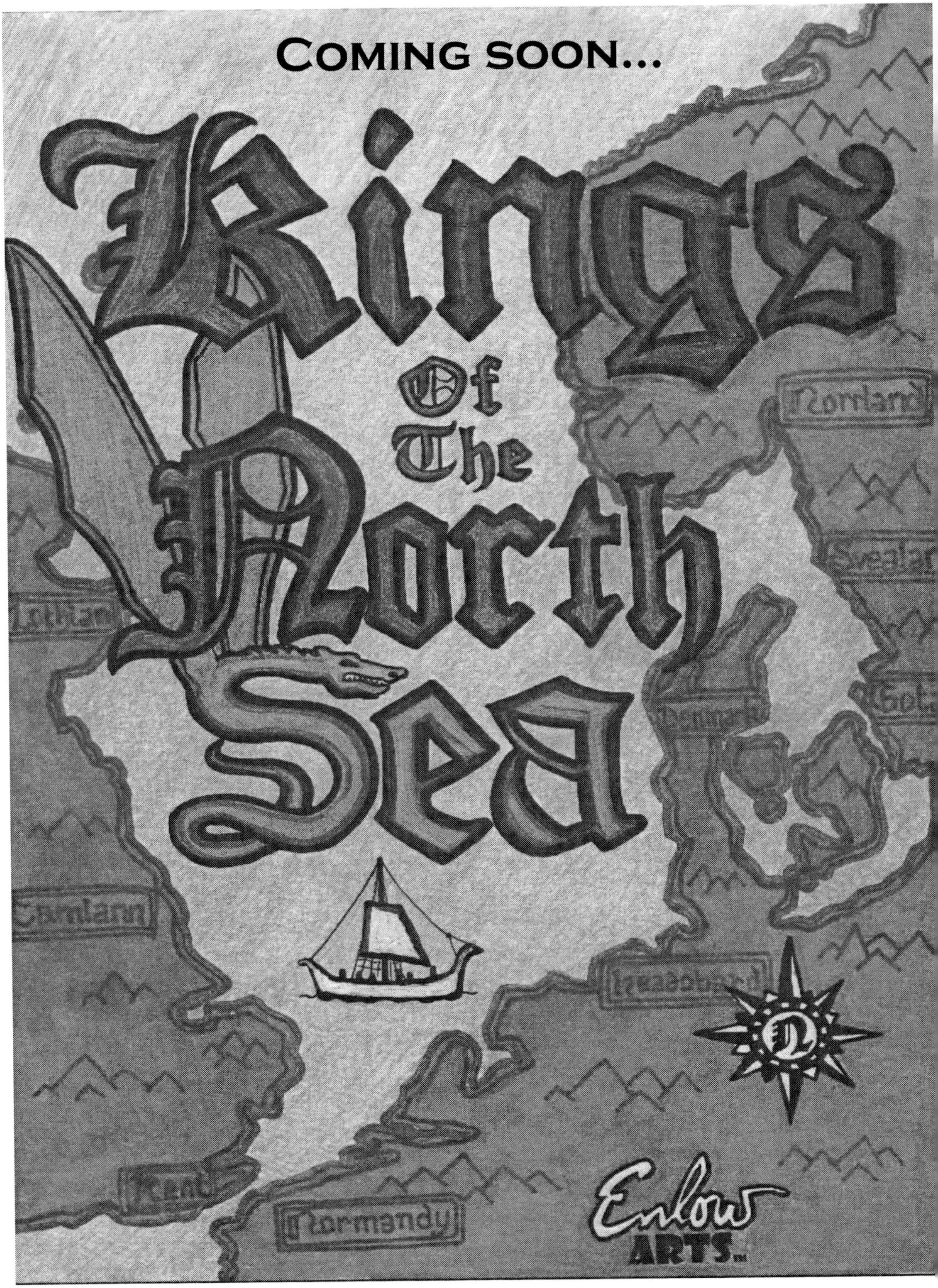
COMING SOON...
Kings of the North Sea
Norrland
Denmark
Kent
Normandy
Enlow
ARTS